PSYCHOLINGUISTICS

A SECOND LANGUAGE PERSPECTIVE

Evelyn Marcussen Hatch

University of California at Los Angeles

NEWBURY HOUSE PUBLISHERS, Cambridge
A division of Harper & Row, Publishers, Inc.
New York, Philadelphia, San Francisco, Washington
London, Mexico City, São Paulo, Singapore, Sydney
1983

Library of Congress Cataloging in Publication Data

Hatch, Evelyn Marcussen.
 Psycholinguistics : a second language perspective.

 Bibliography: p.
 1. Psycholinguistics. 2. Language acquisition.
I. Title.
P37.H34 1983   401'.9   82-8275
ISBN 0-88377-250-7

Cover design by Margot Siegmann

NEWBURY HOUSE PUBLISHERS
A division of Harper & Row, Publishers, Inc.

 Language Science
Language Teaching
Language Learning

CAMBRIDGE, MASSACHUSETTS

First printing: January 1983

Printed in the U.S.A.   7

ACKNOWLEDGMENTS

I want to thank Leland McCleary, Michael Long, Cheryl Brown, and William Rutherford for their helpful comments on the content and style of this book. It would never have evolved without them. And my thanks to Roger Andersen, Brad Arthur, Brita Butler-Wall, Hossein Farhady, Judy Gough, Steve Krashen, Diane Larsen-Freeman, Sabrina Peck, Elaine Tarone, Sandy Thompson, John Schumann, and the participants in my psycholinguistics classes for their contributions. I also want to thank the staff at Newbury House, especially Jackie Sanborn and Elizabeth Lantz, for their advice and comments on my work.

Finally, thanks to the many researchers and publishers for their permission to quote from their studies and reports.

For Susan and Dion

CREDITS

Adams, J. *Donald Copey of Harvard*. Boston: Houghton Mifflin, 1960.

Amastae, J. The acquisition of English vowels. *Papers in Linguistics*, 1978, *11*, 423–458.

Brown, R. *The first language*. Cambridge, Mass.: MIT Press, 1973.

Butterworth, G., & Hatch, E. A Spanish-speaking adolescent's acquisition of English syntax. In E. Hatch (ed.), *Second Language Acquisition*. Rowley, Mass.: Newbury House, 1978, 231–245.

Carey, S. The child as word learner. In M. Halle, J. Bresnan, & G. A. Miller (eds.), *Linguistic theory and psychological reality*. Cambridge, Mass.: MIT Press, 1979.

Cazden, C., Cancino, H., Rosansky, E., & Schumann, J. *Second language acquisition sequences in children, adolescents, and adults*. Final report, U.S. Department of HEW, August, 1975.

Chaika, E. A linguist looks at "schizophrenic" language. *Brain and language*, 1974, *1*, 257–276.

Clark, E. What's in a word? On the child's acquisition of semantics in his first language. In T. Moore (ed.), *Cognitive development and the acquisition of language*. New York: Academic Press, 1973, 65–110.

Clark, H., & Clark, E. *Psychology and language: an introduction to psycholinguistics*. New York: Harcourt Brace Jovanovich, 1977.

Daden, I. Conversational analysis and its relevance to TESL. M.A. thesis, UCLA, 1974.

Eckman, F. Markedness and the contrastive analysis hypothesis. *Language Learning*, 1977, *27*, 2, 315–330.

Ferguson, C. Towards a characterization of English foreigner talk. *Anthropological Linguistics*, 1974, *17*, 1–14.

Gary, N. A discourse analysis of certain root transformations in English. Indiana University Linguistics Club, Bloomington, Indiana, 1976.

Geschwind, N. Specialization of the human brain. *Scientific American*, September 1979, *241*, 3, 180–201.

Goffman, E. Replies and responses. *Language in Society*, 1976, 5, 3, 254–313.

Guilford, J. P. Three faces of intellect. *American Psychologist*, 1959, *14*, 469–479.

Gumperz, J. Sociocultural knowledge in conversational inference. *Georgetown Roundtable on Languages and Linguistics*. Washington, D.C.: Georgetown University Press, 1977, 191–211.

Hakuta, K. A report on the development of the grammatical morphemes in a Japanese child learning English as a second language. *Working Papers on Bilingualism*, OISE, 1974, 3, 18–44.

Hartnett, D. The relationship of analytic and holistic cognitive styles in second language acquisition. Ph.D. dissertation, UCLA, 1980.

Hopper, P. J. Aspect and foregrounding in discourse. In T. Givon (ed.), *Syntax and semantics: discourse & syntax, Vol. 12.* New York: Academic Press, 1979, 213–242.

Huang, J. & Hatch, E. A Chinese child's acquisition of English syntax. In E. Hatch (ed.), *Second language acquisition,* Rowley, Mass.: Newbury House, 1978.

Itoh, H., & Hatch, E. Second language acquisition: a case study. In E. Hatch (ed.), *Second language acquisition.* Rowley, Mass.: Newbury House, 1978.

Johnston, M. V. Observations on learning French by immersion. UCLA, 1973. Abstracted in E. Hatch (ed.), *Second language acquisition.* Rowley, Mass.: Newbury House, 1978.

Jordan, B., & Fuller, N. On the non-fatal nature of trouble: sense-making and trouble managing in Lingua Franca talk. *Semiotica,* 1975, *13,* 1, 11–32.

Kellerman, E. Giving learners a break: native language intuitions as a source of predictions about transferability. *Working Papers on Bilingualism,* 1978, *15,* 59–92.

Kempen, G., & Hoenkamp, E. A procedural grammar for sentence production. *Internal Report 81 FU.03, 81 SO.07.* Vakgroep psychologische functieleer, Psychologisch laboratorium, Katholieke Universiteit, Nijmegen, Netherlands, 1981.

Kernan, K. T., & Sabsay, S. Pragmatics of narrative use by the mildly retarded. Paper presented at the 77th annual American Anthropological Society, Los Angeles, 1978.

Labov, W., & Fanshel, D. *Therapeutic discourse.* New York: Academic Press, 1977.

Lance, D. M. *A brief study of Spanish-English bilinguals: final report.* Research Project ORR-Lib. Arts, 15504, Texas A&M University, 1969.

Levinson, S. E., & Liberman, M. Speech recognition by computer. *Scientific American,* 1981, *244,* 4, 64–87.

Long, M. Input, interaction and second language acquisition. Paper presented at the N.Y. Academy of Sciences, New York, January, 1981.

Luria, A. R. *The mind of a mnemonist: a little book about a vast memory.* New York: Basic Books, 1968.

Miller, G. A. *Language and speech.* San Francisco: W.H. Freeman & Co., 1981.

Miller, G. A., & Isard, S. Free recall of self embedded English sentences. *Information and control,* 1964, *7,* 292–303.

Mulford, R., & Hecht, B. Learning to speak without an accent: acquisition of a second language phonology. *Papers and reports in child language development,* 1980, *18.* Linguistics Department, Stanford University.

Neisser, U. *Cognitive psychology.* Englewood Cliffs, N.J.: Prentice-Hall, 1967.

Neumann, R. An attempt to define through error analysis an intermediate ESL level at UCLA. M.A. thesis, UCLA, 1977.

Olshtain, E., & Cohen, A. Discourse analysis and language learning: speech event sets. Paper presented at AILA, Lund Sweden, 1981.

Peck, S. Child-child discourse in second language acquisition. In Hatch, E. *Second language acquisition.* Rowley, Mass.: Newbury House, 1978, 383–400.

Pomerantz, A. A sequential analysis of interpreting absences. Sociology Department, UCLA, 1978.

Savin, H. B., & Perchonock, E. Grammatical structure of the immediate recall of English sentences. *Journal of verbal learning and verbal behavior,* 1965, *4,* 348–353.

Schane, S. *Generative phonology.* Englewood Cliffs, N.J.: Prentice-Hall, 1973.

Schwartz, J. The negotiation of meaning: repair in conversations between second language learners of English. In D. Larsen-Freeman (ed.), *Discourse analysis in second language research.* Rowley, Mass.: Newbury House, 1980, 138–153.

Scollon, R. A real early stage: an unzippered condensation of a dissertation on child language. In E. Ochs & B. Schieffelin (eds.), *Developmental pragmatics.* New York: Academic Press, 1979.

Shapira, R. The non-learning of English: a case study of an adult. In E. Hatch (ed.), *Second language acquisition.* Rowley, Mass.: Newbury House, 1978, 246–255.

Sher, A. Symmetric predicates: a theoretical and empirical study. M.A. thesis, UCLA, 1975.

Snow, C. The development of conversations between mothers and babies. *Journal of Child Language,* 1977, *4,* 1, 1–22.

Stern, C., & Stern, W. *Die Kindersprache: Eine psychologische und sprachttheoretische Untersuchung.* Leipzig: Barth, 1907.

Stewart, J. M., & Barach, C. A brief memory strategy with distinctive features. *Journal of Psycholinguistic Research,* 1980, *9,* 4, 391–406.

Willis, M. Affixation in English word formation and application to TESOL. M.A. thesis, UCLA, 1975.

Wong-Fillmore, L. The second time around: cognitive and social strategies in second language acquisition. Ph.D. dissertation, Stanford University, 1976.

Yamada, J. On the independence of language and cognition: evidence from a hyperlinguistic retarded adolescent. Paper presented at the International Congress of Child Language. Vancouver, August, 1981.

Yorkey, R. C. *Study skills for students of English as a second language.* New York: McGraw-Hill, 1970.

TABLE OF CONTENTS

PSYCHOLINGUISTICS

A SECOND LANGUAGE PERSPECTIVE

1 Introduction: A Perspective on Psycholinguistics

Psycholinguistics is defined traditionally as the study of human language—language comprehension, language production, and language acquisition. The two disciplines that make up its name, psychology and linguistics, both contribute, but the resulting blend is not always entirely smooth. While psycholinguists from both disciplines have a common goal—understanding how people comprehend and produce language—each pursues it in a somewhat different way. Second language researchers view the field from still another perspective. The assumptions, theories, and methods used by psychologists, linguists, and second language researchers strongly affect the way each defines psycholinguistics.

The linguists' major goal is to discover the systematicity in language and then to write descriptions that capture that systematicity. While they may deny that their descriptions directly correspond to what goes on in people's heads, surely the general processes they describe have some correspondence, however remote or simplistic, to human language production and comprehension. Linguists are interested in the rules of language (its systematicity), and they see language learning, language production, and language comprehension as rule-governed behavior. Therefore, they are concerned not so much with language behavior itself as they are with the organization of the linguistic relationships that underlie language behavior.

Linguists who become psycholinguists expect their new field to verify, psychologically, or biologically, the reality of these underlying linguistic relationships. They believe that, as psycholinguists, they can provide data (on language acquisition, language use, or language behavior) that will support, or at least give them grounds to reconsider, their descriptions of these underlying relationships.

1

Psychologists, on the other hand, turn to psycholinguistics in the hope that it will provide them with a better understanding of human cognition. Their interest in intellectual processes extends to an interest in the processes observed in language learning, production, and comprehension. As psycholinguists, they believe the field should include the cognitive processes involved in language behavior. They assume that such processes as perception, categorization, inference, generalization, retention, and problem solving are of central concern in psycholinguistics, since they believe such processes explain language acquisition and learning in general.

Second language researchers and teachers are also concerned with a variety of issues in language acquisition and language behavior: What is easy, or difficult, in language learning (and why)? Is there a natural order in which structures are learned? How do people learn languages outside the classroom? How is it that some learners, with only minimal second language ability, can still carry on a highly successful conversation while other learners, who score 100 percent on grammar tests, cannot carry on the simplest communication task? Can the traits of good language learners be identified? What factors influence successful second language learning the most? Is second language acquisition the same basic process as first language acquisition? What kinds of models can be proposed to account for lexical retrieval or syntactic construction in language mixing and switching? What models might explain the process of simultaneous translation? Second language researchers believe that psycholinguistics should offer insight into these and many other questions.

Psycholinguists, of course, are interested in what both fields have to say that might shed light on how people comprehend and produce language. Linguists have suggested, through their descriptions, that language is a set of hierarchically arranged subsystems of rules. Psycholinguists have transformed these subsystems into another sort of hierarchy—a set of plans which are related both to the rule systems of the linguists and to the mental processes of the cognitive psychologists. The subsystems, or levels, of linguistic description and psycholinguistic plan levels are:

Linguistic Subsystems	Psycholinguistic Plan Levels
discourse analysis	discourse plans
	intonation plans
sentence syntax	syntactic plans
lexical rules	lexical selection plans
morphophonemic rules	morphophonemic plans
phonology and phonetic rules	phonetic/motor plans

Using the methods of both psychology and linguistics, psycholinguists look for answers to a variety of questions that relate to language behavior. But to do this they have traditionally looked at each subsystem separately, without trying to put all the levels together. Moreover, their approaches to these subsystems differ, depending on whether they have been trained in linguistics or in psychology. As an example, consider the first level, *discourse*. The linguist might be most concerned with whether or not we can even describe discourse as a rule-governed system. Certain discourse units seem to be more amenable to linguistic description than others; for example, the narrative. Having collected narrative data, the linguist would search for common patterns. Most narratives begin with a setting (e.g., "once upon a time," or "last weekend at the beach") which mentions time and place. The description of the cast of characters is given (e.g., "there lived an old man," or "I met this weight lifter"). Once setting and characters are established, the hearer has been "oriented," and the narrative events can be presented in a series of temporally ordered clauses. Then, the resolution is given and a final coda, or moral, finishes off the story (e.g., "and that's why everyone loves the little old man," or "and that's why I don't go to the beach anymore") and brings us back to the present setting. Linguists would include details on the distribution of tense and aspect in verb forms which makes some parts of the action more prominent than others. They would describe ways in which nouns are marked as new or as old information by the change in articles used. They might discuss the role of pronominalization or ellipsis. In the end, they would have a set of "rules of the game." The linguist would eventually develop a formal description of the system underlying the narrative and *then* look for evidence to support that description in the language corpora, both written and oral narratives. This they would consider psycholinguistic validation of one part of the discourse subsystem.

The psychologist, on the other hand, would be more interested in discovering the intellectual processes we use in understanding narratives. Rumelhart (1975), for example, believes that all such narratives are processed as problem-solving reports. In every narrative, the hero/heroine meets a problem. To solve the problem, she or he faces a number of subproblems and either solves or avoids them. Gradually, all the subproblems cumulate in meeting the final *goal* of the story. For example, the cowboy must (goal:) stop the bad guys; the detective must (goal:) find the murderer; Hedda Gabler must (goal:) escape domination. Once we have identified the goal, we then begin to search the narrative for how the hero/heroine solves the problem, i.e., the *plan*. By discovering the goal and the plan, we comprehend the narrative as a problem-solving report.

Now we have two ways of approaching the narrative—one in terms of processes people use in understanding narratives, and the other in terms of how narratives are structured. Both approaches are related to how we understand and/or construct narratives. Linguists can test the structural descriptions of narratives by turning to written and taped data. They can count how many narratives follow the description and try to account for the variation one might expect to find. For the linguist, this would be validation of the description. However, psychologists would not necessarily consider such a validation "psycholinguistics," since it would give little information on whether or not that description is used to either understand or remember narratives.

To test his narrative plan, Rumelhart presented the following story to Ss (S is the abbreviation used for "subject," meaning someone who participates in experiments—usually students in freshman psychology classes.):

There was once an old farmer who owned a very stubborn donkey. One evening the farmer was trying to put his donkey into his shed. First, the farmer pushed the donkey, but the donkey wouldn't move. Then the farmer pulled the donkey, but the donkey still wouldn't move. Then the farmer asked his dog to bark loudly at the donkey and thereby frighten him into the shed. But the dog refused. So then, the farmer asked his cat to scratch the dog so the dog would bark loudly and thereby frighten the donkey into the shed. But the cat replied, "I would gladly scratch the dog if only you would get me some milk." So the farmer went to his cow and asked for some milk to give the cat. But the cow replied, "I would gladly give you some milk if only you would give me some hay." Thus the farmer went to the haystack and got some hay. As soon as he gave the hay to the cow, the cow gave the farmer some milk. Then the farmer went to the cat and gave the milk to the cat. As soon as the cat got the milk, it began to scratch the dog. As soon as the cat scratched the dog, the dog began to bark loudly. The barking so frightened the donkey that it jumped immediately into its shed.

The farmer's *goal* (to get the donkey into the shed) is clearly stated as soon as the setting and the characters have been established. The solution then consists of solving a number of subproblems. Each is set up in a row like dominoes (in temporal sequence). By one touch of the final domino all the subproblems are solved, and the goal is attained.

Now consider a rewrite of the story. The same basic information is presented; the sentences are no more complex than those in the original; the vocabulary is no more abstract; and yet this version of the story is difficult to understand:

There was once an old farmer who owned some very stubborn animals. One evening the farmer was taking a walk when he saw his donkey. The farmer pushed the donkey, but the donkey didn't move. Then he pulled the donkey, but the donkey still didn't move. Then the farmer went to his cow and asked for some milk. But the cow replied, "I would rather have you give me some hay to eat." Then the farmer saw his dog, and he asked him to bark loudly. But the dog refused. Then the farmer went to the haystack and got some hay. When the farmer gave the hay to the cow, the cow gave him some milk. Then the farmer asked the cat to scratch the dog. But the cat replied, "I am thirsty and would be happy if you gave me some milk." So the farmer gave his milk to the cat. As soon as the cat got the milk, it began to scratch the dog. As soon as the cat scratched the dog, the dog began to bark loudly. The barking so frightened the donkey that it jumped immediately into its shed, which the farmer had built at the time he bought the donkey.

If you had not read the first version of the story, you would probably be hard pressed to say what the point of the story is. Even though the setting, characters, and events are given (although not in temporal order), the goal is missing. To be sure that this lack of stated goal did affect comprehension, Rumelhart called his Ss back twenty-four hours after they had read either the first or the second version and asked them to retell the story. In addition, they were asked to scale the story for "comprehensibility." As you might predict, Ss remembered a larger number of propositions from the first version. They also rated the first version as very easy to understand and the second version as difficult.

Owens et al. (1978) believe there is an additional factor in accounting for how people understand such narratives. They propose that a reader's knowledge of a character's motives organizes the way the reader understands the narrative. So they conducted an experiment to test their claim.

They constructed a story about a bland hero/heroine who gets up, makes some coffee, goes to the doctor, then to class, does some grocery shopping, then goes to a cocktail party. The story sounds like a student's response to a language teacher's question: What did you do yesterday? It's a very dull story. One group of subjects heard the story with little information about the hero/heroine. Half of this group read the story about dull, ordinary Jack and half read the story about dull, ordinary Nancy. As you might guess, little of the story was recalled by the subjects twenty-four hours later.

A second group of subjects were presented with "soap opera" information about the hero/heroine. Those who read about Nancy learned about her implied pregnancy—that she woke up feeling sick again, that she was worried about how she would break the news to the professor she'd been seeing, and how she would raise the money. Although the basic story remained the same as it had been with dull, ordinary Nancy, these subjects now remembered all the story details that related to her implied pregnancy. The boring visit to the doctor's office was now remembered as one in which the doctor tells Nancy she is indeed pregnant. In the classroom episode, the professor is remembered as the selfsame professor Nancy had been seeing. When she went to the cocktail party and tried to talk with the neutrally-presented lecturer, readers remembered the incident as one in which the guilty professor intentionally tries to avoid Nancy.

Similarly, when the hero, Jack, was identified as an underweight football player worried about not making the team, the readers remembered the nurse weighing him. The grocery shopping segment is highlighted, and the cocktail party becomes a recounting of all the hors d'oeuvres Jack devoured there. Such story-recall *behavior* is psychological validation that people use strategies such as motive identification as a way of processing narratives.

According to psychologists, then, intellectual processes such as identification of story goal, character motives, and plan are crucial to understanding narratives. Most psycholinguists would accept this, but many believe that the underlying rules of the narrative, as given by linguists, may also help us process narratives, to locate crucial parts of the story rapidly. In other words, the psycholinguist should be able to consider both approaches—the linguists' descriptions of rule systems and the psychologists' tests of mental processes they believe people use in understanding and organizing language.

The narratives presented above were written narratives. Narratives also occur in conversations. If we separate these "stories" from the conversation, we can see how they are organized linguistically, whether they conform with linguistic descriptions, and/or how effective the speaker is in making the goal, motives, and plan clear.

First let's look at data from Kernan and Sabsay's (1978) study of conversations of mentally retarded adults. The story announced by *M* is entitled "a whole buncha troubles." Along with the title, *M* should give an orientation in which place and participants are set. But, notice that the speaker does not seem sure who the cast of characters are nor whether or not his listeners know them (the colons represent sounds held):

M: U::h, I really hate to bring it up but uh (pause) well (pause) I'm thinkin about it uh I'm thinkin about I shouldn't do this shouldn't do that. But uh (pause) again I have to do something. It's either I have to do something or I don't have to do something. That's about as far as it goes. (pause) An there's things like uh (pause) uh well (pause) (softly) what's that guy's name?

MA: Spit it out man.

M: U::h hey man, y'know that guy you used to go with?

LY: What?

M: Remember that guy you used to go with in here?

LY: Who?

M: D.

LY: D who? R?

M: Yeah.

LY: Oh boy. Don't mention it. Bleeh.

M: Sorry about that but he is givin givin me a whole buncha troubles.

It is, of course, possible that this long introduction and the time taken to identify the cast of characters may be a way of capturing the attention of the audience. However, even after the title of the story ("a whole buncha troubles") has been stated, the development of the story itself and the speaker's plan of action is impossible to follow. In the end, the listeners are still asking about the setting and the cast of characters, features usually established at the beginning of such discourse:

M: . . . He said, "Shut up, you." You know what. SOB.

JT: When did this happen?

M: Uh.

JT: Was it recently?

M: Somethin like that.

LY: What did this have to do with D.R.?

M: Well, that's what he does.

Clearly, *M* has difficulty organizing the narrative discourse plan. Of course, we are all better on some days than others in getting our ideas presented in an "ideal" form. Given time to consider and retell his story a few more times, *M* might eventually arrive at a version closer to an ideal organization. We will discuss the many differences that occur in reworked discourse, the differences between planned and unplanned discourse, later on in Chapter 8.

The following narrative was told by an eight-year-old child. The story is not original; she must have heard it several times. While the discourse should, therefore, be closer to the ideal narrative form, there are still problems, as can be seen from the listener's questions. (The numbers in parentheses mark timed pauses; the colon represents a sound held or lengthened.)

Sue: Y'know any other stories?

Mary: Uh-huh. Oh yeh (.5) see, now uh her ma- her mother. Now there was this little /pəkə/ in a in in there was this little /pəkə/ was so small and then he said "When am I gonna grow" "It'll take a little time."

Sue: Mhmm

Mary: N so so then he went outside and den he den he den he den a witch came, he said uh "Pay me:: money or ya won't never grow gra:: gra:::. Give me money:::" So the witch so-

Sue: Wh-wh-wait a minute. The witch said to the little BOY t' give (.2) HER money or (.2) HE would never grow? Is that what?

Mary: No, gum, gum. It's gum.

Sue: Oh, it's gum.

Mary: Yeh.

Sue: (puzzled, soft voice) So the gum won't grow.

Mary: So-so-so he so he started cryin so and then and and then he got bigger and bigger and bigger and bigger and bigger and bigger and bigger (hands close to mouth gradually expand as if blowing up a balloon or bubblegum) and then after he after he stopped cryin, he buried, he buried hisself and and then the witch came back and he said "how did you get so big without givin me any gum?" And then he said "Oh, I'm the biggest /pəkər/ in the whole wide world."

Sue: The biggest what?

Mary: (instructive voice) The pumpkin.

Sue: The biggest PUMkin? Ohh, was he a seed in the beginning? (1.2) Or, or some gum? (1.0)

Mary: (very definite) Well, it's GUM.

Sue: Okay.

Mary: So, so he was, he was about that small as my hand like that.

Sue: Oh, I see, okay and he started crying, all right, and he grew real big. I got that.

Mary: Mmhmm

Sue: N then he buried himself?

Mary: Mmhmm and then the witch unburied him.

Sue: Oh, I see.

Mary: So so he so he said, "I am the biggest /pəkə/ in the whole WIDE WORLD!" So the pumkin buried hisself again and then his mother came back ah at outside and he, and he bin and then he unbury it. And then he see he found this orange thing in it and his mother said, "I told you it would take a little time." "I AM THE BIGGEST /pəkə/ IN THE WHOLE WIDE WORLD!" (giggles)

Sue: (laughing) I don't get it.

Here the problem for the listener does not seem to be so much the overall discourse organization as it is Mary's difficulty in establishing reference. At first it's not clear what a /pəkə/ is except that it's a *he* and has a mother. Then the /pəkə/ seems to be gum, but isn't. Rather, either gum or money would have won the witch's help. True, the temporal sequence of a pumpkin seed being buried and unburied could be clearer, but the basic problem for the listener appears to be the establishment of the cast of characters. A comparison with the linguistic description of narratives can, then, help us locate problems in performance at the discourse level.

Now let's consider the evidence given so far to support the notion of psycholinguistic plans as important in producing and understanding narratives. Among these, only the Rumelhart and Owens studies would likely be considered for publication in many of the journals that include psycholinguistic research. Why is that, since each discusses how people use plans in organizing what they wish to say or in comprehending what others say or write? In most psycholinguistic research, as in psychology itself, hypotheses are made, *S*s are given tasks to perform, and their performance on the tasks can be quantified (number of propositions remembered, number of new propositions added, scaling of comprehensibility of passages, etc.). Thus, performance on a specific task is used to predict behavior in other nontest situations. In the Rumelhart example (about the farmer and the donkey), one behavior, *recall*, is tested as a predictive measure of another mental behavior, *comprehension*.

The narratives presented from child and mentally retarded adult data are *illustrative*. They are evidence in support of psycholinguistic discourse plans, but in a different way. The linguists' test of the adequacy of any description is whether or not it adequately covers the facts in the data and whether or not the description, if used, would regenerate similar forms. When the new data do not fit the description (as they do not in the child and adult narratives given above), there are three possible explanations. First, new data that do not conform to the description may not be an example of what has been described. Second, the description may not adequately describe the underlying characteristics of the structure. Third, we may look at the data as faulty performance data and try to discover where the speaker fails in following the ideal system.

While the child and adult narratives above are taken from natural data, they do not "test" the description of narratives in the tradition of psychology. Rather, they "test" the description of narratives in the tradition of linguistics. This latter tradition accepts illustrative examples as relevant data. The notion of "consulting native-speaker intuition" is, for the linguist, a valid procedure, and researchers are even allowed to create examples to support descriptions (if the examples agree with native-speaker intuition). Certain branches of psychology have an equally long tradition of using illustrative data as grounds for hypotheses which then can be tested in more formal research. Many psycholinguists question evidence that is not based in formal data. It is this difference of opinion regarding appropriate research methods that can be seen by what is and what is not accepted as publishable research by some of the journals. As you can imagine, this creates many arguments among psycholinguists about what does or does not count as evidence, and many more arguments over what kind of evidence one should or should not feel comfortable accepting.

Second language researchers who are interested in the discourse level have looked at narratives of second language learners in several ways. They have followed the arguments about the "universality" of narrative structure proposed by linguists. They have collected narratives of second language learners in both the learners' first and second languages in search of such universal structures. They have also tested learners' abilities to recall narratives that did or did not reflect the language/cultural differences found in narratives of different groups. The data analysis has ranged from anecdotal description to inferential statistics. Many methods have been used and judged acceptable within the field.

Many psycholinguists, like second language researchers, have tried to widen the scope of acceptable evidence and have tried to identify the strengths and weaknesses of a variety of approaches, in hope of selecting the most appropriate research method for each research question. However, it would be absurd to claim that all is peace and harmony within any of these fields. Many researchers refuse to believe that, just because rules can be described, such rules are actually used by learners. It is difficult to convince them that language behavior is rule-governed, at least rule-governed in the form described by linguists. Others refuse to believe that measuring one behavior (such as recall) tells us anything about other mental processes which cannot be observed (such as comprehension). The conflict over what is acceptable evidence is raised again and again every time linguists, psychologists, and second language researchers meet.

However, they do seem to agree on the hierarchical nature of language description. In line with that hierarchy, Chapters 2 through 8 are arranged in a path from phonology to discourse; from the bottom of the hierarchy of plans to the top. This can be misleading in that it obscures the effect that the higher plans have on the lower plans. Although it is clear that plans at higher levels influence plans at lower levels, all levels must be considered simultaneously, even though it may be impossible for us to research more than one level at a time. (Readers who prefer the path to run in the opposite direction should feel free to read Chapters 2 through 8 in reverse order!) Belief in any hierarchical arrangement must be tempered by a willingness to allow the levels to "leak," for none of the levels is impervious. Each is, in turn, affected by the others.

To see why this is so, consider the research now being done on the use of relative clauses by second language learners. These investigations are at the syntactic level. Several researchers have found, among other things, that learners use few relative clauses. When they do, they put more of them in post-verb position than following sentence subjects. There is no obvious explanation for this at the sentence syntax level. However, it is not so surprising when we consult information from the discourse level. The subject position in narratives is usually held by the major character. Once she or he has been identified (and this is usually done with a BE + Pred structure during the orientation section), we know who the subject is. There is no need for further identification (and that is the function a relative clause could have in post-subject position). The major character engages in a series of actions throughout the narrative. These actions affect various people or objects which may need to be identified. And, they may be related to places or times which also may need to be identified. Therefore, given a discourse view, we would expect to find more relative clauses in post-verb position. And, if the story were relatively unrehearsed, we would expect to find a rather small number of relative clauses overall, since much of the work of relative clauses can be presented more easily in other less complex ways.

This influence of one psycholinguistic plan on another is felt at every level of the hierarchy. And the interaction is not entirely one way. That is, lower level plans may have to be consulted in our research at higher plan levels. Consider the following example: If we conduct a research project on the pronunciation errors of second language learners, we may find that our Ss have difficulty producing consonant clusters in English. That information would be crucial when we examine the morphology problems of these same Ss. If the students cannot produce consonant clusters, they may simplify them (by deleting the final consonant) and thus appear not to have acquired the $-s$ endings for plurals, third-person singular present tense, or the possessive. They may also show erratic performance on past tense when it involves consonant cluster production. Therefore, we must remember to consider the possible effects of lower level plans on higher levels as well.

Stacking plan levels like boxes one atop the other also gives the impression that this is a sequential action model, sequential from the top down. Such a model would suggest that one first uses the discourse plan, then the syntactic plan, and so on down. The model need not be interpreted this way. Rather, one might think of teams of planners working in three basic areas: conceptual, formative, and articulatory. The psycholinguistic plan levels given at the beginning of the chapter are one way of further subdividing the work of those on the formative team, for example. Part of the work of the team members at each plan level is independent, each may work on some small part of the total discourse, but much shunting back and forth of the partially formed product must be going on among the team members as well. We will consider such comprehension and production models in Chapter 5. Meanwhile, we will approach the plan levels, and consider the research within each, as though they were independent areas. The reader (and researcher) must remember that they are not.

Language teachers will recognize the hierarchy of plans listed at the start of the chapter as being similar to that of a language teaching syllabus, a syllabus which begins at the lower levels of the plan hierarchy. Most teachers emphasize pronunciation, vocabulary building, and simple sentence syntax in early stages of language teaching. At the intermediate level, students are moved up to work on more complex sentence structures and perhaps on short paragraphs and dialogs. As the class level advances, students are required by the syllabus to move to the top of the hierarchy and organize term papers, present oral reports, worry about style appropriateness, and so on. While the syllabus begins at the bottom of the hierarchy and works up, learners, on the other hand, may be working from the top down. They may be more concerned with discourse organization (establishing a topic, a goal, getting actions in the right order, bridging topics, working out closings, etc.) in order to make what they say/hear/see comprehensible. Given this approach, learners may concentrate on general discourse work, vocabulary, and basic phonology, and pay less attention to syntax and morphology levels. Teachers, as well as researchers, must consider all levels at once, although the focus of teaching (like the focus of research) may concentrate on one level at a time.

In this introductory chapter I have defined psycholinguistics as the search for an understanding of how humans are able to comprehend and produce language. The field uses the strengths of two disciplines, psychology and linguistics. While many of the assumptions, theories, and methods of these disciplines differ, language researchers do not see these differences as insurmountable. Rather, the influence of each field broadens the researcher's understanding of language learning and language behavior. By adding second language research to the field of psycholinguistics, researchers may gain a new perspective on many important issues. In turn, by understanding the work psycholinguists have already accomplished, second language teachers and researchers should gain a new perspective on bilingualism. It is this double perspective which will be maintained in the following chapters.

2 *Phonology*

To know a second language well, we must be able to identify and produce the sounds of the language. Yet, outside the classroom, we are seldom asked to distinguish or produce isolated speech sounds. Rather, it is the total stream of speech that we must comprehend or produce. Language perception and production is an active process which involves all plan levels, from discourse to phonology.

In this chapter we will look at the phonological level and the units linguists have proposed to describe the sound systems of languages. The central question for research is whether or not we use these units in comprehending and producing language. Here, however, I will review the literature only briefly so that we may focus on that which is related to second language acquisition. This focus will allow us to discuss questions not covered in the psycholinguistic literature and also show how second language research can help psycholinguists in their search for evidence to support both linguistic and phonological rules.

Speech error data is one area linguists can turn to for evidence to support their descriptions of language. As we speak, we frequently make phonological errors. The mental program for sequencing sounds may temporarily go awry. Reverend William Spooner became famous for his special talent for slips of the tongue. His errors, speech errors transposing two sounds or two words in utterances (such as "work is the curse of the drinking class" and, scolding a student, "you have hissed all my mystery lectures . . . in fact, you have tasted the whole worm,") are legendary. Natural slips of the tongue support linguistic descriptions of phonology in three areas. Consider first the following.

Phonemic Units

Although it is true that we hear speech as a stream of sound, it is also the case that we can divide that stream of sound into segments. For example, if you were asked how many units there are in the word *can,* you would probably say three. Yet, in listening, it is difficult to say just where each sound begins and ends. As we speak, our tongue moves very rapidly through the positions required to produce the three units. We anticipate the sounds that follow and begin the tongue movement to those positions before finishing the first. Just as we hear a continuum of sound, the tongue is also performing a continuum of motion, rather than articulating each unit separately. Yet, we still feel that we hear and articulate identifiable core segments in each word. These core segments are called *phonemes*, and their function is to contrast forms for meaning. We know that *nip, dip, rip, sip, zip, lip,* and *tip* differ only in the initial segments and that that difference also signals differences in meaning. Therefore, /n, d, r, s, z, l, t/ are phonemes in English. We can also hear that *beat, bit, bait, bet, bat, boot, boat, bought, but, bite,* and *bout* are the same except for the vowel segment. Each word begins and ends with the phonemes /b/ and /t/. The intervening vowels /i, ɪ, e, ɛ, æ, ʊ, o, ɔ, ə, ai, aʊ / are also phonemes.

It could be argued that we are so influenced by spelling that we hear the stream of speech as the number of letters in each word. Core segments, however, are not the same as letters. (e.g., /f/ may be spelled *ph*one or cou*gh* as well as *f*ine). There is no one-to-one correspondence between letters and phonemes. Since the italicized letters in the following words all have the same sound: *s*ugar, ti*ss*ue, lea*sh,* informa*t*ion; and since the sounds of the italicized letters in the following are all different: *s*ugar /š/ , *s*ing /s/, lei*s*ure /ž/, bird*s* /z/; we cannot base identification of segments on spelling.

Students beginning their training as language teachers are usually surprised to find that some of the sounds that are represented by two letters (e.g., *ch* in chip or church, *dg* in ridge or judge, *sh* in ship or shine, *ng* in sing) are actually one, not two, phonemes. We have many theoretical and logical tests to show that these units are valid. Fromkin (1973*a*) and others have established the psychological reality (in contrast to theoretical or logical reality) of the unitness of each individual speech segment (even those represented in spelling with two letters) by collecting and analyzing naturally occurring speech errors of native speakers. Errors such as "chee cane" for "key chain" (/či ken/ for /ki čen/) and "chicken" /čɪkɛn/ for "kitchen" /kɪčɛn/ show that the unit *ch* /č/ is maintained when sounds are transposed. The *c* does not separate from the *h*; *ch* is a unit which cannot be divided. Errors such as "put the white boos in the shocks," for "put the white shoes in the box" show that the unit *sh* /š/ is also maintained—it does not divide into an *s* and an *h*.

Further evidence that phonemic units are separate from the spelling system comes from Cowan et al. (in press) who studied the backward English of AL. AL can, as someone speaks to him, "shadow" what he hears, but not in the usual sense, whereby one repeats what is heard as rapidly as possible. AL can, as he listens, almost simultaneously utter the same sequence of sounds backward. For example, he would say /sip/ "seep" for /pis/ "peace" rather than "ecaep" (the backward spelling). Phonemic units are maintained so that /š/ in "shape" /šep/ becomes /peš/ not /pehs/. For the diphthong /ai/, he does not reverse the direction of the glide but rather retains it as a unit.

Some twenty-seven backward speakers have since been studied by Cowan and his associates. All reported developing this talent for backward speech between the ages of seven and eleven. Some of these, like AL, are phonemic backward speakers while others are orthographic backward speakers, pronouncing letter sequences in reverse order. Two children, one an orthographic and the other a phonemic backward speaker, have also been studied. BW (eight years, ten months) showed the same phonemic sophistication as adult backward speakers. He even retained final /ŋ/ as a unit while most adults did not. "Ring" became /ŋɪr/ while most adults said /gənɪr/. DR (nine years, eleven months) still selected pronunciations of letters that were appropriate for the context. That is, the pronunciations of the letters *g* and *c* are usually /g/ and /k/, unless followed by *e, i,* or *y*. Then, they become /ǰ/ and /s/. DR followed these rules in his backward speech. So again this evidence, along with that from slips of the tongue, shows that it isn't just linguists who analyze the stream of speech into phonemic units governed by context rules. Other people do, too. (Or at least the human brain does.)

From all the possible sounds humans can produce with the vocal tract, each language uses slightly different segments (phonemes) and variants (allophones). For example, English has a series of voiceless segments /p, t, k, č/, which when used at the beginning of words are accompanied by aspiration (pʰin, tʰin, kʰin, čʰin). (You can test this by placing your hand close to your mouth as you say the words. You will feel a puff of air as you articulate the beginning of each word. In contrast, you will not have the same effect with the words s*p*in, s*t*eak, or s*k*in, or for the /č/ in tea*ch*er). This variation in pronunciation of voiceless segments does not occur automatically in all languages. The choice of phoneme segments and their variants differs from language to language. In English we have one /l/ segment, though it is articulated quite differently in the words *l*ight and be*ll*. In Polish, these are two different phonemes rather than one. The /k/ sound in English is also articulated at a slightly different point depending on the following vowel. If you start to say the words "key" and "coffee" (start, but do not say the word) you will feel that the contact point for the /k/ in "key" is much farther forward than the /k/ of "coffee." Yet we hear them as one and the same sound. In Arabic, however, these are two phonemes, /k/ and /q/ (kalb=dog; qalb=heart), and Arabic speakers hear them as two separate sounds.

Since each language has its own set of segments, and we appear to analyze the stream of speech in terms of these segments, one theory of language perception is that, as we learn a language, we construct a set of templates to which we compare the incoming sound signals. If the sounds match the phoneme templates, then we recognize the sound values. However, there are bound to be problems with such matching. Each time we pronounce a segment, it is acoustically never quite the same as the last time. As we have seen above, the actual shape of each phoneme changes according to the environments in which it occurs. The sound to template correspondence, then, could not be like a key and lock, for the key would constantly be changing shape. Not only that; different speakers also pronounce the segments slightly differently. In spite of these individual differences and/or dialect differences in pronunciation, we are still able to recognize the acoustic signal. A strict template hypothesis does not, however, seem to be a valid explanation of how we convert the stream of speech into meaningful segments.

Phonetic Features

Speech error data have also been used to show the reality of phonetic features. Each phoneme can be described as consisting of a set or bundle of phonetic features. For example, the phoneme /p/ might be described in articulatory terms as +stop, +labial, —voiced, etc., while the phoneme /m/ might be described as +nasal, +labial, +voiced, etc. Many phonemes share some features. For example, the phoneme /p/ differs from /b/ only in *voicing*; the vocal folds vibrate when we produce a /b/. Features such as voicing may be misassigned in rapid speech, causing errors such as "glear plue sky" for "clear blue sky," evidence that voicing is a separable phonetic feature. /l/ and /r/ also share features of articulation: They both call for some obstruction of the vocal tract, but not enough to cause friction. They are both called *liquids* for that reason. They are both voiced; our vocal folds vibrate when we make them. When /l/ and /r/ follow voiceless sounds, they are at least partially devoiced (e.g., crown, clown or play, pray). They are also the only consonants permitted after an initial /k, g, p, b/ in English words, so they share certain occurrence rules. /w/ also shares many features with /r/ and /l/. Like /r/, it is rounded—the lips are rounded, and its semivowel quality also makes it similar to the liquids /l/ and /r/.

Teachers working with young children tell us that the r/l/w distinctions are among their most persistent speech articulation problems. Speech error data also show that when adults make errors in articulating these sounds they usually misarticulate only the features that distinguish among them. Errors such as "with this wing I thee red" and "a crump of glass" do happen regularly, but simple feature errors (e.g., "the PLO cr— claimed . . .") are even more common than transposition errors. ESL teachers also know how close these segments are and what difficulty ESL students have detecting the features that separate them. For example, we know that many language groups do not have separate /r/ and /l/ phonemes (Bantu languages, Korean, Japanese, Chinese, etc.). Rather, one is usually a variant of the other (e.g., Korean /l/ becomes /r/ before vowels). Students from these language groups typically have problems in distinguishing the features that separate /l/ and /r/ in English.

Stewart and Barach (1980) note that speakers of various languages attach different orders of importance to the features they hear in the target language. For example, French has a high front, lip-rounded vowel /y/, as in *tu*. While English has high front vowels, and also vowels that have lip rounding, these three features do not combine in one phoneme. So, Stewart and Barach say that

The American student usually solves this dilemma by keeping the lip rounding and the high vowel position and discarding the +front feature resulting in /tu/. This is not the only way to solve the problem. The native speakers of Songhai, a language of Niger, a former French colony in Central Africa, also do not have the high front, lip rounding features together in the same phoneme. They find it easier to retain the high front features and discard the lip rounding with the result that /y/ becomes /i/ (1980, p. 392).

Apparently we can detect the features that comprise sound segments, so perhaps the template hypothesis should be revived. Instead of templates for each phoneme segment, the templates would be for features. The incoming sound stream would then be run through feature-detecting templates that match and identify the features. Templates matched for +voiced, +labial, +stop would yield the phoneme segment /b/. If +stop, +labial, +voiced, +aspirated were detected, this should yield /p/; and if rules were attached to the detectors, then the /p/ would be identified as in initial position. Since careful articulation at slow speed is more likely to produce a closer match to template values, perhaps the addition of a set of speed rules (which would change values in the signal in predictable ways) would help patch up the hypothesis, taking care of some of the matching problems. Even with some flexibility built into a matching model, there would still be no one-to-one correspondence with the acoustic signal. Yet, feature detection does seem to play a part in our perception of messages, as shown in many of the examples given so far in this chapter.

Sequence of Sounds

In addition to providing evidence both to support the phonemic status of sounds in any particular language and for features, speech errors provide important evidence in a third area. Certain speech errors seldom, if ever, occur—evidence that validates linguistic rules on permissible sound sequences. Anyone trying to learn Vietnamese knows that it is difficult for Americans to pronounce words that begin with /ŋ/. We may end words with /ŋ/ in English (e.g., sing or bring), but it's not a possible initial sound for words in English (and thus difficult for Cowan's backward speakers to produce). It's unlikely then that an English speaker would ever make a speech error substituting an /ŋ/ for some other sound at the beginning of a word. Conversely, as ESL teachers know, Spanish speakers have problems with initial s-clusters in English (e.g., star, school) for it's not a permissible sequence in Spanish. To make such clusters fit the permissible sequence of sounds of Spanish, learners break up the cluster in some way (e.g., ɛstar for star or sɛteks for steaks). Hyltenstam (personal communication) notes that Finns learning Swedish have difficulty with Swedish clusters but solve the problem more often by dropping the initial consonant (thus, "skriva" becomes "riva" and "smor" becomes "mor").

Ladefoged and Broadbent (1957) tried to provoke perception of clusters that are impossible in English. They asked American Ss to listen to words presented simultaneously through headsets. One nonsense word, for example, "tass," was presented to the S's one ear and another, for example, "tak," was presented to the other ear. Listeners reported hearing either "task" or "tacks." If the onset time for "tass" was set slightly ahead of "tak," listeners would report "task." If "tak" was set slightly ahead, listeners reported hearing "tacks." A nonsense word "lanket" was then presented to one ear and "banket" to the other. No matter how the onset time was adjusted, listeners continued to report that they heard "blanket," never "lbanket." We seem to "hear" what we have learned are permissible sequences of sounds in our language. (Actually, an initial liquid +stop cluster would be unlikely in any language.) Since English has a large number of consonant cluster sequences (compared to most languages), this may be an important experiment for language teachers to think about. Do foreign students "hear" only combinations that are permissible in their first language, or do they quickly become sensitive to new sequences and process them easily? We will return to this question in a moment.

Of course, in real life we seldom listen to isolated words over headsets. Nor do we listen to sounds in isolation. The psycholinguistic literature shows that surrounding context plays an important part in processing speech sounds. To test this, Ladefoged and Broadbent asked Ss to circle the word they thought they heard (bit/bet/but/bat), which followed an instruction sentence ("please say what this word is"). When instructions were given at high pitch, the Ss reported hearing the high vowel in "bit." That is, they used pitch of previously presented information in "hearing" the vowel that followed, no matter which of the four words was presented.

Warren and Warren (1970) had Ss listen to a tape, which was spliced so that various words could be used to conclude the sentence: "There's a (cough) eel on the (axle/shoe/orange/table)." Asked to report what they heard, Ss filled in the appropriate sound according to the last word given. That is, they thought they heard wheel, heel, peel, or meal, depending on the final word—even though the first part of the tape was always the same. Context does shape our perception of discrete sounds. Still, redundancy helps, so we should do even better when people don't cough while speaking to us.

The above are examples of but a few of the many studies done in perception and production of speech sounds. Based on many such studies, a number of competing hypotheses regarding perception—such as the template and feature detection hypotheses—have been proposed. Another popular hypothesis is that we have an internal "speech synthesizer" which adjusts to the speaker's language, dialect, rate, voice quality, and so on. (Thus we avoid some of the problems of the template matching hypothesis.) This is called the "motor theory of speech perception." It suggests that as we listen we synthesize the motor movements of the other's speech. If we took this literally, it would mean that our synthesizer mouths the incoming data; that, figuratively, we talk to ourselves subvocally while listening to others talk. (Production and comprehension models would then be the same.) This would imply that we couldn't understand speech that we couldn't internally produce ourselves. We may want to take the hypothesis less literally, since we know that second language learners can easily understand the differences between ship and sheep in context, though they may not be able to produce the difference. As second language learners we understand much that we cannot produce. However, we may understand by overriding the phonological synthesizer using one of the higher level plans giving syntactic or discourse information.

Investigators of the phonological systems of second language learners have also looked to the research on speech errors, but errors in a different sense. Some of the errors are systematic phonological errors made consistently in the attempt to speak the new language. Others are less systematic, and some are even slips of the tongue. Four proposals, investigated in second language research, account for these errors: (1) contrastive analysis, (2) reactivated L1 phonological processes, (3) natural phonology and universal syllable structure, and (4) inter-language variable rules. Each proposal takes the accuracy of the linguistic units we have discussed as a given, yet each supports (or argues against) parts of rules or descriptive units proposed by linguists.

Contrastive Analysis

We all can identify, more or less accurately, a Japanese "accent," a Spanish "accent," or an Arabic "accent." It may appear that learners are simply transferring the pronunciation rules of the first language to English. Many teachers (and some textbook writers) believe that all learners need to do is learn the new sounds—those they cannot transfer from the first language. That transfer, however, is not as simple as it might appear. Correspondence between phonological systems can be extremely complicated.

Linguists have written descriptions of the sound systems of a variety of languages, and many of these have then been contrasted with English (for an example of contrastive analysis at its best, see Stockwell, Bowen, and Martin, 1965a). Contrastive descriptions allow us to predict pronunciation difficulties for learners, and a number of suggestions have been made for a hierarchy of difficulty based on the kinds of correspondences found between the native language and the target language. The accompanying table is an adaptation of a chart presented by Clifford Prator (personal communication, 1964), based on Stockwell's description of correspondences in Tagalog and English. (For another more complex hierarchy, see Stockwell, Bowen, and Martin, 1965b, p. 284).

The ideas presented in such hierarchies of difficulty are intuitively appealing. All ESL teachers know that certain sounds are more difficult for their students than others, and the hierarchy gives us a better understanding of why this may be so. The easiest sounds to produce should be those where there is strong correspondence in the two languages. The most difficult should be that where the mismatch is most complex. A number of studies have been done to see whether or not errors predicted by contrastive analysis actually occur, but the hierarchy itself has never been empirically tested.

As teachers, we know much about many languages, not because we have been exposed to those languages but because we are so attuned to the pronunciation problems of our students. If you know what your Japanese students' pronunciation of English sounds like, you know something about the

Table 1 Hierarchy of Difficulty

Ease–Difficulty (0–5)	Category	Num. Relationship Native Lang. → Target Lang.	Learning Process	Example
	Overdifferentiate:			
4	New category	0 → 1	Learn new item	Germans add /θ, ð/
3	Split category	1 → 2, n	Make new distinction	Japanese /l/ must split for /l, r/
	Underdifferentiate:			
2	Absent	1 → 0	Avoid production	Arabic Ss need not produce ʧ
1	Coalesced	2, n → 1	Overlook distinctions	Thai /θʰ, θ/ becomes /θ/
	Parallel:			
0	Transfer, no difference in shape or distribution	1 → 1	Transfer	Swedish /m/ to English /m/
3	Reinterpret shape or distribution differs	1 → 1	Give familiar item new shape or position	French dentals to alveolars

Japanese sound system. If you know what a Persian accent in English sounds like, you know something about Persian. Certain parts of the accent may stand out to you more than others, and the reverse can be said for learners—certain differences of the target language are more salient to them than others.

Child second language learners often show an almost immediate awareness of sound differences in the new language. Ravem (1974), observing his two Norwegian children acquiring English, noted that they did not hesitate to use Norwegian words in their early English utterances, but that they always changed the pronunciation of the Norwegian words to the way that word would be pronounced if it were English. That is, when they are unable to produce "real" English, they simply used Norwegian, overlaying it with the intonation and sound system of English. This is a very common phenomenon. Children often play at "speaking Spanish" and "speaking Russian" and believe they are, in fact, speaking those languages when they are simply speaking English but adopting Spanish or Russian phonological features. Jordens (personal communication) gives some interesting data on a Dutch child's performance in German. While her German was fluent, she sometimes used Dutch words, but added German pronunciation features. For example, she said "er geht verstopfen" using the Dutch word "verstoppen" in place of the German "verstecken" (meaning "to hide"). What is especially interesting about this is that it shows an "awareness" of an historical difference in the evolution of German and Dutch. About 800 A.D., German voiceless stops became either fricatives or affricates in certain environments. So, German /p/ became /pf/ while Dutch /p/ remained /p/, leaving a regular apposition of these sounds in Dutch and German cognates:

Dutch—paal, pond, kloppen
German—pfahl, pfund, klopfen

This child wasn't around in 800 A.D., nor does she read texts on historical linguistics; nevertheless, she has, figuratively, "heard all about it" and so tries to make Dutch pass for German by applying the rule.

In spite of all this supporting evidence for transfer and awareness of contrasts between the two languages, many studies have shown us that contrastive analysis alone cannot totally predict the ease or difficulty students have in perceiving or producing sounds in the new language. For example, Johansson (1973) studied the phonological errors of adults learning Swedish. Her twenty students were from a variety of first languages (Czech, Danish, English, Finnish, Greek, Hungarian, Polish, Portuguese, and Serbo-Croatian). While many of the phonological errors could be attributed to the first language and predicted from contrastive analysis, others could not. Some were over-generalizations of Swedish sounds; others could best be explained as approximations to the Swedish sounds. Johansson also suggested that certain Swedish sounds are intrinsically difficult to produce, and that this acts independently of interference, though interference may also reinforce the difficulty of sounds for the learner.

If, however, the contrastive analysis hypothesis is at least partially correct, we are still left with the problem of interpreting what it means. If there is interference, where does the interference take place? Does it mean that the learner is unable to intake, "hear," the incoming material accurately? Does it mean that the learner is able to hear accurately but is unable to analyze the system underlying what is heard? Does it mean the learner can hear and analyze, but that the motor commands for production don't work to match the analysis? Or does it mean that everything works except that when the motor commands go to the articulators, they are somehow resistant (frozen from overuse in L1 patterns) to the commands?

Some research along these lines has been done. Early research (Eimas, 1974) suggested that young children are sensitive to sound differences; They can hear differences that are not part of the system in their emerging phonology. Heart rate studies of very young infants have also shown that they are quite sensitive to novel sounds—that is, they are able to make fine phonetic distinctions between similar sounds. Adults were thought to be much less sensitive to differences that are not part of their language system. The Ladefoged and Broadbent study, mentioned earlier in this chapter, and Abramson and Lisker's study (1970) show that adults appear to "hear" in terms of the phonological system of their native languages; a finding that makes sense in light of the relatively unsuccessful attempts of many adult learners to acquire a nativelike accent in a second language. More recent research (Eilers, Wilson, and Moore, 1979), however, has shown that adults can distinguish sounds (e.g., differences in voice onset time), differences that are not part of their system. Therefore, we would expect that it is *not* that learners are *unable* to *hear* accurately.

Does it mean that the learner is able to hear accurately but does not *analyze* the material accurately? Does the learner convert the input using first language analysis? According to Trubetzkoy, "the sounds of the foreign language receive an incorrect phonological interpretation since they are strained through the 'phonological sieve' of one's own mother tongue" (1939, p. 52). A good deal of evidence supports this possibility. Arabic speakers appear to analyze English /θð/ as /s/ and /z/ and fail to distinguish /p/ from /b/. (In fact, one of my former students who writes me appends a "b.s." at the end of his letters.) Japanese students appear to analyze English /r, l/ in terms of Japanese. And it works the other way around for English speakers learning Arabic or Japanese. For example, Japanese has two variants of the phoneme /s/, [š] and [s]. Romaji, an orthography for writing Japanese in Roman characters, gives separate letters to these two allophones of /s/. This is probably because the Westerners who devised this romanization of Japanese heard them as phonemically distinct, as they are in English, and so gave them separate letters. Yet, all of these examples could be evidence of *production* difficulties rather than interference at the *analysis* level in *perception*.

Does it mean that learners are unable to produce the right commands for articulation? Perhaps the difficulty is in organizing the correct production plans.

Many second language learners report that their production does not match what they "hear in their heads." As a child, my son referred to his friend Violet as Biolet yet would protest vehemently if I called her Biolet. He could hear and process a difference which he could not produce. In Arabic, I can easily hear that my pharyngeal consonants do not match my interior model for those particular sounds. Briere (1966), however, found that American university students could produce the distinctions among Arabic pharyngeal consonants (probably by kinesthetic cue) even though they could not hear the differences among them.

Does it mean that learners are able to hear, analyze, and send out appropriate commands for articulation, but that the articulators are somehow resistant, "frozen," and don't respond? This seems highly unlikely. However, most adult second language learners do seem to feel that practice in articulating sounds, like other physical exercises, helps them to finally automatically produce sounds which were first learned through kinesthetic cues.

These studies have given us some initial clues to the nature of phonological interference. But the clues tell us that, somehow, all and none of the guesses about the nature of interference are correct. We need to learn much more if we are to feel comfortable when talking about the actual meaning of phonological interference in second language learning. It is clear that transfer/interference is an important source of error, but where and when it occurs, physiologically, is not clear.

Reactivated L1 Processes

When we look at second language data, we often see striking parallels with that of child first language learners. For example, adult second language learners often produce ungrammatical utterances such as "I no want" or "me sing," forms that also occur in data of children learning English as their native language. One might wonder, then, whether the learning of second language phonology recapitulates that of the child learning the sound system of a first language. D. K. Oller (1974) surveyed the somewhat sparse L2 English phonology literature, and compared the data from these studies with that of child language in three areas: simplification of consonant clusters, dropping of final consonants, and deletion of weak syllables. These processes are common in child phonology (e.g., "blue" pronounced as /buː/, "big" pronounced /bɪ/, and "banana" pronounced /nænə/). Oller found very different forms in the data of L2 English learners. Consonant clusters were not simplified in the studies he reviewed (however, see data from Finnish learners of Swedish given earlier in this chapter for counter examples). Rather, they were broken up and a vowel inserted (e.g., "tree" became /teri/). Vowels were added following final consonants (e.g., "big" became /bigu/). Weak syllables were never deleted. Finding little similarity between L2 phonology errors and the developmental forms used by child L1 learners, Oller suggested that the differences might be due to a number of factors (including L1 influence). For example, it may be that literate adult learners feel each letter must be pronounced, so few deletions would occur. He also noted that many L2 errors were the result of attempts to produce open CV (consonant + vowel) syllables, a common syllable pattern in most languages.

However, we should also remember that children acquiring first language phonology are learning how to control the vocal apparatus. For example, they acquire stops before fricatives, probably because it is easier to completely stop the oral cavity than it is to modify the shape just enough to produce friction in the appropriate place. Children also have problems sustaining voicing at the ends of words. This may be due to the physiological difficulty in building up enough pressure to continue vibrating the vocal folds. For the child, devoicing and dropping or weakening final consonants may be a matter of not yet having full physiological control. Physiological ease/difficulty may be an important factor in L2 phonology, especially for very young second language learners. (Itoh's 1978 study of a two-and-a-half-year-old Japanese child's acquisition of English phonology shows his problem with fricatives in both languages. Celce-Murcia's 1978 case study of her child acquiring French gives a delightful example of avoidance of difficult fricatives, leading to French-English creations such as pied-ball for football.)

In another case study of a six-year-old Icelandic child acquiring English fricatives, Mulford and Hecht (1980) first checked to see whether a contrastive analysis transfer hypothesis, or an L1 developmental hypothesis (based on the ordering of fricatives by child first language learners supplied by Olmsted, 1971), could best predict the Icelandic child's errors. The data are shown in Figures 2.1 and 2.2.

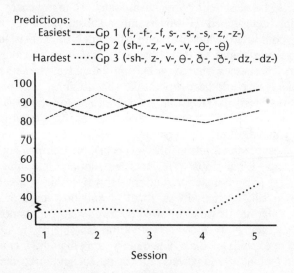

Figure 2.1 Developmental Hypothesis

Predictions:
        Easiest -----(s-, -s-, -s, f-, -f-, -f)
              -----(v-, -v-, ð-, -ð-, -ɵ-, -ɵ)
        Hardest ·····(z-, -z-, -z, sh-, -sh-, -dz, -dz-)
        (note that affricates are omitted)

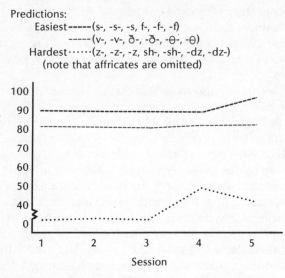

Session

Figure 2.2   Transfer Hypothesis

The data match the contrastive analysis transfer hypothesis better than the developmental hypothesis. However, if we look at the substitutions the child used for these particular problematic sounds, developmental claims could be made. For example, final /z/ was pronounced as /s/ by the child. Devoicing of final consonants is a common process for Icelandic consonants. However, it is also prevalent in child language data. Final /z/ pronounced as /s/ is acceptable in many adult speech styles as well. Neither interference nor developmental processes could be claimed as *the* causal factor. In many cases, errors were doubly or triply determined. However, only a subset of the possible developmental errors could also be linked to contrastive analysis. That is, in many cases (e.g., affricate weakening so that "cheese" /čiz/ was pronounced /ši:s/) developmental processes shared with first language learners rather than contrastive analysis could best explain the substitutions.

While the Mulford and Hecht paper does not go into detail regarding the rest of the child's developing L2 phonology, they mention that similarities with child L1 phonology may best predict substitutes used for fricatives (and contrastive analysis may best predict *where* errors will occur); but this may not hold true for other consonants. Final stops were devoiced (doubly determined as a child language process and a transfer prediction). However, they were also aspirated (e.g., "big" as /bikʰ/, "bread" as /bretʰ/, and this could only be due to interference. Velar nasals were followed by a velar stop, a phonotactic rule in Icelandic (e.g., "going" as /gowiŋk/, "sitting" as /sitiŋg/). Again, transfer must be used to explain the data. The quality of the liquids (*l, r*) also matched their values in Icelandic, and vowels retained the Icelandic accent flavor even a year after observations began. Mulford and Hecht suggest a continuum by which one could roughly account for the influence of transfer versus developmental patterns on second language phonology:

Vowels   Liquids   Stops   Fricatives & Affricates

transfer dominates   developmental predominates

They caution their readers to remember that this is only one case study; that there is always variability in each *S*'s data and among *S*s; and that the models in the input to this child must also be considered in accounting for errors and substitutions.

While definitions of "ease" for child first and second language learners may be similar, the definition of "ease" for the older child and adult is likely to be at least somewhat different. Adults must learn to articulate new sounds and make fine adjustments in articulating similar sounds. However, they have already learned to control the vocal apparatus well. We should not be surprised, then, that Oller found no strong evidence for the claim that the order of acquisition of sounds for adults in second languages might be the same as that of child first language learning.

Natural Phonology

Some segments and phonological processes are almost universal. For example, almost all languages have a series of voiceless stops, /p, t, k/ . /c/, an alveopalatal stop, appears much less frequently. This is probably because it is much more difficult for the tongue muscles to effect a full closure of the vocal tract in this area than for the dental, bilabial or velar positions. /t, p, k/, therefore, are more "natural" than /c/ and should be acquired earlier than /c/ by learners of languages that have this full series. It is also more "natural" that languages have voiceless than voiced stops, for it takes extra glottis control for the vocal folds to vibrate when the air is stopped in the oral tract. Conversely, it is more natural to have voicing for sonorants (the vowels, nasals, and liquids) where the vocal tract is not stopped. So, for languages with voiceless but no voiced stops, it is quite common that these voiceless stops become voiced between vowels.

The dental/alveolar area seems to be an easy, natural place of articulation. Most languages have dental or alveolar stops. Most languages have fricatives and for these the most common is the alveolar /s/. Similarly, most languages have an alveolar nasal /n/. Again, this seems to be related to ease of articulation in the dental and alveolar area.

Schane (1973) lists the following examples of natural segments and processes: (The notes in parentheses have been added to clarify the prediction of ease or difficulty of particular sounds for second language learning.)

1. Among three-vowel systems, *i, a,* and *u* are more natural than *I, æ* , and *o.* (ESL students should have more errors for *I, æ* , and *o* than *i, a,* and *u.*)

2. Languages with front rounded vowels also have front unrounded and back rounded vowels. (In learning such languages as French or Danish, it should be easier to learn the front unrounded and back rounded than the front rounded vowels.)

3. Languages that have nasalized vowels also have oral ones. (It should be easier to learn the oral vowels of languages such as French than the nasalized series.)

4. Among stops, *p, t,* and *k* are more natural than *p, t,* and *c.* (In learning languages such as Russian, it should be easier to learn *p, t,* and *k* than *c.*)

5. In child language, fricatives emerge after stops. (ESL learners should have more difficulty with fricatives than with stops.)

6. Languages with affricates also have stops and fricatives. (In English /č, ǰ/ should be harder than stops and fricatives.)

7. Anterior consonants emerge before nonanterior ones. (The dental and alveolar consonants should not be difficult.)

8. Languages with voiced obstruents also have voiceless ones. (Voiceless stops should give learners less trouble than voiced stops.)

9. Languages with labialized consonants also have plain ones. (Regular consonants should be easier to produce than their labialized counterparts.)

10. A rule that nasalizes vowels before nasal consonants is more natural than one that nasalizes vowels in word final position.

11. For obstruents to become voiceless in word final position is more expected than for obstruents to become voiced in that environment. (Devoicing of voiced final consonants should be expected in the speech of ESL learners.)

While some sound segments are more universal than others, they need not always be easy for the second language learner. It may be that the first language and the second language both have, say, the voiceless stops /p, t, k/, but that does not mean that the phonetic quality of the stops will necessarily be identical. For example, the French dental /t/ and the English alveolar /t/ are not exactly the same. English and Swedish may both have final voiced stops, but the amount of devoicing of the stop may be different. Korean and English may both have an aspirated series of initial voiceless stops, but the degree of aspiration is different. For this reason, comparisons of the phonetic value must be considered not only in doing contrastive analysis but also in evaluating natural phonology as an explanation of second language data.

In addition to the naturalness of segments, there are a number of natural processes likely in phonology. For example, it is common for nasals to take the articulation position of the following consonant. For example, in English, the nasal in the negative prefix *in-* (*in*accurate, *in*decisive) becomes /m/ before bilabials (*im*possible) and /ŋ/ before velars (at least for some speakers), as in *in*correct. Before liquids, they may even lose their nasal quality (illegal, irregular, rather than inlegal, inregular). As noted by Schane in item 11 above, it is quite common to have devoicing or weakening of consonants in word final position. Consonant clusters are also frequently simplified (one or the other of the consonants being dropped). Assimilation of segments to agree with neighboring sounds is a common process. These processes, then, should not be especially difficult for learners since they are associated with natural physiological processes.

Many of the natural rules for modification of articulation during rapid speech have to do with the natural move toward an open CV syllable. It has been suggested that all languages share a basic open syllable structure. It is the only syllable type that occurs in all languages. Some languages elaborate on the CV syllable much more than others.

In all languages, rapid speech may result in changes which move toward this basic CV syllable. Rapid speech changes nasal position and results in simplification of consonant clusters, in vowel reduction, and in liaison. This can easily be shown for English:

1. *nasal position &*   si/yə/n/tẽ/mĩ/nəts   See you in ten minutes.
   V nasalization   CV/CV/C/CV/CV/CVCC

                          ɪ/kæ̃/pɪ/dən   It can't be done.
                          V/CV/CV/CVC

2. *cluster simplification* gɪ/mi/ðə/ki   Give me the key.
                             CV/CV/CV/CV

3. *vowel reduction*   i/pʊ/tə/tã/nəs/kar   He put it in his car.
                       V/CV/CV/CV/CVC/CVC

4. *liaison*   dɪ/di/faɪn/dit   Did he find it?
                CV/CV/CVC/CVC

It has also been shown that, in addition to simplification of syllable structure due to speed, the speech of English speakers while under stress or when tired also moves toward this basic CV syllable structure. Tarone (1976) suggests that some of the errors of second language learners might be due to the natural pressure to use open CV syllables in the new language. Second language performance is also a stressful situation for many learners, so even though they may have consonant clusters in their first language, learners may be prone to produce CV syllables in English. Interlanguage data should be very rich in CV syllables.

To test this hypothesis, Tarone conducted a study asking six Ss from three language backgrounds (Hong Kong Cantonese, Brazilian Portuguese, and Korean) to tell a story about a set of pictures presented in a story sequence. The taped data was transcribed in narrow phonetic transcription for analysis. Unlike Oller, Tarone found that these learners did delete final consonants, producing CV syllables where CVC syllables were called for. They also produced CV syllables by adding V's to clusters. The two Portuguese speakers added vowels to consonant clusters (epenthesis) to produce CV syllables more frequently than they deleted C's. The Cantonese and Korean students used both final C deletion and vowel insertion equally often in order to produce CV syllables. A final strategy used by subjects was the insertion of glottal stops to separate lexical items when the second word began with a V (again maintaining the basic CV syllable).

Tarone then looked at the syllable structure of Cantonese, Korean, and Portuguese. She found that Korean is closer to English in syllable structure elaboration than either Cantonese or Portuguese. The Korean students made fewer English syllable errors than the other subjects. Though Cantonese and Portuguese have more open CV syllables than English, clusters are possible across word boundaries. Once an exhaustive list of possible consonant combinations within and across syllables for each of the three languages was drawn up, Tarone was able to see which errors could be accounted for as native language transfer or interference and which could not.

Tarone's findings can be summarized as follows: First, the syllable structure of learners of English is often quite different from that of English speakers. Learners use both epenthesis (addition of vowels to break up consonant clusters) and consonant deletion to maintain a CV syllable structure. The first language seems to relate both to the preference of one strategy over another and to the number of errors made. The dominant process influencing syllable structure for these learners appears to be language transfer, although less than half of one of the Korean S's errors could be accounted for in this way. A preference for the open CV syllable must operate as a process independent of language transfer (though it may be reinforced by transfer).

Researchers who like to draw parallels between second language acquisition and descriptions of pidgins may want to add natural phonology and the move to open syllables to their discussions, since they may be characteristic of both. There are, however, obvious problems with naturalness theory applied to acquisition research. As Anderson (1980) has pointed out, languages do, with depressing regularity, include *un*natural rules as well. Recent studies (e.g., Bach and Harms, 1972) have, as Anderson suggests, shown a disconcerting tendency for natural rules to be replaced by "crazy" rules. Why this should be the case is not clear. Instead, natural rules should prevail. Still, it does appear that some sounds are difficult, if not impossible, to produce and do not appear in most languages. Labiodental stops, as Ladefoged (1980) says, could only be made by people with no spaces between their teeth. Yet, if naturalness alone were to determine which sounds are produced in languages, eventually all languages should have uniform inventories of sounds. That is not the case. As both Ladefoged and Anderson state, phonological universality and naturalness probably reflect a natural balance between the demands of speech production, the physiology of the human vocal tract, perception, the physical acoustics of sound transmission in air, structural properties of the auditory system, learnability, memory, and other cognitive factors.

Just as phoneticians question the power of naturalness theory, Tarone and other researchers suggest that learners' errors in the target language phonology cannot be accounted for by natural phonology or natural phonological processes alone. However, such processes *are* important and must be considered along with contrastive interference theory.

Interlanguage as a Set of Variable Rules

In ESL pronunciation classes, we usually diagnose students' problems in pronunciation by a combination of error and contrastive analyses, then turn to an instruction program that works on segmentals in initial position, then final position, and then medial position of selected words. When students are able to produce the sounds at least part of the time, we may give them feedback information on some sort of scale like: very wrong—not so wrong—almost right—right. We are aware that they still make errors, yet we see the errors as random and unsystematic. We may be puzzled when learners are not consistent in articulating problematic sounds. Why should they backslide once they are able to produce the sound?

Dickerson (1975) has applied the notion of variable rules to account for seeming inconsistency in second language learner data. She tape-recorded ten Japanese ESL students once each quarter (three times during the university academic year) as they read lists of words, read dialogues, and spoke spontaneously. She then transcribed the tapes in phonetic detail. Since all students showed a high frequency of error on /r, l, z/, their production of these three sounds was analyzed over time.

Dickerson found that all ten students had problems with the same sounds. Further, they all used the same pronunciation variants; variants which were influenced by the sounds that follow. For example, four environments were found that affected the pronunciation of /z/ : (1) /z/ followed by a vowel; (2) /z/ followed by a consonant other than those listed under 4 below; (3) /z/ followed by silence; and (4) /z/ followed by /ɵ, ð, t, d, č, ǰ/ . The easiest environment was 1 and the most difficult, 4. For each subject a bar graph was drawn to show the percent of occurrence for each of the variants for Time 1, Time 2, and Time 3. When it was followed by a vowel, students generally used the correct form /z/. In environment 2, three variants appeared: /s, ǰ, z/. The students gradually improved so that /z/ became the preferred form by Time 3 and /ǰ/ dropped out entirely, leaving /s, z/ in competition in that environment. In environment 3, most of the students used the unvoiced /s/ for /z/ at the ends of words. This gradually changed so that at Time 2 the two forms appear to be approximately of equal frequency, and at Time 3, /z/ gained in prominence. In cnvironment 4, five variants were used: /ɵ, s, ǰ, z, ž/. By Time 2 only /ɵ, z, ž/ were used; and the percentages shifted to about 60 percent accuracy of /z/ at Time 3. These estimates are based on a bar graph for one student which is cited as being representative of the findings in the report. While all students did follow this progression, there were differences among the students. That is, some students began with a higher percent correct in each of the environments, and some students also made more rapid progress than others. Improvement occurred in all environments over time.

The practical implications of Dickerson's work are important. First, she believes that teachers' and students' attitudes about pronunciation errors would change if they saw that correct/incorrect variation is not random but conditioned by linguistic environments. Teacher and student expectations would also change since they would expect this variability. Third, she believes that the identification of variable rule environments would help in the evaluation of student progress. Teachers would see that students are not stubbornly resisting instruction but that they are, instead, actually making progress in pronunciation of problematic sounds.

The theoretical implications are also important because the environments shown in variable rules are not random. Is it possible to predict the environments on some basis, perhaps by physiological difficulty of articulation? We already know that certain segments are likely to be more difficult than others. Schane's natural rules for devoicing of final stops and for nasalization relate to environments as well as to the segments themselves. Additional predictions on the ease/difficulty of consonants in (1) initial position, (2) between vowels, and (3) in final position could be made. The ease/difficulty of single segments in these positions could then be contrasted with the same segments in consonant clusters in each of the positions. The difficulty of the clusters themselves could also be predicted on the basis of the complexity of the surrounding consonants and the transitions required in articulating the cluster. A number of interesting predictions might be made in terms of natural phonology and environments. They could be opposed to a purely contrastive analysis set of predictions and tested. Then a combination of naturalness and contrastive difficulty could be made and a new hierarchy of difficulty, perhaps with better predictive power, could be proposed.

Students' variable performance might also be influenced by the formality of the speech situation. Most people articulate more accurately or carefully in formal rather than informal situations. Ma and Herasimchuk(1971), investigating the pronunciation of Puerto Rican Spanish-English bilinguals, showed, for example, that English /r/ followed by a consonant was articulated more accurately in formal than informal contexts. The use of /ə, ø/ for /r/ increased with informality of the speech situation:

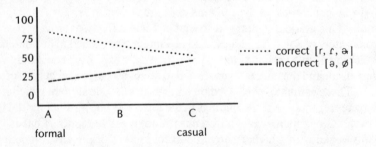

Figure 2.3   Accuracy of /r/

Schmidt(1977) also showed that Arabic Ss' pronunciation of the English *th* sounds became more accurate when they were given a formal task(reading word lists), rather than an informal task(conversation).

Since the formality of the speech situation may change the degree of accuracy with which particular sounds are produced, teachers should consider this factor in evaluating the performance of their students. Students may be more likely to articulate accurately when doing a formal task in class than in conversations with teachers outside class.

It is not clear, however, that formality of the speech situation will invariably cause the learner to use more accurate forms. Beebe (1980) considered the production of English /r/ by nine Thai speakers. She found that the social weight of the particular sounds in first language speech styles might also influence second language production. For example, in informal conversational contexts, initial /r/ was pronounced correctly in 38 percent of all occasions. In formal tasks it was produced correctly only 9 percent of the time. This is because the most *correct r* for initial position in Thai according to Royal usage is a trilled *r*. The formal trilled *r*, therefore, has high social value in Thai. In the English data of her Thai speakers, the trilled *r* did not occur once in the informal conversational data, while students attempted to produce it consistently in the formal tasks. Social value attached to particular forms in the first language is, therefore, another variable to consider when attempting to explain second language data.

Influenced by Dickerson's work, Gatbonton (1978) suggested that a diffusion model, rather than variable rules, better explains language learner phonology. When Labov proposed variable rules for first language data, the basic principle was that certain pronunciation variants would be favored by a given context. Bickerton (1973) suggested that variable rules were not appropriate when describing learner data, for there, old rules are gradually replaced as the new rule is acquired. As the new rule comes in, the old and new may both appear in the same context for a time. The learner gradually acquires a form—that is, a new form appears, competes with an old form, and then replaces it (as shown in Table 2 where 1 = old form and 2 = new, correct form). The environmental categories (only three are presented in the table; more or fewer might occur in the data) show where variants occur. The rows indicate the

Table 2   Diffusion Model

Stages	Environmental Categories		
	A	B	C
Acquisition phase:			
a	1	1	1
b	1,2	1	1
c	1,2	1,2	1
d	1,2	1,2	1,2
Replacement phase:			
e	2	1,2	1,2
f	2	2	1,2
g	2	2	2

1 = old form; 2 = new form.

different stages learners may go through as they acquire the target sound. Only incorrect variants (1's) are found at stage a, and only correct variants (2's) are found in the final stage. Between the initial and final stages, the correct forms are shown as they appear in the acquisition phase and then as they take over all environments in the replacement phase.

Testing the model, Gatbonton found that it fit the English performance of twenty-seven French Canadian adults who were ESL learners. The three sounds examined were /ð/ (the *th* in "brother," "seethe," etc.), /θ/ (the *th* in "teeth," "think," etc.), and /h/ (as in "behind," "he," etc.). The Ss read word lists and two diagnostic paragraphs. They were also taped in natural spontaneous speech settings. The environment categories for each phoneme were specified and each learner was placed on the scale as having all correct, all incorrect, or a combination of correct and incorrect. The model specifies that "... for each individual some environmental categories are ordered, so that mastery of target sounds is characterized first by the gradual acquisition of correct variants across these categories and then by the gradual elimination of incorrect ones in exactly the same orderly manner. Individuals could, in principle, differ in the precise ordering of the categories." (Gatbonton, 1978, p. 344)

The diffusion model differs from variable rules in that it emphasizes the gradual replacement process rather than investigating errors in general. No a priori predictions are made as to the environment nor the hierarchy of difficulty across environments. This is not a model in which an hypothesized order of difficulty is first set up and then tested. Rather, the model predicts difficulty by establishing the order or scale. In this model one searches for a scale (the gradual move from incorrect to correct) and then tests the scale to discover the systematicity of the progression; so it is important that research also describe precisely how "scalable" the data actually are. Unfortunately, in the studies mentioned so far this has not been done.

Amastae (1978) combined implicational and diffusion models in his investigation of the accuracy with which nine fluent Spanish-English bilinguals used certain English vowels. His implicational scale for the nine Ss shows an error hierarchy as shown in Table 3 (where 2 = standard form only and 1 = variation between standard and other forms).

The easiest, or most correct, was /o/ and the most difficult, /ɪ/. Theoretically, a S who got /æ/ correct should also have /o/ correct; a S who got /ʊ/ correct should get /æ/ and /o/ correct, etc. Notice that S2 contradicts this principle. Since /ɛ/ is correct, she should have also produced all others below /ɛ/ without difficulty. However, the easiest phoneme, /o/, was missed. Similarly, if a S got only one item correct, it should be an /o/; two correct should be /o/ and /æ/, etc. S8 contradicts this by getting /ɪ/, the hardest, prior to getting /ʊ/ and /ɛ/. So, while the data is a close match to the ideal model, it is not an exact match. A coefficient of reproducibility (which gives us a first approximation as to how close to the ideal prediction the data sample is) of .96

Table 3 Implicational Scale for Vowels

S	/o/	/æ/	/U/	/E/	/I/
9	1	1	1	1	1
8	2	2	1	1	②
7	2	2	1	1	1
6	2	2	2	1	1
5	2	2	2	2	1
4	2	2	2	2	1
3	2	2	2	2	1
2	①	2	2	2	1
1	2	2	2	2	1

shows us that the difficulty order of the items can be predicted. (This figure is obtained by dividing the total number of errors—the two circled—by the total number of responses (see Table 3), 9 Ss × 5 vowels or 45, and then subtracting this from 1. So. 2/45 = .04 and 1 − .04 = .96.)

Table 4 is a diffusion model chart set up for the vowel data. Amastae placed S9 at the end of the replacement phase (the S was using a mixture of correct and incorrect forms for all vowels). Ss 7, 6, 5, 4, 3, and 1 were placed in the acquisition phase since for some vowels they consistently used correct forms. Ss 8 and 2 did not fit the model since they did not produce the vowels in the order predicted by the model (S8, 22XX2, and S2, X222X).

This study is interesting precisely because it raises so many questions. For example, how variable are the X's? If a S got /æ/ correct 10 percent of the time, it's an X; if a S got /æ/ correct 90 percent of the time, it's still an X. Much information has been lost on how close each S was to a 1 or a 2 for each vowel.

Table 4 Diffusion Model for Vowels

	OW	æ	U	E	I	
Interference phase	1	1	1	1	1	
Replacement phase	X	1	1	1	1	
	X	X	1	1	1	
	X	X	X	1	1	
	X	X	X	X	1	
	X	X	X	X	X	S9
Acquisition phase	2	X	X	X	X	
	2	2	X	X	X	S7
	2	2	2	X	X	S6
	2	2	2	2	X	S5, 4, 3, 1
	2	2	2	2	2	

1 = incorrect; X = variation; 2 = correct

Percentage data with cutoffs set at 60, 70, or 80 percent correct might give us more accurate information on the actual ordering of these vowels. Second, Amastae points out that he did not include all problematic vowels so that /u, ə, ʌ, ɔ, e/ should be added. He expects, however, that /u/ and /e/ would cluster with /o/—that is, would be learned early and that /ɔ/ would cluster with /ɛ/. With a larger range of vowels and more Ss, true scalability of the data would be easier to assess. Amastae also notes that he did not statistically examine the position, that is, the environments in which the vowels occurred. This, given the findings of previous research, would also be important in any attempt to establish scalability of the order in which vowels are acquired.

In spite of these problems, Amastae draws some interesting hypotheses about the data in his attempt to show underlying similarities with first language data, and how the data might also be related to markedness theory (which is linked to natural phonology). In the L1 studies he cites, /ɪ/ and /ɛ/ and /ʊ/ seem to appear late in child language. In misperception studies, he points out that adults have been least accurate in consistently interpreting /ɪ, ɛ, a, ɔ, ʌ/. This may be due to intrinsic vowel length (Peterson and Lehiste, 1960, have listed /i, ʊ, ə, ɛ, o/ as shortest to longest). In terms of language universals, the most commonly occurring vowels are those of the five-vowel triangle /i, e, a, o, u/. It isn't clear from the Stanford Archive data display that the order is statistically similar to those of child language, misperception orders, or to this second language data. Nevertheless, there appears to be some similarity among them. Amastae then relates this to markedness theory.

The test for markedness supposedly rests on its psychological reality. That is, the less marked an element is the easier it should be to acquire (child language and second language data), and the more natural (more universal and simpler in terms of articulatory effort) and the more neutral the form should be. Having looked at the vowel data from child language, and at the frequency with which these particular vowels occur as phonemes or as variants of phonemes in the languages of the world (Stanford Archives), and at his second language data, Amastae felt that there were strong similarities. Based on this, he turned to the rules for markedness in generative phonology. These rules already show that /a/ is less marked than /æ/ so /a/ should be learned before /æ/ (as it is in Amastae's data). As you can see in Schane's list in the preceding section, /i/ should be easier than /ɪ/. Amastae proposed new rules which would also show that /ʊ/ is less marked than /ɛ/ or /ɪ/ and that /ɛ/ is less marked than /ɪ/. The form of the proposed rules is not important here. The proposed change of rules for markedness, however, shows that second language data can be a rich source against which theoretical linguists can test and evaluate their descriptions of phonology.

Eckman has proposed a "markedness differential hypothesis" which combines the strengths of contrastive analysis and markedness theory. He believes that problems in second language learning can be predicted by comparing the two languages, but that:

a. Those areas of the target language which differ from the native language and are more marked than the native language will be difficult.
b. The relative degree of difficulty of the areas of the target language which are more marked than the native language will correspond to the relative degree of markedness.
c. Those areas of the target language which are different from the native language, but are not more marked than the native language will not be difficult. (1977, p. 321)

This modification of contrastive analysis to include markedness theory should be important to language teachers who are truly interested in the natural order in which sounds of new languages might be learned and in the explanations or reasons behind that order. However, as Rutherford (1981) has pointed out, the markedness differential hypothesis for contrastive analysis assumes (as does error analysis) that the proof of difficulty is the making of errors. This is not necessarily true, since many learners have difficulty with sounds they make correctly. A second problem is that the hypothesis can only make statements about areas where markedness relationships have been made specific.

A final note on variable rules and the diffusion model (which also applies to the use of variable rules and implicational scaling elsewhere for both syntactic and phonological rules): When adopting methods we must be very careful to carry out the statistical procedures on which they rest. We must also take care to report the procedures we use. None of the papers discussed above report on the scalability of the data, although Amastae does, at least, include the coefficient of reproducibility. Unless the data is scalable, the statistics reported are meaningless. This does not mean that the data in these studies are not scalable. It only emphasizes the importance of including this information (a coefficient of scalability over .60) in reporting findings. For further discussion of this issue, see Hatch and Farhady, 1982.

Suprasegmental System

So far in this chapter we have looked at the research on isolated speech segments, features, and syllable structure. Overlaying the segmental speech units is the suprasegmental system. This system includes pitch, stress, intonation, and tone. Much information is conveyed by the suprasegmental system. Some of the information is linguistic. Differences in intonation tell us whether an utterance is a statement or a question. Intonation also delineates units within an utterance. In written text, linguistic information given in speech by intonation curves is marked by periods, question marks, and commas. Stress differences in utterances also give us meaning differences, such as the following example from Bruder and Paulston (1976):

> You didn't EAT that watermelon, did you?
> (No, I gave it away.)
> You didn't eat THAT watermelon, did you?
> (No, I ate the other one.)
> You didn't eat that WATERmelon, did you?
> (No, I ate the banana.)

Students from syllable-timed languages (e.g., Spanish) find such contrasts in stress difficult to manage. More difficult in suprasegmentals, however, may be the mastery of tone. Many university students who begin to study Chinese or other tone languages simply cannot believe that tone plays such an important role in language. Apparently it is extremely difficult for adults to acquire this part of the new language system.

Beyond linguistic information, the suprasegmental system also gives us information on personal variables such as age, sex, and perhaps temperament and character of the speaker. It may also give us sociolinguistic information, information on where speakers are from, their social membership, their status, or the formality they think situations have. It also gives us expressive information, information on the speaker's emotions, feelings, moods, conviction, sincerity, and so on. The suprasegmental system may also give message-bound meaning (e.g., accidents such as "oops"). Finally, intonation may tell us about the function of a statement—whether a statement (for example, Crystal's 1969, "This is the third time he's been to see me this week") is a complaint, an announcement, a doubt, a suspicion, and so on.

Psycholinguists have conducted a number of studies trying to mask out message information, leaving only the basic intonation and other suprasegmental system information. Little work, however, has been done in this area with second language learners. Before proposing research involving second language learners, Gasser (1979) suggests that first we must discover whether or not native speakers can reliably identify the differences signaled by the suprasegmental system of the language. He asked English speakers to listen to sentences such as "I'd like to talk to you" and to judge from the suprasegmentals whether the speaker's status was higher or lower than, or the same as, the addressee's. He also used such sentences with different suprasegmental overlays to try to discover whether or not native speakers could identify the formal, informal, or sexual relationship between speaker and addressee. He used sentences like "Your paper's really interesting" to tap Ss' recognition of and agreement on conviction, sincerity, faked conviction, lack of conviction, and sarcasm. He tested Ss' agreement in their judgments of boredom, irritation, exasperation, distaste, hatred, sadness, resignation, worry, fear, guilt, happiness, relief, amusement, confidence, interest, admiration, surprise, puzzlement, and uncertainty, by having them listen to such sentences as "There's that little dog in the garden again" as well as the "I'd like to talk to you" sentence (with different suprasegmental overlays).

Gasser's Ss agreed in their judgments of speaker-listener status and the formal and sexual relationship of speaker and listener. They also agreed on conviction and faked conviction, but disagreed on sarcasm (confusing it with faked conviction). They agreed on some of the "emotion" items and not on others. They confused guilt with uncertainty, surprise with happiness. In a similar experiment Egan (1980) tape-recorded the utterance "On Sunday" using seventeen different intonation curves. He then had fifteen native speakers of English rate each utterance as (as not) appropriate on a six-point scale with a list of descriptors. Since there were so many descriptors, Egan used factor analysis to group them. The results are shown in Table 5 (the titles for the factors are Egan's).

Table 5 Factor Clusters

Credence	Option	Salience	Arousal	Weak belief
sure	hopes	amused	surprised	thinks
believes	wants it to be	concerned	can't believe	suspects
doubts	bugs her	worried	excited	orders
wonders	fears	glad		
asking	glad	bugs her		
knows	requests	fears		
requests	excited			

In a second experiment, Egan had fifteen additional native speakers of English listen to the "On Sunday" tape while looking at pairs of descriptors and judging the speakers' "frame of mind" on the descriptors according to the intonation. Multidimensional scaling techniques resulted in groups similar to those discovered through factor analysis.

While Egan was able to identify five factor groups as important for the assignment of meanings to intonation, the study gives little information on how uniform *S*s' judgments were. It is surprising (and happy), in one sense, that Gasser found as much agreement as he did, since Bolinger (1961) and others have pointed out that the signals are seldom clear or unambiguous. Labov and Fanshel, in fact, think this is a plus:

Speakers need a form of communication which is *deniable*. It is advantageous for them to express hostility, challenge the competence of others, or express friendliness and affection in a way that can be denied if they are held explicitly to account for it. (1977, p. 46)

If suprasegmental cues were completely explicit, we might have trouble denying—that we didn't mean X the way it sounded. However, if native speakers can agree as much as Gasser has suggested on the meanings conveyed by the suprasegmental system, the next question is whether L2 learners also recognize the meanings of suprasegmentals. That is, are the meanings universal? Gumperz suggests they are not:

The . . . incident . . . took place in London on a bus driven by a West Indian driver/conductor. The bus was standing at a stop, and passengers were filing in. The driver announced periodically, "Exact change, please," as London bus drivers often do. When passengers who had been standing close by either did not have money ready or tried to give him a large bill, the driver repeated, "Exact change, please." The second time around, he said "please" with extra loudness, high pitch, and falling intonation, and he seemed to pause before "please." One passenger so addressed, as well as several following him, walked down the bus aisle exchanging angry looks and obviously annoyed, muttering, "Why do these people have to be so rude and threatening about it?" (1977, p. 199)

The bus driver wasn't really annoyed nor did he intend to be rude. The driver should have used rising intonation on "please." The intonation was (using British English rules) interpreted as excessively direct and rude. Another example from Gumperz shows how important the suprasegmental system can be for the second language learner:

In a staff cafeteria . . . newly hired Indian and Pakistani women were perceived as surly and uncooperative by their supervisors as well as by the cargo handlers whom they served. Observation revealed that while relatively few words were exchanged, the intonation and manner in which these words were pronounced were interpreted negatively. For example, a person who had chosen meat would have to be asked whether he wanted gravy. A British attendant would ask by saying, "Gravy?" with rising intonation. The Indian women, on the other hand, would say the word using falling intonation: "Gravy." We taped relevant sequences, including interchanges like these, and asked the employees to paraphrase what they meant in each case. At first the Indian workers saw no difference. However, the English teacher and the supervisor could point out that "gravy" said with falling intonation means "This is gravy" and is not interpreted as an offer but rather as an announcement. (1977, p. 208)

For the women, falling intonation was the normal way of asking questions to make an offer, and no rudeness or indifference had been intended. Happily, following practice and change in intonation, improvement was also found in the attitudes of the clients toward the Indian workers, and the women no longer felt that they were being discriminated against (a natural reaction to the behavior their "rudeness" provoked).

It has become a cliché to say that the suprasegmental system is more important in second language intelligibility than segmentals. One may have learned the segmentals well but, because of stress and intonation, be virtually incomprehensible. The suprasegmental system is a higher-level plan than the segmental plan. Stress placement and the intonation curves determine how various words within the sentence will be pronounced. That is, we do not select a word from our mental dictionaries, decide how to pronounce it, and then say it. We organize entire phrases, and the suprasegmental system tells us which words will receive stress (and therefore full vowel value) and which will not (where vowels will be reduced). Fromkin has suggested that the intonation plan depends on syntactic structure rather than on individual words. Her speech error data shows that the intonation contour of utterances often remains the same as it is in the intended message before words are disordered.

In the intended utterance "Seymour sliced the salami with a knife" the highest pitch would be on knife. In the disordered sentence (Seymour sliced the knife with a salami) the highest pitch occurred on the second syllable of "salami." Thus, the intonation of the original sentence was maintained, evidence that intonation must be constructed prior to articulation and depends on the syntactic structure. (Fromkin, 1973a, pp. 115)

While it seems more plausible that intonation depends both on discourse and on syntactic plans, whatever the order of plans within the hierarchy, differences in meaning signaled by stress, juncture, and intonation are important in second language learning. Consider the difficulty we have in disambiguating utterances such as: "What did she find out there?," "They arrived late today," "I couldn't recommend him too highly," and "We prefer reading to music." Without the suprasegmental cues, it is impossible to interpret such sentences accurately. If the suprasegmental system gives the same reading for each meaning of the sentence, we can only understand if we go to context (the discourse plan) for information.

Within the phonological level, we can summarize that the study of speech errors has given linguists evidence to support many of the units of language descriptions. The early analysis of error data of second language learners, since it focused on error, led naturally to a study of interference/transfer. The subsequent shift from simply looking at errors to studying the changing phonological system of the learners as they acquire the target language has led us to a richer understanding of possible sources of error beyond those of transfer and interference. The investigation of naturalness and markedness in phonological theory may reveal much of value to second language researchers. Nevertheless, at the phonological and suprasegmental levels, contrastive analysis does have some predictive power. We are left, though, with the intriguing question of what "interference" really is, where (physiologically) it occurs and when (linguistic environments) it occurs. Given the many unresolved questions on the development of sound systems in a second language, and given the availability of a variety of second language learners to help us answer our questions, we can expect to learn much from new research in this area.

The study of speech errors, however, tells us little about listening comprehension or the role of phonology in that process. While several hypotheses have been made on how we comprehend the stream of speech, none are very appealing. Levinson and Liberman (1981) are not the first to say that it is much more difficult to build a speech analyzing computer to *comprehend* language than a speech synthesizer to *produce* language. They found it impossible to build templates for either phonemic or distinctive features and to expect the computer to analyze incoming speech in terms of those templates. The distortion of each sound by the surrounding sounds makes the template-matching task impossible. They found it easier to build *word* templates and have the computer match these to process incoming data (though this works only when the number of words to be recognized is fairly limited). Many problems are involved in using the word as the basic unit of analysis, as is made clear in the following chapters. Thousands of templates would have to be stored, and the problems in word retrieval would be immense. We know that we must be using some system at the phonological level for part of our language proooooing, but how we do this is yet a mystery.

To understand a new language, and to speak it well, we must use all levels in the hierarchy of plans. Accuracy at each level is important. However, just how important each level is to comprehension and production of language is not yet known. The phonological level and the suprasegmental system must play important parts in both comprehension and production, especially when one is learning a second language. Thus we find that second language data is a valuable source for psycholinguists who search for evidence to support (or to contradict) their linguistic claims about the phonological systems of language.

3 *Morphology*

If you opened a psycholinguistic dictionary looking for the word "wug," you might find it described as a little creature created by Jean Berko-Gleason. You would not be surprised, should you look, to discover no separate listings for wugs, or wug's, or wuggy. Each of these "words" means something slightly different, yet they are semantically related. If there are no such entries in the dictionary, it is because we can predict the variants. We know the "rules" of affixation that let us form new words from old. It is unlikely that our mental dictionaries would have entries for each of the following as separate words: write, written, writes, writing, wrote. It seems much more likely that we have one form and a set of rules to produce the others. Yet, what evidence is there that this is so?

One source of evidence is language acquisition data. Berko devised an ingenious method of testing production of affixes by preschool, first grade, and adult native speakers of English. The test consists of a set of pictures illustrating nonsense words. The point of using nonsense words is to be sure the children did not simply memorize the various words with their morphological endings intact. The test consists of twenty-seven items, each testing a particular morpheme rule, similar to the following examples (for exact items, see Berko, 1958).

This is a wug. Now there are two of them. There are two. . . ? (wugs /z/ voiced form of plural)

This is a bird who knows how to rick. It is ricking. It did the same thing yesterday. What did it do yesterday? Yesterday it. . . ? (ricked /t/ voiceless form of past tense)

This is a nizz. Now there are two of them. There are two. . . ? (nizzes /əs/ form of plural)

This is a frog who knows how to mot. He is motting. He did the same thing yesterday. What did he do yesterday? Yesterday he. . . ? (motted /əd/ form of the past tense)

This is a little wug. What would you call such a small wug? It's a. . . ? (wuggy, wuglet—diminutive)

This wug lives in this house. What would you call a house a wug lives in? It's a. . . ? (wughouse, wug-home, wugwam—noun compounding)

This is a blick. Now there are two of them. There are two. . . ? (blicks /s/ voiceless form of plural)

The *S*s were twelve adults and fifty-six children from preschool and first grade groups. The results clearly support the claim that children have a set of internalized rules for forming plurals, possessives, *-ing* continuous, past tense, and present. There were differences between the preschool and first grade groups, mainly on rules for forming plural and past tense forms that require an additional syllable (e.g., *nizzes, motted*). Adults also made a few errors on the production of these same rules (e.g., *wugzez hat*).

Using Berko's test and the Spanish version by Kernan and Blount (1966), Marilyn Adams (1972) tried it with bilingual *S*s, Mexican-American children in the Los Angeles area. Sample Spanish items follow:

las tifas

Esta es una tifa. Ahora hay otra. Hay dos de ellas. ¿Hay dos. . . ?

Este es un hombre que sabe ticar. Está ticando. ¿Cómo se llama un hombre que tica?

El hombre tica. Mañana lo hará. ¿Mañana, el. . . ?

About the same time, Swain, Naiman, and Dumas (1972) constructed a French version of the Berko test and gave it to Canadian children attending a French immersion kindergarten. Sample French items follow:

Voici un gof. Maintenant voici deux. . . ?

Voici un homme qui pole. Hier el a. . . ?

Voici une fille qui est cherte. Voici aussi un garçon qui est. . . ?

Voici un homme qui dape. Demain il va. . . ?

Voici un homme qui va tifer. Maintenant il. . . ?

These studies are evidence that children follow internal rules for morphology in both their first and second languages. Following these studies, many other studies have reported on the acquisition of such rules by second language learners (cf., Natalicio and Natalicio, 1971; Martinez-Bernal, 1972; Johnson, 1973; Heckler, 1975), using variations of the Berko model of nonsense words as stimuli.

Speech error data are also evidence that affixes are psychologically separate units and that we use rules to apply them to particular lexical items. Fromkin (1973*b*) found that native speakers of English do make slips of the tongue in applying these rules. They said such things as motion*ly* for motion*less*, blood*ent* for blood*y*, sequenc*ingly* for sequent*ially*, explanat*ing* for explana-*tory*. This is evidence that we do not have separate entries in our mental dictionaries for each of these forms, but rather use rules for applying affixes; and when rushed or tired we make errors in applying them.

Error data also show us something of the reality of rules of affixation in second language learning. The following errors were found by Nemser(1971) in compositions of Hungarian college students: *cruelism* for *cruelty, enviness* for *envy, hungriness* for *hunger, alienatedness* for *alienation, ignoration* for *ignorance, destroyation* for *destruction, deconcentrate* for *dilute,* and others such as *inferiorate* and *dissatisfactional* which have no direct equivalent. Hungarian has many more affixes, and affixes are more productive, more regular than in English. It should not be surprising, then, that Hungarian students try to transfer this productivity to English morphology.

Linguists as well as language learners have difficulty deciding on the exact relationship among lexical items that are related by affixation. When the system is regular, as in the inflectional system, the problems do not seem so immense. As linguists, we feel comfortable with rules for forming plurals and possessives, rules for forming continuous aspect, and rules for forming past tense. As teachers, we also feel we are on solid ground, for the inflectional system appears to be regular. But, as shown in the errors of Hungarian students above and similar data on Arabic students (Al-Naggar, 1977), derivational affix rules in English are not as regular, as productive, or as easy to learn as we might wish.

Derivational Morphology

While most derivational affixes can be used occasionally to form new words, only certain affixes are highly productive; for example, *un-* and *re-* can be widely used. Some affixes come and go in vogue (e.g., *-teria* as in *cafeteria, bookateria, chocolateria, washateria,* or *-nik* as in *beatnik, TVnik*). Others are highly productive but only in one small domain (e.g., *-ese* for language or a group, as in *journalese, educationese, TESLese*).

The boundaries of even the most productive affixes are difficult to define. For example, *-able,* as in *washable,* is now so productive that we can easily use it to form new words such as *doable.* However, Thompson (1974) points out that -*able* is not productive for two-word verbs (*pickup-able, *talkable to). We may use it for *listenable* but not *listen toable or *listenable to, and the problem for the learner and linguist is to discover the extent to which such affixes can be applied.

Second language learners are faced with having to develop a feel for just how productive affixes are, *and* they must also decide on which form of the affix to use. For example, there are several negative prefixes (*dis*honest, *in*tolerable, and *un*happy). Marchand (1974) claims that the distribution of these prefixes is different and thus at least partially predictable. For example, *un-* is used for everyday reversible verbs (*undo, unworkable*) and reversible verbs derived from nouns (*unbutton, unzip*). *Dis-* is used especially with verbs beginning with *en-* or *in-* (*disengage, disinfect*). Marchand believes that *de-* is replacing *dis-* and is especially productive with verbs ending in -*ize* and -*ify* (*declassify, demoralize*).

However, in cases where a semantic distinction exists, all three competing forms may be retained for the same lexical item (*unconnected, disconnected; unclassified, declassified*). *De-, dis-,* and *un-* compete in ablatives (*deplane, disbar, unhorse*) and privatives (*deflea, disarm, unnerve*). Another negative prefix, *non-*, Algeo (1971) claims, has both pejorative (*nonbook, nonevent, nonmusic*) and neutral, unemotional qualities (*nonobedient* versus *disobedient, noninspired* versus *uninspired*), and is used as a prestige marker (*nonsalaried, nonprofit*), and for euphemisms (*nonsuccess, nonreader*). Zimmer (1964), on the other hand, believes that *non-* is neutral rather than pejorative while *un-* and *in-* are judgmental (e.g., *unAmerican* versus *non-American*).

As Mackay and Baerwitz (personal communication) suggest, when two negative affixes can be used with the same word (*unmeasurable* and *immeasurable, uninterested* and *disinterested, displace* and *misplace, unmoral, immoral,* and *amoral*), we have a natural area for native speaker error. Historical change in word meanings takes place relatively rapidly for such pairs, although, as Marchand points out, competing forms will be retained if the semantic distinction is clear.

Not only do different morphemes cover the same semantic relationship, but also one affix may have several meanings (e.g., /šən/ in *application, congregation, production,* etc.). Thompson (1974) gives examples that show we are not always able to find the base form from which the new forms are supposedly derived (e.g., *aggressive* and *aggressor,* but no *agress; tenacious* and *tenacity,* but no *ten*). Do we have to propose a nonexistent form in order to derive the existing ones? Thompson also points out that most people will agree that *wetten* and *hotten* in the pattern of *moisten* sound better than *stickyen* and *thinnen* using the same pattern. If we have such intuitions about forms we have never heard before, those intuitions must be based on (unconscious) rules, but we do not know what they are. (For perhaps the best framework for the regularities of nonproductive or occasionally productive affixes, see Jackendoff, 1975.)

Learners are further confused to find that neither the meaning of *ignorant* nor that of *ignorance* can be discovered simply by recognizing them as forms related to *ignore,* nor is *considerate* the attribute of one who *considers.* Learners and linguists may find some affixes so erratic in behavior (e.g., *-ity* in *readability* versus **blameability*) that both may wonder whether affixes are truly derivational at all—whether one form really is derived from the other. Theoretical arguments on this issue are ongoing.

Willis (1975), interested in productivity of derivational affixes, constructed four tests to discover how native speakers use affixes to produce new words. Here are a few examples from her test.

To her disgust a female Bruin fan has been deemed a Bruin _____ (ette, ess) by a well-known chauvinist.

My grandmother thinks everyone is trying to kill her and get her money. She doesn't even have any money. She's really (super, hyper, ultra, maxi) _____ paranoid.

You got $1,000 from your great-aunt? We had to pay that much for my uncle's debts. Talk about (dis, mis, un, de) _____ benefitting someone.

Willis found that native speakers deemed acceptable a wide variety of affix patterns, further psychological evidence for at least some of the hunches expressed by Algeo and Marchand. Following her analysis, Willis surveyed teaching materials to see how affixation was presented in ESL texts. She found, unfortunately, little systematic discussion of derivational affixes. Highly productive affixes were neither stressed nor opposed to less productive affixes. She therefore proposed a sequenced presentation of derivational affixes based on productivity and arranged by levels (beginning, low intermediate, high intermediate, and advanced classes). Within each level, the affixes are sequenced as semantically and formally easy, semantically easy and formally difficult, semantically difficult, affixes with small domains or infrequent use, and finally competing or closely related forms. Such information should be valuable to ESL textbook writers and language teachers, particularly if future research shows that the ease or difficulty of acquisition follows her categorization.

Inflectional Morphology

We still await research on how well second language learners understand and use productive derivational affixes in English. Inflectional morphology, on the other hand, has been of central concern to second language acquisition researchers. This is not surprising, since much has been written on the acquisition of morphology by children learning English as their first language, and since one of the basic questions in second language research is whether first and second language learning processes are, in fact, the same.

Berko has shown that children by the first grade do have a set of rules for the major inflectional affixes. Other first language researchers have been interested in tracing the gradual development of those rules in the language of young children. In order to trace the acquisition of such morphemes, longitudinal data had to be obtained. Speech samples were usually collected at two-week intervals during play sessions with the child. Once the data had been obtained and transcribed, the researcher could look for patterns of development over time. Writing of first language learners' acquisition of morphology, R. Brown said:

> ... a set of little words and inflections begins to appear: a few prepositions, especially *in* and *on,* an occasional article, an occasional copular *am, is,* or *are,* the plural and possessive inflections on the noun, the progressive, past, and third person indicative inflections on the verb. All these, like an intricate sort of ivy, begin to grow up between and upon the major construction blocks, the nouns and verbs, to which Stage I is largely limited. However, in the course of Stage II we have only the first sprouting of the grammatical morphemes. Their development is not completed within the stage but extends, for lengths of time varying with the morpheme. (1973, p. 249)

In order to trace the intricate twining of the ivy of morphology in child language, Brown, Cazden, and deVilliers (1974) devised a methodology for data analysis. The morphemes to be investigated were listed and all examples pulled from the data transcripts. The researchers then counted the number of times each morpheme was used correctly in an obligatory instance. When the learners produced the morpheme at a level of 90 percent correct over three consecutive data-gathering sessions (e.g., over six weeks), they were said to have acquired that morpheme. Using this method, Brown rank-ordered the acquisition of a variety of inflectional affixes and some grammatical markers, such as articles and prepositions, in the developing language of three first language learners (see Table 1).

Researchers in second language acquisition wondered, then, if the same acquisition order of these morphemes would be revealed if they looked at second language learner data. Using observational data on an eight-year-old Japanese child learning English, Hakuta (1974a) scored the morphemes shown in Table 2. These were scored, using the procedure described above, and then ranked in the order they were acquired by his second language learner. Table 1 also compares the ranks obtained by Brown and Hakuta.

Observational studies of child language have a number of built-in problems. One of these is time. Researchers cannot obtain data all at once, since they are usually unable to observe more than a few children at a time. Obtaining acquisition data on the development of a morphological system may require a very long period of observation (sometimes years); and an even longer period of time must be spent on accurately transcribing the data. In the end, even though working with hundreds of utterances for each child, researchers sometimes worry about how generalizable findings from individual case studies are, and if they can legitimately compare acquisition orders of individual children. Fortunately, cross-sectional data can validate longitudinal data (just as observational data can validate the findings of the cross-sectional research).

In a cross-sectional study, deVilliers and deVilliers (1973) elicited spontaneous speech data from twenty-one children, comparing the *accuracy* order for the group of children at *one* time period with the *acquisition* order

Table 1 Morpheme Rank Orders in Several Studies

Brown's Longitudinal Order		deVilliers and deVilliers		Hakuta		Dulay and Burt (1974)	
n = 3		n = 21		n = 1		n = 115	
1	Pres. Prog.	2	Pres. Prog.	2	Pres. Prog.	1	Art.
2.5	on	2	Plural	2	Copula	2	Cop.
2.5	in	2	on	2	Aux.	3	Prog.
4	Plural	4	in	4.5	in	4	Plural
5	Past Irreg.	5	Past Irreg.	4.5	to	5	Aux.
6	Poss.	6	Arts.	6	Aux. Past.	6	Reg. past
7	Uncontr. Cop.	7	Poss.	7	on	7	Irreg. past
8	Arts.	8.5	3rd Pers. Irreg.	8	Poss.	8	Long plural
9	Past Reg.	8.5	Contr. Cop.	9	Past Irreg.	9	Poss.
10	3rd Pers. Reg.	10.5	Past Reg.	10	Plural	10	3rd Pers. Sing.
11	3rd Pers. Irreg.	10.5	3rd Pers. Reg.	11	Arts.		
12	Uncontr. Aux.	12	Uncontr. Cop.	12	3rd Pers. Reg.		
13	Contr. Cop.	13	Contr. Cop.	13	Past Reg.		
14	Contr. Aux.	14	Uncontr. Aux.	14	Gonna Aux.		

Bailey et al.*		Larsen-Freeman		Rosansky*	
n = 73		n = 24		n = 6	
1	Pres. Prog.	1	Pres. Prog.	1	Pres. Prog. ING
2	Plural	2	Cop.	2	Short Plural
3	Contr. Cop.	3	Art.	3	Pro. Case
4	Art.	4	Aux.	4	Art.
5	Past Irreg.	5	Short Plural	5	Cop.
6	Poss.	6	Reg. Past	6	Aux.
7	Contr. Aux	7	Sing.	7	Poss.
8	3rd Pers. Pres.	8	Past Irreg.	8	Past Irreg.
		9	Long Plural	9	Long Plural
		10	Poss.	10	Past Reg.
				11	3rd Pers. Reg.

*The rank numbers do not represent true ranks but rather listings which reflect the Group Means for each morpheme. In addition, the Rosansky data should *not* be interpreted as anything more than a list, since her contention is that the Group Means and the rank order obscure the variability present in the data.

found by Brown for his three subjects in his longitudinal study. They found that the accuracy order data correlated highly with that found in the observational data (see Table 1).

Following the deVilliers and deVilliers model, Dulay and Burt carried out a series of studies using accuracy data rather than acquisition data. With Hernandez, they developed a set of seven cartoon pictures and a series of questions (*Bilingual Syntax Measure*, 1973) to help them elicit spontaneous speech data from bilingual children. The questions and pictures provoke responses which should contain most of the morphemes described by Brown, yet give a wide range of possible responses, allowing for fairly natural spontaneous speech. For example, in response to a picture of a very fat man and the question "Why is he so fat?," the child might say: He ate too much; he doesn't exercise; he ate a lot of junk; he not on weight watchers.

Table 2   Morpheme List

Morpheme	Form	Example
Present Prog.	-ing	My father is reading a books.
Copula	be, am, is, are	Kenji is bald.
Aux. (Prog.)	be, am, is, are	She's eating a money.
Past Aux.	didn't, did	Margie didn't play.
Prep. in	in	Policeman is hiding in K's shoes.
Prep. on	on	Don't sit on bed.
Prep. to	to	He come back to school.
Poss.	's	My father's teacher.
Plural	-s	My hands is dirty.
Art.	a, the	She's in a house.
Past Reg.	-ed	The policeman disappeared.
Past Irreg.	go, went	She came back.
3rd pers. reg.	-s	This froggie wants more milk.
3rd pers. irreg.	has, does	She has mother, right?
Gonna Aux.	am, is, are	I'm gonna died today.

Using this instrument in their Sacramento study (1973), Dulay and Burt looked for an accuracy order of morphemes of children whose first language was Spanish. They found that, while there were similarities in the data of their second language learners and the first language data, the correlation was not statistically significant. They attributed this to the greater cognitive development of the second language learners. They argued that we should expect differences since the child is already mature and has acquired one language. They next looked at the accuracy order of morphemes for two language groups—learners whose first languages were Spanish and Chinese (the 1974 study). They found the order of morpheme accuracy to be the same for the two groups, as shown in Figure 1. This led them to suggest that, at least for child second language learners, first language transfer/interference is unimportant in the acquisition of morphology.

Fathman (1975) asked a similar question in her research. She developed a test, the SLOPE (Second Language Oral Proficiency Exam), to elicit specific grammatical forms, including inflectional morphemes. Using her test, she compared the responses of sixty Korean and sixty Spanish children learning English (ages six to fourteen years). Her basic research questions were whether or not first language related to order of acquisition, and whether or not age and learning situation influenced the order or general overall accuracy. The only area that showed a significant difference between the two first language groups was the article (t-test, p=.01). A trend toward difference was obtained for: possessive, comparative, superlative, and plural irregular. On the basis of her test, differences attributable to first language did show up, though perhaps not as strongly as one might have predicted. Unfortunately, direct comparisons cannot be drawn to the Dulay and Burt work since different morphemes were elicited and the test situation was more controlled.

Bailey, Madden, and Krashen (1974) replicated the Dulay and Burt studies with adult second language learners from a variety of first language groups.

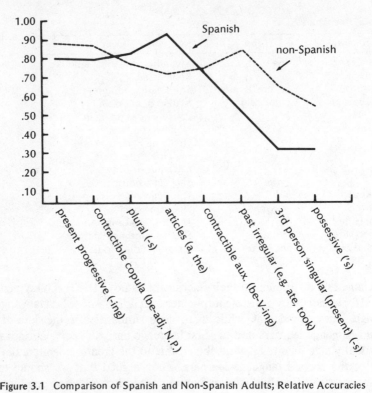

Figure 3.1   Comparison of Spanish and Non-Spanish Adults; Relative Accuracies
for 8 Functors

Using the Bilingual Syntax Measure, they found an accuracy order which correlated highly with that of the child second language learners (see Figure 2). This led Dulay and Burt and Bailey, Madden, and Krashen to suggest that, regardless of age or first language, second language learners of English acquire these morphemes in a "natural order."

Larsen-Freeman (1975) also tested adult second language learners and found a healthy correlation of accuracy with child second language learners when the data were obtained on the Bilingual Syntax Measure. However, the accuracy order on other tasks, using other instruments, did not reach the same level of significance, but rather varied with the task. This led her to suggest that we should be cautious in interpreting our results and in claiming an invariant order for morpheme acquisition.

All of the morpheme research has come under careful scrutiny. It has been clear from the outset that we need to know whether accuracy orders are necessarily evidence of acquisition orders. In some cases we need to know more about the children being tested. Were they bilinguals born in the States or the children of newly arrived immigrants? We need to know more about the scoring procedures. For example, looking at a picture book, the investigator might ask the child learner, "What does the little boy do?," and the child might respond,

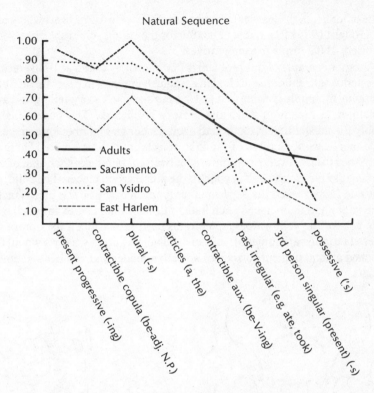

Figure 3.2 Comparison of Child and Adult Relative Accuracies for 8
Functors

"jumping, jumping, jump!" Is the response an obligatory instance of present
tense-*s,* since the investigator has set up that context in the question? Or is it an
obligatory instance for present progressive, since the picture shows ongoing
action? Are there two correct and one incorrect uses of present continuous, or
three incorrect uses of present tense-*s*? Either many arbitrary decisions must be
made or much data must be discarded as ambiguous.

We also need to understand what the criterion level of 90 percent or 80
percent correct means. Even perfect performance can be deceptive. If we count,
for example, all instances of *be* as copula, we may find that the learner has
produced the copula correctly in 90 percent of the obligatory cases. A closer
look, however, may reveal that only *is* has been used (e.g., this *is,* that's, it's).
With child *S*s, all the copulas may be I'*m,* and this/that *is.* There may be no
examples of *are, was,* or *were.* Yet the learner is credited with acquisition of the
copula.

It is possible to score morphemes as acquired when, in fact, the function of
the morpheme has not been acquired. For example, many learners produce
large numbers of-ING verb forms in the beginning stages of learning. In counts,
the morpheme may appear in 90 percent of the obligatory instances for -ING.

On the other hand, the learner may also use -ING verb forms everywhere else as well. Gough (1975) found this to be true for the Iranian child she observed. He even used -ING forms for imperatives!

Another example of this problem is that shown by Plann's (1976) research. She tested Anglo children enrolled in a Spanish immersion program on Spanish inflectional morphology using four tasks: a puzzle task, a story-telling task guided by pictures, a repetition task, and a story retell task. The puzzle task was possibly the most efficient method to elicit gender and number agreement. The puzzle pieces were pictures of familiar objects in various colors. There were twenty-four pieces, twelve masculine and twelve feminine gender, half of which were singular pieces and half of which were plural group pieces. The child, given the puzzle frame, asked the experimenter for each of the puzzle pieces pictured on the paper and then placed each in the puzzle frame. For example, the child had to ask for the yellow dogs (Quiero los perros amarillos), the orange turtle (Quiero la tortuga anaranjada), and so on. Table 3 shows what we would find if we looked at total percent correct for adjective gender and number agreement in this data.

If we looked only at masculine singular, we might think that almost all children had "mastered" the rule for masculine singular agreement of adjectives. However, if we look at the adjectives that should have been marked as feminine singular, we find that the children also used masculine singular for the feminine. Plann's confusion matrices for verb endings and noun article and noun

Table 3 Gender and Number Agreement

Grade	Masculine Singular	Masculine Plural	Feminine Singular	Feminine Plural
4	96%	69%	51%	50%
3	94	61	40	45
2	82	77	32	31
1	90	68	33	9

adjective agreement morphemes illustrate the point that Mikeš (1967) and others tried to make to researchers years before: We should not claim acquisition of morpheme forms until those forms appear in contrast to others in their class.

The scoring method obscures use of a form when it should not be used and whether all variants of a form are produced or only one. It also prevents us from seeing what acquisition looks like below the 90 percent criterion level. That is, the criterion treats all performance above that level as "acquired" and everything below it as "not acquired." This leaves us with no information about the 0–89 percent range.

To solve this problem, R. Andersen (1977) suggested using a Group Range Method for scoring, a method which looks at variability within data. In Table 4 you can see the percentage of subjects (eighty-nine Spanish speakers learning English at the university level; data from compositions) who used any particular morpheme correctly 90–100 percent of the time, 70–80 percent, and so on. It thus shows us the percentage of learners who never make an error in using the morpheme, the percentage of learners who never use the morpheme correctly, and percentages of learners at points in between. The morphemes are ranked in an accuracy order from left to right. Andersen found a significant correlation with rank orders in the previous studies, but his method gives us much more information because it allows us to see important individual patterning within the data.

Another question can also be discussed in light of Andersen's findings. Researchers of child language chose a particular list of morphemes and grammatical markers to study for the reasons quoted above (Brown, 1973). Naturally, language researchers who were interested in comparing second language data with that of first language learners used the same list. However, in taking over this list of morphemes for second language research, we have

Table 4 The 1–99 Percent Range of Morpheme Use Expanded into Intervals

Percent	Cop.	Aux.	-ING	Past Ir.	Past Reg.	Perf. have	3rd Pers.	Perf. -en
100	90	51	41	24	15	11	3	6
90–99	4	2	7	7	5	0	3	0
80–89	4	13	13	14	5	3	7	1
70–79	1	4	5	8	7.5	3	3	1
60–69	1	5	8	10	15	3	7	3
50–59	0	7	1	1	7.5	4	7	4
40–49	0	2	4	6	7.5	1	1	1
30–39	0	1	2	4	5	3	7	3
20–29	0	2	6	11	12.5	7	5	6
10–19	0	5	5	4	5	11	10	9
1– 9	0	0	1	1	0	0	5	1
0	0	7	6	10	15	53	42	64

Andersen, 1977.

grouped together morphemes that should not be treated as one and separated morphemes that should have been grouped. For example, Andersen shows that collapsing articles into only one category covers up variability of performance on definite/indefinite/∅ article accuracy. His learners did much better on definite articles than indefinite, and much better on *the* than on zero articles. Huebner (1979) also convincingly argues against an order of acquisition method for interlanguage analysis. Using what he calls a "dynamic paradigm" approach, he is able to show the distribution of *da* (definite article), *a,* and ∅ in the language of his subject, "Ge," across four longitudinal tapings spanning one year. This analysis shows a gradual shifting from a topic prominent (Hmong-like) system to a subject prominent (English-like) system. While an order of acquisition approach used on this subject's data would lead one to believe that learning had stopped or fossilized for articles, the dynamic paradigm approach shows how the learner's unconscious hypotheses about the target language change over time. The differences detailed by Andersen and Huebner reveal language transfer/interference as an important factor—a sharp contrast to findings of no first language interference when the articles are grouped together.

While there are problems in scoring morphemes, and problems in the criterion level being insensitive to variation, there are even more objections to the analysis of rank orders. The differences between the morphemes, once they are rank ordered, are assumed to be equidistant. That is, the difference between ranks 1 and 2 is assumed to be the same as that between ranks 5 and 6, and so on. If you look at mean scores presented in many of the studies, and then at how close or how far apart each of the pairs are in the ranks, you can see that the orders are not composed of equidistant ranks. Imagine a hypothetical case: Japanese students have mean scores far apart on copula and articles, yet they still rank 2 and 3 in accuracy; while Persian students have mean scores close together for the same morphemes which also rank as 2 and 3. The differences, depending on the statistical tests used, could be obscured in the analysis.

Further, Rosansky (1976) has shown that the correlation figures for cross-sectional studies are very confusing when subjected to fine-grained analysis. She first noted that the Dulay and Burt Sacramento sample obtained an order which correlated with the 1974 Spanish sample but *not* with the 1974 Chinese sample. This makes little sense since the Spanish and Chinese samples in the 1974 study were highly correlated and cited as evidence that native language of the learner was unimportant in the acquisition of syntax. Rosansky next found that the order of morpheme acquisition of the six Spanish speakers in the Cazden et al. study (1975), collected in observational sessions rather than cross-sectionally, correlated with the Dulay and Burt, the Bailey et al., and the Larsen-Freeman Bilingual Syntax orders. However, it also correlated with deVilliers and deVilliers's first language order. Since none of the other studies correlated with the first language order, again the interpretation of the correlations in all these studies is open to question. Rosansky's conclusions are that individual variability gets washed out little by little through each step of the analysis and the correlations in the end are meaningless.

A final problem with the order of acquisition methodology is this: Set cutoff points allow us to believe that each rule is acquired and applied (at some percentage value) across the board. In the acquisition of phonology we know this is not the case. Learners can often produce sounds correctly in one environment, say, at the beginning of words, before they can accurately produce them elsewhere, say, in consonant clusters. We don't expect that all sounds will be produced in all environments equally well. If a learner has "acquired" /r/ at an .80 level, we can easily make predictions as to where the /r/ will not be produced accurately. The question is whether we can do the same thing for morphology. The methodology suggests that if a learner produces -ING at the 20 percent (or 80 percent) level, then *any* verbs in *any* context could be marked with an -ING 20 percent (or 80 percent) of the time.

Evidence against this view of blanket acquisition and application of rules is emerging gradually. Antinucci and Miller (1976) pointed out that the past tense appears only for certain verbs, not all verbs, in the early stages of first language acquisition. Bloom et al. (1980) looked at longitudinal data from four child first language learners and found that the inflections -ING, *s,* and irregular are differentially applied. Their assumption is that this organizational work is at least as important as the meanings of the inflections for determining their acquisition. These children applied the inflections much more frequently to action verbs (e.g., *run, go*) than to state verbs (e.g., *sleep*). Even within the action group differences were found. Simple action verbs and locative action verbs were most frequently inflected. The locative action verbs are those where the goal of the movement is a change of place (e.g., Gia ride to playground). Inflections were much less frequently applied to the category of mover locative action, where the pre-verb noun is both the recipient and initiator of the action (e.g., Tape recorder go in there), or the category of the agent locative action (e.g., I put a car under bridge). This order of application of verb inflections was consistent across Stages I, II, and III (stages defined according to the mean length of utterance of each child). This research suggests that acquisition of rules (at least in first language acquisition) is more than the analysis of the function of an inflection and of its form; this information must also interact with the organization of the lexicon itself. As the learner organizes the lexicon, the inflections are differentially applied according to the evolving lexical system.

In second language acquisition, Huebner's (1979) research also shows that articles are not learned as units and applied at a set percentage level across the board. At Time 1, three weeks after arrival, Ge, the Laotian learner of English mentioned earlier, used *da* (the) to mark nouns as specific and known to the hearer in some cases and not in others. *Da* was used least frequently in subject position. For example, Ge said:

chainis tertii-tertii fai. bat jaepanii isa twentii eit.
(The) Chinese (man is) 35. But (the) Japanese is 28.

Huebner suggests that Ge's interlanguage, like his native language, is topic prominent, and that topics most frequently fall in subject position. Topics are assumed to be "old information" (that is, known to the hearer). Their "known" quality is not in doubt. In other positions Ge more frequently used *da* to remove that ambiguity, thus marking the noun as definite and known:

> gow howm, isa plei da gerl.
> (When we) went home, (we would visit) the girls.

As the learner gradually reorganized his interlanguage system from a topic to a subject system, his use of both definite and indefinite articles began to change. Again, the order of acquisition methodology must be revised and refined if we want to show that the variability reflected in percent correct scores is not random. A finer analysis, of course, will reveal once again that none of the plan levels (phonology, morphology, lexicon, syntax, or discourse) is completely independent of the others. Huebner's data, like that of first language researchers, shows how strongly the organizing of the lexicon affects the acquisition of inflectional morphology.

Despite all these problems with research methodology, an analogy can still be drawn between comprehension and production processes in phonology and morphology. One may believe that contrastive analysis and transfer/interference can best account for some of the data (just as in phonology). One may also believe in a "natural" ease/difficulty scale for morphemes, just as one may believe in naturalness rules in phonology. A series of naturalness statements for morphemes might include the following:

1. Bound morphemes are more difficult than free morphemes (see Vihman, 1980; Krashen, 1977). As mentioned in Chapter 2, stress is most universally placed on the penultimate syllable. Therefore, affixes are not perceptually prominent; they do not "stand out" in the stream of speech. Free morphemes can be learned as lexical items, whole words, rather than as affixes.

2. Affixes that are phonologically stable should be easier to learn than those that have several forms. For example, -ING (invariant /ɪŋ/) should be easier than the plural, possessive and 3rd person singular (s, z, əz) variant forms.

3. Affixes with clear semantic function should be easier than those that have no clear function (e.g., plurals and possessives should be learned before aspect).

4. High frequency affixes within any language should be learned before low frequency affixes (e.g., plurals before aspect).

5. Affixes that affect the phonological form of the word stem should be more difficult than those that do not change the stem.

6. Categories most universally marked by morphology should be easier than those least universal.

7. Inflections should be applied more accurately to action verbs and to highly concrete, "visual" nouns than to state verbs and abstract, difficult-to-visualize nouns.

8. Inflections should be applied more accurately where the organization of first language lexical categories can be transferred to the second language.

Intricate organization in sharp contrast to first language organization should make application of inflectional rules difficult to accomplish across the board.

If naturalness theory for morphology can be hypothesized, it might help to explain the apparent mismatch of acquisition of form and function in second language morphology. As noted by Gough, Plann, and more recently Olshtain (1979), second language learners frequently use forms before acquiring their functions. In most first language acquisition literature, it is assumed that the acquisition of function precedes the acquisition of form. For example, children mark their utterances as referring to past time by using adverbs like *yesterday* before they acquire the regular past tense morpheme. It is not clear that this occurs in second language acquisition. The overuse of -ING by second language learners is a case in point.

In Olshtain's case study of Orly (a six-year-old Hebrew speaker learning English in California), the -ING affix appeared long before its function was acquired. To test for accuracy of function, Olshtain asked Orly questions related to a picture-series story: "What is happening here?," "What do you think is going to happen next?," "What was happening when . . . ? ." Her responses showed she had no difficulty with the tense required (past, present, future), but she had no notion of aspect. In a translation task, Orly was asked to translate Hebrew sentences into spoken English. The sentences contained contexts suitable for present and past in both simple and progressive forms. Orly used progressive for all present and a mixture of simple past and progressive for the past. Asked to do a completion task, she filled in all blanks with the simple present. Asked why, she said that putting in two words would make it "look longer." Shortly thereafter, when the progressive function was acquired, she was easily able to correct her previous errors. When asked why the progressive was used in some cases and the simple tense in others, she replied "because it's better this way."

To summarize, if the form is naturally easy, it may be acquired early even though its function is not known. On the other hand, if the function is clear (e.g., plurality), it may *not* be acquired early *if* the affix is not regular. The free morpheme of number (2, 3, 4, etc.) should be easier than the plural affixes. The comparative -er should be easy semantically but may not always be acquired early because of the difficult articulation of /r/ in English. In other words, the naturalness rules for morphology may have to be stated in terms of if/then statements, and orders may have to be assigned to each of the rules as well.

As with phonology, problems in second language morphology may be doubly determined. For example, Hebrew, Orly's first language, does not have progressive aspect, so her problems with the function of -ING may be partially due to her first language and partially due to "natural morphology" predictions. Difficulty of some morphemes may be triply determined. That is, if the word stem ends in a consonant and the plural affixes add an /s/ or /z/, the cluster may be difficult for the learner to articulate—though the /s/ cluster should be easier than the /z/ cluster. Ease/difficulty of articulation, ease/difficulty of morphological processes, and first language interference must all be considered if we are to understand the use of morphological markers by second language learners.

Finally, individual strategies of learners may also result in different orders of acquisition of morphemes. Rosansky has suggested that most of the individual variability in the acquisition of morphology has been washed out by the statistical procedures used in analyzing the data. When individual variability can *not* be traced to the learner's first language, to natural difficulty of particular morphemes, or to special input to which the child might be exposed, then individual learning strategies might give us the answer. A first step in this direction is Vihman's paper (1980) on the "whole word approach" of an Estonian child, Raivo, in acquiring English and Estonian morphology. His resistance to bound morphology is similar to that of many adult learners of English, and it contrasts with that of two other Estonian children mentioned in her report. The majority of young language learners, with the exception of Raivo, appear to be sensitive to the rules for affixation; young children appear to eventually match the morphology of the new language. For some older second language learners, the acquisition of morphology can be important when they recognize the social consequences of errors. For many others, however, morphology is the "icing on the cake," fairly far down the list of any hierarchy of importance in the plans:

> Zoila: . . . I never using this little, little words.
> Rina: Like what?
> Zoila: "Ah," "and" "and" "that," "/em/" " /ipidit/," you know? "If," /bin/, /it/ sometimes XXX. Well, maybe because I no study . . . never . . . and only hear the people and . . . and talking.
> Rina: Yeah, but people talk with these words.
> Zoila: Yeah, pero /es, eh/ I'm hear and put more attention the big words. You know and . . . something "house." I know "house" is the "casa" for me. And /es es/ and little words is no too important for me.
>
> (Shapira, 1978)

Both the rules of phonology and the rules of affixation appear to be learned relatively quickly and well by child learners living in the country where the second language is spoken (given they interact with children who are native speakers of the language).

The phonological and morphological levels are the most automatic plan levels—levels we think about least. For many, though not all, adult second language learners, the phonological level seems to be the most resistant to change and therefore more prone to "interference" from the first language. While very young children in the early stages of second language learning misapply affixes of one language to lexicon of the other language, it seems more likely that this is a temporary transfer until the affixes of the new language are found and rules internalized for their formation. Given sufficient exposure to the language, they do acquire the forms. Most adults are much more likely to settle for, as an example, an unmarked verb or a Verb + ing and never bother with the rest of the verb tense/aspect system. Why should these two plan levels— phonology and morphology—be so much more difficult for the adult learner to acquire than the higher plan levels?

In contrast, there is little evidence that adult learners have the same difficulty with derivational affixes. Is this evidence that the derivational system itself is not a system at all but that there are, instead, individual lexical items which happen to contain identifiable affixes? Is the discrepancy between acquisition of inflectional and derivational morphology by adults evidence that the inflectional system is really part of the phonological component, while the derivational system (if there is one for the L2 learner) is a sublevel of the lexical component? Most linguists would agree with such an analysis from theoretical and logical evidence. It is not clear, however, whether this is the best interpretation of the psycholinguistic research on morphology.

In this chapter, as in the phonology chapter, I have suggested two major explanations for acquisition data—a "naturalness" order (which is based on perceptual saliency, frequency, invariance of forms, clarity of semantic value, phonological difficulty, and universality) and first language interference. Doubly determined errors are expected to be more problematic than those that can be traced to one factor alone. It also appears that age of acquisition may have some influence on the acquisition of the inflectional system of morphology. It is not clear whether this is truly due to age and the automaticity of inflectional morphology (as compared with derivational morphology) or to differences of frequency of input to adult and child learners. This final issue will be discussed in more detail in Chapters 8, 10, and 11. However, this disparity of acquisition of inflectional versus derivational affixes by second language learners gives extra fuel for linguists' arguments on the lexical nature of derivational affixation in contrast to the morphophonemic nature of inflectional morphology.

4 *Lexicon*

In Chapter 2 I mentioned that Levinson and Liberman found it much easier to use the word as the basic unit for their language comprehension model. Yet every time we say a word it is not an exact phonological copy of the word the last time we said it. Different speakers say words with slightly different pronunciation, and yet we recognize that the words are the same. Even Hellion, a monkey, trained to aid in the care of a paraplegic patient, can react to one-word commands by different speakers at different pitch levels and with slightly different pronunciation. Whether the trainer, the nurse, or the patient says "spoon," Hellion the monkey knows she is to feed the patient. How is it possible that monkeys and computers can recognize scores of isolated words, and humans recognize thousands of words which appear in the stream of speech? This chapter is concerned with this question and the research on methods of lexical storage and retrieval.

Lexical Features

For a moment, think of the lexical level as a data bank filled with key-punched data cards. Each lexical item is a card containing punches for various pieces of information about the word. A word like "cat," for example, might have a hole punched for +animal; it might also have a hole punched for +Noun; it might also have a hole punched for +furry. If we are trying to find a word for something that's furry, we could do a quick run through all the cards in our lexicon, pulling out all those with the hole punched for that feature. That might lead us to make errors like "coat" or "bear" or even "rabbit" for "cat." More punches are needed if we want to retrieve only "cat."

Evidence supports such features, both in developmental studies and in lexical retrieval research. Developmental data show that children often take one feature of an object, and then, wherever that feature occurs, they use the word they know that has that feature. For example, Leopold's bilingual child,

58

Hildegard, used *tick-tock* first for a watch, then generalized it to all clocks, then gas meters, a fire hose wound on a spool, and a bath scale with a round dial. The feature must have been dial shape. She used the "furry" feature of texture, "wau-wau," first for dog, then toy dog, then slippers, then a picture of a man wearing a fur coat (Leopold, 1939). E. Clark (1973) gives examples of overgeneralization related to movement, size, and sound. The overgeneralizations related to shape, as shown in Table 1, are much more numerous.

As we learn more about how far we can "stretch" lexical items, we build up a cluster of features which help us differentiate words one from another. Does that mean the card gets repunched each time we get new information about the word? Or do we get a new card each time we use/hear/read the word in a way that gives us new information about its features?

From speech error data we see that a major key punch must be for a word's syntactic class, because when we make a lexical error we usually substitute a word with the same part of speech. Very seldom, if ever, do we try to substitute a verb for a noun or an adjective for a noun. Maratsos (1978) has shown that children are quite good at maintaining formal syntactic categories across semantic lines. That is, they don't make errors like "he's angrying" or "you're mistaking" (errors that are fairly common for adult second language learners, as shown in the Nemser data in Chapter 3). Therefore, children must be sensitive not only to word class, that is, the part of speech, but also to the subclasses into which words fall. Certain subclasses appear to be learned later than others. Bowerman (1974), for example, found that as her daughter Christy began to acquire causative verbs (e.g., "He warmed the bottle," *causing* the bottle to become warm), she made errors using causatives for verbs not in the causative subclass:

> How would you flat it?
> (said while trying to flatten a piece of paper)
>
> Down your little knee.
> (said while trying to push her sibling's knee down)
>
> I'm singing him.
> (said while pulling a string to make a puppet sing)

Figuratively, her data card needs an additional punch with information on the causative subclass.

Another source of information on the way lexical items are stored and retrieved is the way we temporarily forget words. When we forget a word—or never really knew it—we may still be able to call up some of its features (either semantic or phonological). We have all had the experience of not being quite able to remember a word ("it's right on the tip of my tongue"). Usually we remember something about it. For example, a colleague of mine came into my office one day and asked for the name of the man who wrote a book with McIntosh and Strevens. He only remembered that it began with an "H" (Halliday, as a matter of fact). In his case it seems that all the lexical features

Table 1   Some Overgeneralizations Related to Shape

Source	Lexical Item	1st Referent	Extensions and Overextensions
Chamberlain and Chamberlain	mooi	moon	cakes, round marks on window, writing on window and in books, round shapes in books, tooling on leather book covers, round postmarks, letter O
Gregoire	wawa	dog	small white sheep
Guillaume	nenin (breast)	breast, food	button on garment, point of elbow, eye in portrait, face of person in photograph
Idelberger	bow-wow	dog	fur piece with glass eyes, father's cufflinks, pearl buttons on dress, bath thermometer
Imedadze	buti	ball	toy, radish, stone spheres at park entrance
Leopold	tick-tock	watch	clocks, all clocks and watches, gas-meter, fire hose wound on spool, bath scale with round dial
Lewis	kotibaiz	bars of cot	large toy abacus, toast rack with parallel bars, picture of building with columns
Lewis	tee (Timmy)	cat	dogs, cows and sheep, horse
Pavlovitch	wau-wau	picture of hunting dog	small black dog, all dogs, cat, woolen toy dog
Pavlovitch	deda	grandfather	picture of Vul Karadzic, photos of grandfather and King Peter of Serbia
Pavlovitch	kutija	cardboard box	match box, drawer, bedside table
Pavlovitch	gumene	coat button	collar stud, door handle, light switch, anything small and round
Pavlovitch	bebe	reflection of self in mirror	photo of self, all photos, all pictures, all books with pictures, all books
Pavlovitch	vata	door	shutters in window
Rasmussen	vov-vov	dog	kitten, hens, all animals at zoo, picture of pigs dancing
Taube	ball	rubber ball	apples

E. Clark, 1973, p. 80.

were retrievable, present, and ready for use, but most of the phonological information had been temporarily cut off—except for the initial consonant. Does this mean that the cards are somehow arranged in a dictionary alphabetized by first letters or sounds?

Brown and McNeill (1966), interested in the Tip of the Tongue (TOT) phenomenon, selected from the Thorndike-Lorge (1952) list words with very low frequency. Definitions were read from the dictionary for each word, and *S*s were asked what they thought the word was. This produced for some *S*s a TOT state, and they were then asked to write down what they could remember of the word. When the target was a "flat-bottomed boat used in rivers and along the coast in Southeast Asia," *S*s wrote words like: *saipan, Siam, Cheyenne, sarong, sympoon, sanching, houseboat, barge, junk.* Yarmey (1973), realizing that people's names are often difficult to recall, used photos of famous people instead of definitions to produce the TOT state. The data from such studies show that we most frequently remember the first sound of the word, and sometimes the number of syllables, the stress, and the final sound as well. Less often do we recall the next to the last sound, the third from the last, or affixes. Why should this be so? What happens to the middle parts of words—is the card not punched for them, or is it just lightly penciled in?

To show you more clearly how words may be stored, let's try to replicate one of Baker's (1974) tasks. As soon as you read the words below, try to think of as many like words as you can that have the same initial, medial, or final sound:

Group 1:	same vowel sound as the word given		
	bone	tick	cake
Group 2:	same initial consonant		
	boy	fan	cone
Group 3:	same final consonant		
	rim	mass	cab
Group 4:	same number of syllables		
	survival	desk	hippopotamus
Group 5:	same medial consonant		
	final	mileage	ladder
Group 6:	same part of speech		
	sit	yellow	quick
Group 7:	same last syllable		
	hunter	photo	lesson

Stress and rhyme probably influence the number of words you think of in many of the categories. At least I imagine that, in order to get the same medial consonant, and the same vowel, you relied on rhyme with the test word. Again, what happened to the medial parts of words in your recall? Were your cards clearly punched for them?

The TOT phenomenon relates to what teachers often call passive versus active vocabulary. What do we mean when we claim to teach vocabulary for recognition? Do we expect enough punches will be made to allow us to match up meanings, but not enough to allow us to retrieve the words completely? How many times must we use/see/hear a word before it's really active? Are words learned in the oral/aural mode punched more or less completely than words learned by reading?

Children have often been called word-learning wizards, yet the word-learning process may take them a very long time. Carey and Bartlett, in their classroom research, found that one experience with a word, or at most a few experiences, sufficed for preschool children to get a partially etched color word. They call this "fast mapping." The children needed further (and often protracted) experience with the word to get it fully represented. They believe the child, learning a new color word, not only must find its place in the overall lexicon, but also must restructure the color lexicon to find the right place for a color like, say, olive (that it's neither green nor brown). Given the initial speed in fast mapping of the new color word, they found that slow mapping was indeed slow. However, as they say:

Suppose that, on the average, six months is required for the full acquisition of a new word (surely an underestimate, as we will see). If the child is learning nine new words a day, then he is working out the meanings of over 1,600 words at a time. This fact is a clue to the real significance of the fast mapping. What is included in that initial mapping—that the new word is a word, along with some of its syntactic and semantic properties—must allow the child to hold onto that fragile new entry in his lexicon and keep it separate from hundreds of other fragile new entries, and it must guide his further hypotheses about the word's meaning. (Carey, 1978, pp. 274–275)

Once a lexical item is fully etched, however, there is another issue to be faced—the number of cards we need in the lexicon; that is, whether for a noun compound we need one word or two. In the preceding chapter I mentioned Berko's test of morphology. Within that test she also asked children to give the derivational history of noun compounds. In answer to a question like "Why is a blackboard called a blackboard?," children replied "Because you write on it," not that it is a board that's black; Thanksgiving was called Thanksgiving not because you give thanks but because that's when you eat turkey; and Sunday was called Sunday because that's when you go to church. This suggests that at least some compounds are acquired as single lexical units—not as two words plus rules for combining them. Speech error evidence, however, shows that we do make errors in compounds (e.g., "Oh, I see you're not wearing your swimming pool (suit)"), so compounding may be a real process. It seems that some compounds are single lexical items, while others truly are formed by compounding two words. Again, let's try one of Baker's tasks to see how easily compounds can be retrieved. Try to think of as many compounds as possible as soon as you read the word:

First part of the compound given, supply the second part:

mince _____   shell _____
door _____   drift _____
apple _____   rattle _____

Supply the first part of the compound:

_____ meat	_____ fish
_____ knob	_____ wood
_____ sauce	_____ snake

In making compounds it seems much easier to use the first part than the last part (once we equalize for number of possible compounds for each part). This suggests that many are probably lexicalized as one item. Some compounds, however, seem to be much less lexical and more truly compounding; for example:

made-up example	uncalled-for remark
overheated engine	invited guests
check-cashing service	fast-moving events

For more examples, consult the lists in Rutherford (1968). Stress in American English seems to fall on the first member of the compound when it is a lexical unit; so this occurrence is often used to test whether a word is lexical or a true compound. *Toothbrush, basketball,* and *mailbox* are lexical. Why *chocolate cake* and *cherry pie* should still have stress on the second part is puzzling. Still, once a compound has become a real, single lexical item, the stress appears to shift to the first part of the compound.

Let's summarize and elaborate on some of the claims presented thus far. *First,* there is evidence that our mental dictionaries must code lexical items for *syntactic class*—parts of speech. In addition to studies already cited, further evidence shows that the brain differentially organizes lexical items in this way. Language disordered, aphasic patients often are able to recall many nouns but few verbs. Word association studies (e.g., Luria and Tsvetkova, 1968) have shown that aphasic word associations are much stronger for nouns and their attributes (adjectives) than for verbs. Whitaker (1975) found that if such *S*s were given words to use in sentences, they used the given words as nouns whenever possible. Given *read, S*s might use a much less frequent noun and create an utterance concerning a *reed.* During the initial stages of first and second language learning, nouns are acquired in much greater numbers than are verbs. The syntactic category must also be marked by certain selectional restrictions. Thus *weigh* as a verb would be coded to show that it cannot be selected if the focus of the sentence is to be passive. (*Five pounds was weighed by the sugar.) And *speak* would be coded so that only a human noun could precede it.(*The bicycle spoke is just as ungrammatical as *The blackboard spoke when *spoke* is a verb). Syntactic class, both part of speech and selectional restrictions, must be one of the major organizational categories by which we select and retrieve lexical items.

Second, storage must also be by *semantic features.* It appears that there are several organizing semantic classes. Baker, in the study mentioned previously, found that "parts of the body" responses were given to the word "hand." An "edible" class included vegetables and fruits, and color words formed a group.

There was a category for humans, for birds, and for insects. In the Yarmey experiment it appeared that even proper nouns were recalled by such semantic features as profession and location of the person (along with phonological cues). There is anecdotal evidence that professional jargon is stored differentially as well. While such studies have not, to my knowledge, appeared in print, there have been case reports; for example, a pharmacist being unable to retrieve pharmaceutical terminology. These terms gradually but permanently became lost to him, while the remainder of his vocabulary appeared to be untouched. When tired or under pressure, people have difficulty recalling names. As an ardent birdwatcher I have had the same problem with this special terminology— calling out *thrasher* when I meant *flicker*, or *sparrow* for *swallow*. This seems quite normal to me since I can, at other times, easily retrieve these words.

In addition to major semantic classes, there is also some evidence that time and space may be one category; that they are not entirely separate. Nooteboom (1967) found such space/time slips of the tongue as "the two *contemporary*, er, sorry, *adjacent* buildings," "the *singular*, sorry, the *present* time," and "*during* the apparatus, er, *behind* the apparatus." Another example of this space/time category is the hospital spokesman who, reporting on President Reagan's emergency operation, said the incision was "about six month—six inches long."

And *third*, a major lexical classification seems to be *phonological shape*. From the results of the lexical experiments mentioned earlier, Baker concluded that the lexicon is indexed so that words beginning with the same initial consonant sound constitute a subgroup. However, number of syllables and middle and final consonants do not constitute *major* subgroups. Although we may agree with Baker's conclusions, it is also clear that stress and final sounds must be part of the retrieval system. Otherwise it would not be so easy for us to find rhyming words (excluded from Baker's analysis).

Word retrieval, then, involves these three major factors—phonological, semantic, and syntactic. Retrieval is seen as matching the lexical features with sentence syntax, pulling up phonologically listed words that have the syntactic and semantic features we want, sorting these in some buffer zone, and building a syntactic plan for them (or putting them into slots in the output of the syntactic plan, depending on your view of which comes first, syntax or lexicon).

Second Language Lexicon—Models

If the organizational models given here accurately describe storage and retrieval of words in a first language, will they also do so for bilingual lexicons? Do bilinguals punch two cards for each referent, while monolinguals punch one? Do bilinguals punch one card for "table" and another for "tarabeeza"? Or do they add another punch to the "table" card which says that the phonological features for "table" in Egyptian Arabic should give "tarabeeza"? There is some information to support the second alternative.

In observational studies of children learning two languages simultaneously, we often find the child learner playing with translation equivalents of lexical items, requesting translations of new words, and even commenting on the restrictions of a lexical item in one language as compared to the same word in the other language. Eva, a six-year-old Hungarian learning French (Kenyeres, 1938), was astonished that *seven* and *week* were not the same word in French—as they are in Hungarian. Louie, a French and German bilingual (Ronjat, 1913), began giving word pairs (*oeil, auge; oui, ja*) at twenty months. From then on, he constantly elicited equivalents. At thirty-six months, for example, he asked his mother, "Mama, puree de pommes de terre, wie heisst?" After he learned "Gefullte Tomaten," he asked his father, "Comment tu dis, toi?" to get "tomates farcies." Hildegard (Leopold, 1939) also elicited alternate forms, but on occasion she tried either to change the pronunciation to that of the other language (e.g., using "stimming" for playing the piano but pronouncing the *st* cluster as the English *st*), or to create a parallel form. For example, she created "Butterfliege" from butterfly for Schmetterling. Louie produced "Laden von Hut" on the format of "magasin du chapeau" for Hutladen. These examples suggest that the child learner may simply be punching one card with two phonological representations. However, there is a good deal of evidence against this notion as well, some of it from word association studies.

If words in two languages for the same lexical item are stored together in a bilingual lexicon, then one would suppose that all the data about the item would be shared by both languages. We would expect the learner to give similar word associations for the lexical item in each language. To test this, Kolers (1963) had university students (in the U.S.) from Thai, German, and Spanish first language groups give word associations under four conditions: (1) native language stimulus word and native language associations; (2) English word and English associations; (3) native language word and English associations; and (4) English word and native language associations. Examples are given in Table 2.

Table 2 Sample Word Associations

English–English		English–Native Language	
table	dish	table	silla
boy	girl	boy	niña
king	queen	king	reina
house	window	house	blanco

Native–Native Language		Native Language–English	
mesa	silla	mesa	chair
muchacho	hombre	muchacho	trousers
rey	reina	rey	queen
casa	madre	casa	mother

Kolers, 1973.

His *S*s gave very similar word associations as long as the stimulus word was a concrete noun, and especially if it could be manipulated as well. They gave fewer similar associations when the stimulus word was abstract, emotionally loaded, or imagery prone. Does this mean that all concrete words are in one lexicon while everything else is listed in separate dictionaries according to the language—or that one card has an L2 tag with specific association rules attached?

Word association studies conflict somewhat with word recall experiments. In recall experiments, the S sees lists of words in either one or two languages—for example, Lambert et al. (1968) gave bilinguals lists of words in English and in either French or Russian (whichever was the S's first language) to remember. In such recall experiments the words are sometimes presented in either all L2 or all L1 lists, sometimes in half L1 and half L2 lists, and sometimes the language of the words is randomized in mixed sets. Dalrymple-Alford and Aamiry (1969) gave Arabic-English bilinguals lists of words to recall. The first list was a set of words of body parts and animal names: *sheep, tiger, camel, dog, hand, eye, neck,* and *nose,* and the Arabic equivalents of *cat, cow, horse, lion, ear, mouth,* and *head.* The second list was the Arabic equivalents of the English words and the English equivalents of the Arabic words on the first list. Each list was organized in two ways: (1) *language* structured, so that the English words occurred in one block followed by the Arabic words, or vice versa, with animal/body part alternating within the block; and (2) *category* structured, so that all animals were given with alternating English and Arabic words and then all body parts given, again with alternating English and Arabic words. After viewing all sixteen words on the first list, Ss had one minute to recall as many words as they could, a procedure repeated in four trials. The findings of most recall tests show that bilinguals use categories more than language to retrieve words. It suggests that, rather than go to a box labeled, say, "French," to look for the right card, we go to an index of cards for, say, "animal," and (figuratively speaking) look there for the right words. The Dalrymple-Alford and Aamiry findings are consistent with this—recall by categories is more natural to bilinguals than recall by language. However, the Dalrymple-Alford and Aamiry analysis showed that language-category clustering, rather than either category or language by itself, facilitated retrieval. To be sure of this, that it was the *combination* of language and category, they then constructed a trilingual word list, using *socks, hat, mouth, neck, cow, camel, ceinture, souliers, oreille, nex, chein,* and *mouton,* and the Arabic equivalents of *glove, shirt, eye, head, horse,* and *mouse.* The three categories were apparel, animals, and parts of the body (each category having two words from each of the three languages). Six different arrangements of the eighteen words were made so that no two adjacent words belonged to the same category or the same language. Again, the results showed that the main organizational principle in recall is category *and* language, not language or semantic category alone.

To explain the results, we assume that the association network between words in the same category within a language is stronger than the network between words in the same category but in different languages, or in different categories but in the same language. If a student is asked to respond with a translation equivalent, he or she can do so very quickly. However, if recall is based mainly on word association, it follows that there would be a tendency to produce sequences of words from the same language and category, rather than to produce words consecutively from the same language but a different category, or from the same category but a different language. Therefore, we might hypothesize that we go to the category box in our data set and find it subdivided, say, into a set of English words and a set of Spanish words with some sort of cross-reference system.

Unfortunately, it's not that simple, since the recall studies conflict with the word association studies. Kolers believes that words such as *horse* and *cheval* really represent the same underlying meaning; but Dalrymple-Alford and Aamiry claim they are synonyms with nonidentical underlying representations. MacLeod (1976) turned to the *savings* literature as a way to test this conflict. "Savings" works like this: *S*s are asked to learn number-word pairs, such as 56-car. Usually sixteen to twenty pairs are given. Later, when asked to recall the pairs, *S*s will have forgotten some of them. New words are then substituted for those forgotten. If the new word is related to the forgotten word, some savings in learning can occur. In other words, there is *some* residual memory of the first word, although not enough to allow the *S* to recall it. The accompanying diagram shows that, in the studies on savings, subordinates and superordinates (e.g., *Buick* and *vehicle* for *car*) result in strong savings (S). No reliable savings (NS) has been found, however, for antonyms, synonyms, or associates of the target item.

(Superordinate)
VEHICLE (S)

TRUCK (NS) ——— CAR ——— AUTO (NS)
(Associate)   (Synonym)

BUICK (S)
(Subordinate)

Since "no savings" has been found for antonyms or synonyms or associates, it should be possible to set up an experiment to test whether or not savings occurs for *horse* and *cheval,* and thus discover if they are likely synonyms.

MacLeod had French-English bilinguals learn a list of twenty number +word combinations. Five weeks later, the *S*s were asked to recall the list again in response to the number portion of each pair. All the missed items were then presented again under one of four conditions: (1) the same word in the same language, (2) a different word in the same language, (3) the same word in the other language, or (4) a different word in the other language. Following a short interval (when *S*s had to count backward by 3's from 100), the *S*s were retested. The *S*s did perform better on the follow-up test if the same word in the same ᴀge were given. They did next best if the translation to the other language ᴡᴇre given. However, the difference in savings between original language and translation was not significant. The savings was the same. Since savings was found for translation as well as for the original word, MacLeod believes that translation equivalents are not synonyms but are identical.

In a second experiment, MacLeod asked four groups of Ss to view words flashed on a screen. Each group was asked one of the following questions as the words were shown: Is the word in English? Is the word in French? Does this word represent something living? Does this word represent something nonliving? After the last word on the list, the Ss were asked to recall the words; then they were to look at the list of words, both French and English, and circle the language in which they thought each word had been presented. Words that were recalled were words in the language in which they had been presented (only three of the 273 items recalled were in the wrong language); so language retention was excellent. Those Ss who had been asked the meaning-focused questions ("Is this word LIVING/NONLIVING?") recalled more words than Ss who had been asked the language identity questions ("Is this word in LANGUAGE X?"). Once more it appears that the primary indexing is by category, not language. Furthermore, recovery of the language tag cannot occur at all unless meaning is retrieved. According to MacLeod, "The principal conclusions to be drawn are that a word is represented in a bilingual's memory as a language-free semantic trace, and that input language is attached, perhaps in the form of some kind of language tag, to that semantic trace." (1976, p. 362)

Having reread MacLeod's experiments several times, I still find them puzzling. In the first experiment, savings was not checked in all positions (superordinate, subordinate, associate), only in synonym relationship. Since savings was found for the translation equivalents, MacLeod claims they are identical rather than synonymous. We might just as logically argue that they are either superordinates or subordinates. That is, "tarabeeza" might be a kind of "table" for me, or "table" might be a kind of "tarabeeza" for an Egyptian student learning English. So first we need to know whether superordinates and subordinates and associates in the second language would also give us savings on other-language words. The experiment should be reconstructed with a second language word (other than translations) in each of the four positions, to see whether or not savings can be found on any of the positions. Second, in the word association literature, we find bilinguals give very similar word associations for nouns that are concrete and highly visual. The words used in MacLeod's experiments (*bird, dog, gift, window, tree, boy, house,* etc.) seem to be mostly of that sort. If differences are to be found, we should try abstract nouns, or nouns with heavy emotional loading, since these are the words for which different associations are found. However, these Ss did remember the language of the word over a long period of time. This in itself is surprising. In monolingual recall experiments, Ss seldom remember the exact form of the syntax (grammatical structure), though they do recall the underlying message (meaning). Bilinguals who switch language during conversations are often asked to remember which language they used to say parts of their conversations and are unable to recall the languages accurately. Why bilinguals would remember in which language words have been presented is a puzzle. In line with other recall literature, bilinguals, like monolinguals, should remember the word meaning but not the language in which it was presented. This finding needs further study.

Since we do find differences in word associations along a concrete to abstract continuum, we might consider for a moment just what "concrete" means. For many learners, recall seems to be in terms of visual pictures stimulated by the word. For example, given the word *car,* we may visualize our favorite blue Volkswagen; or we may visualize a crowded freeway with "frames" flipping through Buicks, Chevrolets, Hondas, and so forth. For some, a word draws up an image that is incomparably vivid and stable. And for some, the image is also linked to sensations of splotches, lines, or haze, and even taste, sensation, and smell. Luria studied an extraordinary mnemonist. This person, who had an incredible memory, changed fairly abstract words and numbers into visually concrete images. As Luria's subject describes it:

When I hear the word *green,* a green flowerpot appears; with the word *red* I see a man in a red shirt coming toward me; as for *blue,* this means an image of someone waving a small blue flag from a window . . . Even numbers remind me of images. Take the number 1. This is a proud, well-built man; 2 is a high-spirited woman; 3 is a gloomy person (why I don't know); 6 a man with a swollen foot; 7 a man with a mustache; 8 a very stout woman—a sack within a sack. As for the number 87, what I see is a fat woman and a man twirling his mustache. (1968, p. 31)

When asked to remember long lists of words or numbers, the subject took a mental "walk." As he mentally strolled down some road or street of his childhood, he would distribute his word images at houses, gates, and store windows. This technique, converting words to images, explains how Luria's subject could so easily reproduce a series of words from start to finish, or in reverse order; and how he could so easily name the word that preceded or followed any other word or number in the series. All he had to do was take his walk again, starting out at either end of the street. When asked to begin in the middle, he would first find the image asked for and then, by noticing what was on either side of it, continue to recall the rest of the list.

Other learners, especially sensitive to the sounds of words, find some words in the new language especially pleasing and "right" for the referent; others sound disgusting or completely "wrong." Whatever we may say about the arbitrariness of word form, these feelings are still there for many learners. Children love to play with the sounds of words, repeating them over and over with slight variations in form. Many adults also report doing this type of sound play subvocally. Again, Luria's mnemonist talking about sounds of words:

Then there's the word "pig" (Russian: svinya). Now I ask you, can this really be pig? Svi-n-ya—it's so fine, so elegant. . . . But what a difference when you come to khavronya (Russian: sow) or khazzer (Yiddish: pig). That's really it—the kh sound makes me think of a fat greasy belly, a rough coat caked with dried mud, a khazzer. . . . But take the word samovar. Of course it's just sheer luster—not from the samovar, but from the letter s. But the Germans use the word Teemaschine. That's not right. Tee is a falling sound—it's here! Oi! I was afraid of that, it's on the floor . . . So how could Teemaschine mean the same thing as samovar? (1968, pp. 87–88)

In general, researchers believe that visual associations are helpful in learning second language vocabulary, but the findings conflict. Atkinson (1975) used the visual approach to teach vocabulary. For example, to learn the German *ei* for *egg,* students were asked to visualize an eye inside an egg. Other types of associations may be made by learners. It appears that beginning learners use more "sound-alike" associations for vocabulary items, intermediate learners use more structure associations, and advanced learners appear to use a wide variety of associations with heavy use of context (cf., Henning, 1973; Cohen and Aphek, 1979). Cohen and Aphek (1980) looked at the kinds of associations used by English speakers studying Hebrew. They found some first-language associations (e.g., *nadir* "rare" associated with English "dear"—"it's dear to me because it's rare") and some cross-language associations (e.g., *hardama* "anesthetics" associated with the French word *dormir* "to sleep"). They also found onomatopoeic associations (e.g., *lifom* "to beat as heart" associated with the sounds "pom, pom") and associations to letters in the word (*rovtsim* "flop" using the "m" at the end of the word to associate with *mita* "bed" which begins with an "m"). In these studies researchers disagree on how effective it is to have students make such associations as a way of learning new vocabulary. While most agree that teaching some associations does result in better retention, there are studies that fail to confirm the technique as being more effective than other methods (cf., Willerman and Melvin, 1979). Cohen and Aphek also caution that we need to look at which students profit most from such instruction. It is quite likely that different types of association training (e.g., visual association, sound of word association, word spelling association) may have different degrees of effectiveness for different students. The Cohen and Aphek study is filled with interesting speculations which deserve further investigation.

Second language learners, especially adults, are sensitive to the differences in the range of word meaning, to sound similarities, and to differences in word forms as well. Bowen and Haggerty (1971) looked at the distribution of the word *hacer* in Spanish to English *do/make,* etc. If we are to believe that there is only one card for *hacer* punched for all these collocations, then how many subpunches for the second language must there be? Or is each polyseme punched on a separate card? We might think of polysemes as analogous to color hues. If you think of the range of hues you accept as being red, the range must be very wide indeed. Yet, given these hues as color chips, you will arrange them as most to least redlike in some way. There is a "core" chip you will choose as the real red. In the same sense, you can select *core meanings* of polysemes. Consider the following list from Caramazza and Grober (1976):

Two parallel *lines* never meet.
They were arrested at the state *line.*
Please *line* up the blocks.
Would you read over the actors' *lines.*
What *line* of work are you in?

Most people will choose the first example as the most "core" meaning for *line*, then the second, and so on.

While children learning two languages simultaneously have given us a great deal of data on overextension of meanings along semantic feature lines (see Clark, 1973), older second language learners seem overly cautious. Kellerman and Jordens, in a series of papers, give us empirical evidence to support the notion that second language learners' willingness to transfer meanings of L1 words to L2 words is systematic, not random, and that it relates to the concept of "coreness." They hypothesize that we are more likely to transfer the core meanings of words if we believe they may be universal in some sense. If the new language is thought (by learners) to be fairly similar to their own, the learners may try to transfer more of the meanings. If the languages seem very unrelated, learners may be less willing to attempt transfer of anything but core meanings. Let's consider Kellerman's example word *breken* (Dutch for *break*). If we were learning Dutch, we would probably believe that we could use *breken* in a sentence about breaking a cup or breaking an arm. But would you be willing to try it for "he *broke up* with Alice" or for "the strike *breakers*"? If you think you might risk using *breken* for these, let's consider a language very different from English. Say you learned the Japanese word for *break* and knew you could use it for "break a teacup." Would you use it for "breaking waves" or "broken heart"?

To test for psychological reality of coreness for lexical items, Kellerman (1978) had students sort cards with sentences using *breken* in Dutch, their first language. Dutch *S*s were presented with seventeen cards on which were written the following sentences:

1. De golven braken op de rotsen.
   (The waves broke on the rock.)
2. De lichtstralen breken in het water.
   (The light rays refract in the water.)
3. Hij brak zijn been.
   (He broke his leg.)
4. 't Kopje brak.
   (The cup broke.)
5. Na 't ongeluk is hij 'n gebroken man geworden.
   (After the accident, he was a broken man.)
6. Zij brak zijn hart.
   (She broke his heart.)
7. Hij brak zijn woord.
   (He broke his word.)
8. De man brak zijn eed.
   (The man broke his oath.)
9. Welk land heeft de wapenstilstand gebroken?
   (Which country has broken the cease fire?)
10. Sommige arbeiders hebben de staking gebroken.
    (Some workers have broken the strike.)

11. Nood breekt wet.
    (Necessity breaks law—a saying)
12. Dankzij 'n paar grapjes was 't ijs eindelihk gebroken.
    (Thanks to a few jokes the ice was finally broken.)
13. 'n Spelletje zou de middag enigszins breken.
    (A game would break up the afternoon a bit.)
14. Zij brak 't wereldrecord.
    (She broke the world record.)
15. Zijn stem brak toen hij 13 was.
    (His voice broke when he was 13.)
16. Zijn val werd door 'n boom gebroken.
    (His fall was broken by a tree.)
17. Het ondergrondse verzet werd gebroken.
    (The underground resistance was broken.)

(As you read through the list, you may have been surprised to find parallels in meanings of *break* and *breken* that you did not predict as possible.) After finding that students were able to agree on some sense of coreness for *breken*, Kellerman ran his major experiment. Three groups of students (210 Dutch secondary and university students learning English, eighty-one third- and fourth-year English majors, and forty Dutch university students studying German) were asked to read sentences that used *breken*, judging whether or not they thought these meanings could be transferred from the native language to the target language they were studying. Their rank orders for judgments of transferability were then correlated to judgments of coreness. A healthy relationship was found.

The problem of how to define coreness led Jordens to do a follow-up study. He asked one group of native speakers (n=29) to rank sets such as the following for the most normal (core) to least normal (noncore) meanings:

He laid his cards *face* down on the table.
They disappeared from the *face* of the earth.
The stone hit him in the *face*.
If you want to save *face*, stay away from the meeting.
After cheating on the test, Chris was ashamed to show his *face*.

A second set of native speakers (n=25) were asked to rank the same sets of sentences on how idiomatic they believed the sentences to be. Finally, a third group of Ss (n=22) were asked whether or not they thought the polysemes ("face" in the above example) would be translated by the same word in each of the sentences. For example, given a sentence like "This is a very high mountain," we know that *high* would be *alto* in Spanish, *haut* in French, *hoch* in German. How likely would it be that *high* would have these same translations in:

This fence is six feet *high*.
He did it in a *high*-handed manner.
How long have you been in *high* school?
It's *high* time we started.
The cost of living has reached a new *high*.
Fasting gives you a natural *high*.

*S*s in the Jordens study were also asked to give any reasons they might have formulated for their judgments on translatability of the words. Almost all responses of *S*s in group 3 showed they were aware that they avoided transferring words in idiomatic expressions. Their rankings correlated highly with the rank orders of the second group and less well with the rank orders of the first group.

Together, the Kellerman and Jordens studies present us with a puzzle to pull apart. Kellerman found a strong correlation between coreness and transferability. However, when searching for the attributes of coreness, he found that concrete meanings are not necessarily all more transferable than abstract meanings, so coreness is not simply concrete versus abstract. High imagery also might be an attribute of coreness, since it correlated with judgments of coreness. Yet, there was no correlation of note between high imagery and transferability. Metaphorical extensions of core meanings were judged as dissimilar to literal core, yet might be more transferable than literal meanings judged less dissimilar. So, Kellerman found no *simple* relationship between linear distance away from core and transferability. Jordens's preliminary results suggest that transferability may relate more to judgments on how idiomatic the use may be, perhaps even more than with judgments of coreness. This ongoing research is extremely interesting since the notion of core/noncore (related to naturalness theory as unmarked/marked or language neutral/language specific) has been proposed as important in predicting ease of learning as well as transferability.

The psycholinguistic literature presented here does not allow us to make strong recommendations about teaching vocabulary in second language classrooms. However, many useful pedagogical suggestions have been made by researchers (see Celce-Murcia and Rosensweig, 1979). We may advise teachers to either use or not use available cognates (e.g., English *carrot* and French *carotte*), and to either avoid or emphasize false cognates (e.g., "We should pretend to study" Spanish *pretendir = try*). We may decide that we need to be sure that vocabulary gets thoroughly "punched" for part of speech, for semantic features, and for collocation sets. To do that we may use what Carton (1971) calls *inferencing*. Examples of such procedures appear in Yorkey (1970):

We had a whoosis.
A tropical fish
An eggbeater
A leather suitcase.

If we add "but the handle was broken," we can narrow the possible answers down to two—the eggbeater or the suitcase. If we add "so we had to beat the eggs with a fork," we can arrive at the correct answer, eggbeater. In examples such as:

The night was so _____ that not a sound could be heard.
(quiet, beautiful, dark, dangerous)

we can select the correct alternative from the context. If we don't know *banished* in the following passage, we can find a definition elsewhere in the paragraph:

The ruler was so cruel and dishonest that after the revolution he was banished. A few members of the Senate opposed the decision, but the majority voted that the ruler should leave the country forever. (killed by stoning, sent away or exiled, imprisoned or jailed, punished by whipping)

Work on inferencing has been at least partially tested by Johnson (1977). Her work shows that individual students have strong personal preferences for conscious study to acquire vocabulary. Some like dictionary work, some keep vocabulary lists, some prefer to learn new words from written text and others from conversations. Some students like to guess meanings while others have a very low tolerance for the uncertainty that guessing provokes. In other words, the picture that emerges from the psycholinguistic literature is extremely complex and the pedagogical work on vocabulary teaching in the classroom shows high variability in lexical strategies of adult second language learners.

Yet, it is the lexical level that adult second language learners claim is most important. When our first goal is communication, when we have little of the new language at our command, it is the lexicon that is crucial. If we can but find the words, we know we can take care of our immediate needs. The words (along with all the gestures we have to help us get meaning across) will make basic communication possible. As Krashen has often pointed out, learners don't carry grammar books around in their pockets, they carry dictionaries. It is not surprising, then, to find that much of early conversations are "negotiations of meaning" (see Schwartz, 1980). Once the learner and the addressee are sure they have the right word in mind, the conversation can continue, since much of the rest can be guessed. Basic communicative competence is largely concerned with the strategies learners use to solicit the vocabulary they need in order to get meaning across—as we shall see in Chapter 7. Therefore, this is one of the most important plan levels for the second language learner. After a period when research on the lexicon was largely neglected, this plan level may become one of the most researched areas of second language acquisition. In so doing, the research may follow that of psycholinguists who are now devising ways to test the adequacy of linguistic grammars that are lexically driven.

5 Syntax and Sentence Comprehension Models

As communicators, we must somehow express our thoughts in language; we must be able to change thoughts and the relationships among them into linearly ordered utterances. Conversely, as listeners, we must somehow, from linearly ordered utterances, arrive at the thoughts that underlie them (hopefully the same ones that the speaker has in mind). In language production, sentence syntax allows us to choose just how we wish to present our ideas in linear sequence.

Suppose we went to the Sunkist track meet to watch the runners from the San Fernando Valley Track Club. We are surprised to see a very chubby high school girl beat all the San Fernando runners in her event. We might combine these elements into a statement: "A chubby, teenage girl beat San Fernando's runners." We might, however, combine them as "The woman who outdistanced the San Fernando runners was younger, and chubby too," or "The runners from San Fernando were outdistanced by a chubby, high school girl," or a number of other paraphrases. Indeed, we might even make each proposition a simple sentence and string them together one after another. We wouldn't, though, because we know that others would rightfully become impatient if we said: "We went to a track meet. Sunkist sponsored the track meet. San Fernando has a track club. We watched some runners . . .", etc. It might take hours to get to the point. It is much more efficient simply to combine many of the propositions into one utterance.

Syntax allows us to present simple propositions or to combine them in many ways. To combine them, we may use *conjunction* (I went to the race *and* I saw Frank Shorter), *relativization* (The woman *who won the race* . . .), or *complementation* (We were amazed *that the chubby teenage girl beat everyone*). Syntax allows us to expand utterances via *recursive* elements (e.g., recursive relative clauses such as "This is the man who ran the race that set the record that nobody has broken . . ."). It allows us to shorten output by deletion of *redundant* elements (Sue Petersen entered the marathon and Sue Simms *did too*. Sue Simms didn't win the marathon but *neither did* Sue Petersen). In other words, syntax gives us a variety of ways to present propositions. The form we choose depends on many things, not the least of which is our desire to be understood (or perhaps not to be understood).

It seems that, if our goal is to be understood, we should use the simplest syntactic arrangement possible, keeping our utterances short as well. After all, the more we elaborate on a sentence, the longer and more complicated it gets. When this happens, the more there is for our listeners to hold in short-term memory. Yet much of our elaboration is apparently an attempt to be clear. If we say, "The woman beat the runners," we may be asked, "What woman?" or "What runners?" To make reference clear, we may add information to identify the runners or to identify the woman. Yet, in doing so, we increase both sentence length and syntactic complexity. There is no one-to-one relationship between complexity and comprehension. More complexity can mean greater comprehensibility, though we soon reach a point of diminishing returns if we continue to add more and more information to each utterance.

Transformational Grammar and Complexity

What is the relationship between syntactic complexity and comprehension? Psycholinguists, captured by early forms of transformational grammar, believed they had a way to measure sentence complexity and a way to check it against comprehension. At that point in theory development, propositions were expressed by simple "kernel" sentences. A series of transformations could be applied to these kernel sentences. Psycholinguists equated these transformations with mental processes. The larger the number of transformations, the more difficult the sentence should be. Thus, a number of experiments were done involving the kernel sentence and its transformations.

To test the notion that number of transformations equals number of mental processes involved in deciphering meaning, Savin and Perchonock (1965) had *S*s listen to a series of sentences, illustrated in Table 1.

Table 1   Complexity and Recall

Kernel Sentence	Words Recalled
The boy has bounced the ball.	5.27
Transformations:	
P—The ball has been bounced by the boy.	4.55
N—The boy hasn't bounced the ball.	4.44
Q—Has the boy bounced the ball?	4.78
NQ—Hasn't the boy bounced the ball?	4.39
PN—The ball hasn't been bounced by the boy.	3.48
PQ—Has the ball been bounced by the boy?	4.02
PQN—Hasn't the ball been bounced by the boy?	3.85

P = passive; N = negative; Q = question.

Each sentence was followed by a list of eight words. The Ss were instructed to recall the sentence verbatim and as many of the words as possible. The figures in Table 1 show the mean number of words recalled following each sentence type. The rationale was that, since each transformation took up mental processing effort, the greater the processing effort (that is, the larger the number of transformations), the less space would be left for storing and remembering the words that followed. The results of the experiment appeared to confirm equating number of transformations with sentence complexity.

These early experiments soon came under attack. Psychologists pointed out that, as the number of transformations increased, sentence length also varied, so the results could just as easily be accounted for by the length of the utterance. Others suggested that it is not the number of operations, but rather that there may be something intrinsically more difficult about some of the transformations. For example, in the negative sentences it is difficult to know what is being negated (it wasn't the *boy* who . . . ; it wasn't the *ball* that . . . ; he didn't *bounce* it, he kicked it, etc.). Others said that passive is difficult only because the focus changes from the subject to the object. Since agents—the "doers"—usually appear in the first noun phrase (NP) of the sentence, one would expect lower scores when the object is placed there instead. About this time, linguists decided that the passive should not be considered a transformation at all but, instead, should be part of the Aux rewrite rule (though they have since changed their minds many times on the location of the passive rule). More importantly, linguists had by then modified the grammar so that transformations included any structural change used to modify phrase structure in the transformational component. In that case, the numbers of transformations psycholinguists used in such test sentences were not the same as those in linguistic descriptions. In addition, Sachs (1967) showed that form is not stored in memory once sentence meaning has been processed. Although her Ss recalled sentence meaning, they did not recall syntactic form. She found that, after 7.5 seconds, recognition for syntactic change dropped to chance level. Formal structure, in other words, is held for only a brief time and then vanishes. This contradicted Savin and Perchonock's conclusion that we remember and store sentences in kernel sentence form along with tags for transformations.

Syntactic Processing

Obviously, in comprehending sentences, we do use syntactic organization to some extent. We do not process the following sentences, all of which have similar surface structure, in the same way:

Dion will make a $\begin{cases} \text{wonderful film.} \\ \text{wonderful film editor.} \\ \text{wonderful bilingual.} \\ \text{wonderful mixture.} \end{cases}$

ESL teachers who were using slot-filler drills at this time often assumed that, since such sentences as those represented above were similar in surface structure, they should be drilled together. So, a moving slot drill might have looked something like this:

The	boy	is ready to work.	(eat)
"	"	" " " eat.	(soup)
"	soup	" " " ".	(chicken) (*The soup eats.)
"	chicken	" " " ".	(ambiguous structure)

Since the surface structure is not an adequate representation of the syntactic relationships shown above, how do we arrive at sentence meaning? If we use syntactic rules to understand sentences, how do we do this?

Table 2, adapted from Clark and Clark (1977), presents the syntactic approach to sentence processing.

These proposed strategies assign a great deal of importance to function words as signals of how to break up the utterance into constituents. What evidence is there that we really do this? Ammon (1968) looked for evidence to support syntactic processing using a "probe word technique." He presented Ss with sentences such as:

> The polite actor thanked the old woman
>   1   2   3   4
> who carried the black umbrella.
>   5

After hearing the sentence, and others of various structure types, the Ss were asked questions such as, "What's the next word after *old*?." Time of response and accuracy were measured. Ammon found that when the word given was in position 1 (*polite*) or 3 (*old*), the Ss recalled the next word more accurately and more quickly than when the word was 5 (*who*), 2 (*actor*), or 4 (*woman*). The lowest accuracy and the longest time readings came at the major constituent break between NP's and VP's, the next between NP and relative clauses, and the least between Adj and N. This agrees with the notion that *polite* (below) is being syntactically bracketed with *actor, old* with *woman*, and so on.

((the) ((polite) (actor)))/(thanked ((the) ((old) (woman)))/(who . . .))))

Such bracketing looks very similar to the immediate constituent diagrams of grammarians. And, it matches the processing model in Table 2 fairly well. However, like most tasks that we hope test the processing of input, it relies on production; and unless we process and produce language in the same way, the results may say more about production than comprehension.

A second source of evidence of syntactic processing is the "click experiment" of Ladefoged and Broadbent (1960), Fodor and Bever (1965), and Garrett et al. (1966). In this procedure Ss were presented with sentences such as:

> O-pen road-side mar-kets   dis-play tas-ty pro-ducts
>   −7   −4   −2 −1 0 +1 +2   +4   +7

Table 2 Syntactic Processing

1. Whenever you find a function word, begin a new constituent larger than one word. This gives you the beginning of a constituent.
    a. When you find a determiner or quantifier, begin a new NP (noun phrase).
    b. When you find a preposition, begin a PP (prepositional phrase).
    c. When you find a definite pronoun, begin a new NP.
    d. When you find an aux verb with tense, begin a new VP (verb phrase).
    e. When you find a relative pronoun, begin a new S (sentence).
    f. When you find a complementizer, begin a new S.
    g. When you find a subordinating conjunction, begin a new S.
    h. When you find a coordinating conjunction, begin a new constituent similar to the one just completed.
2. After identifying the beginning, look for content words for that type of constituent.
    a. After identifying a determiner or quantifier, look for a N to close out the NP.
    b. After identifying a prep, look for the NP to close out the PP.
    c. After identifying a pronoun, close out the NP.
    d. After identifying a tense Aux, look for a main verb to close out the V.
    e. After identifying the relative pronoun, look for a sentence with one NP missing.
    f. After identifying a complementizer, look for a S.
    g. After identifying a subordinate conjunction, look for a S.
    h. After identifying a coordinate conjunction, look for content words of the same kind as those identified in the previous constituent.
3. Use affixes to help decide whether a content word is a N, V, Adj, or Adv.
4. Look for number and kinds of argument appropriate to any V found.
5. Try to attach each new word to the constituent that came just before.
6. Use the first word of the clause to identify the function of the clause in the sentence.
    a. If it begins with a subordinate conjunction, it's an adverbial clause subordinate to the main clause.
    b. If it begins with a relative pronoun, it's a relative modifying the N.
    c. When the clause begins with a WH word, it is a WH question.
    d. When the clause begins with a complementizer, it's a sentence functioning as a NP.
    e. When it begins with an Aux verb with tense, it's a yes/no question.
    f. When a clause begins with a main verb in the infinitive, it's an imperative.
    g. When a clause begins like a WH question but doesn't have subject and verb inverted, it is an exclamation.
    h. When a clause is not classifiable by any of the above, it's an assertion.
7. Assume the first clause is the main clause unless it is marked at or prior to the main verb as something else.

Clark and Clark, 1977, pp. 57–70.

and were told that they would hear a "click" (noise burst) somewhere in the sentence. They were to report where they heard the click. *S*s tended to move the click from where it actually occurred to the major constituent boundaries. Clicks placed near the major break (0), for example, were heard as occurring at the 0 position. Clicks should be heard as though they were at constituent boundaries if linguistic units are impervious to outside interruption. Reports of clicks at constituent boundaries, then, should be evidence that people (as well as linguists) analyze sentences using syntactic groupings.

The click experiments also came under attack. The procedure originally involved hearing the sentence, writing the sentence down, and then marking where the click was heard. But by the time the Ss wrote the sentence down, it was difficult for them to remember just where the click occurred, so the center was the safest guess. This procedure was changed so that the Ss heard the sentence and also saw the sentence printed in front of them. Psychologists still objected, saying one might hear a click toward the middle of the sentence simply because one could not differentiate where in real time it occurred (unless there are pulse-timed beats). To show that click placement near constituent breaks had little to do with syntactic processing, psychologists presented Ss with various types of noise and showed that Ss tended to hear clicks in the center of non-language sample items. Of course, this stimulated psycholinguists to test sentences with major sentence brackets near the beginning or end of sentences.

In addition to probe word and click experiments, a number of experiments on "right branching" relative clauses have been cited as evidence for the syntactic processing model. Miller and Isard (1964) worked out a series of sentences each twenty-two words long containing relative clauses of various types:

1. She liked the man that visited the jeweler that made the ring that won the prize that was given at the fair.
2. The man that she liked visited the jeweler that made the ring that won the prize that was given at the fair.
3. The jeweler that the man that she liked visited made the ring that won the prize that was given at the fair.
4. The ring that the jeweler that the man that she liked visited made won the prize that was given at the fair.
5. The prize that the ring that the jeweler that the man that she liked visited made won was given at the fair.

Reading through the sentences, most people find them progressively difficult to process. And more and more of the relative clauses are left branching (that is, the missing NP in the relative clause sentence is not the same as the noun to which it is attached). To process these, we can't use the strategy in Table 2 which says that a relative clause is about to begin and instructs us to look for a missing NP. Such a strategy may allow us to begin and close brackets, but it doesn't tell us how we can attach the remainder to the preceding constituent. We can try to do this for sentence 5 above, but most people fail and therefore consider the sentence ungrammatical or at least incomprehensible.

There are a number of problems with this sentence processing model. It is incomplete; for example, it disallows the processing of questions of the "You want some coffee?" type (see rules 6e and 6h in Table 2). This could easily be fixed by adding other subrules for processing. Sentences such as those cited earlier (Dion will make a wonderful film/bilingual/film editor) would all have to be bracketed in the same way. That is, the model has all the problems that led linguists to abandon straight constituent structure grammars. Perhaps even more critical is the importance the model gives to function words in processing of input. If these are the flags that tell us when to start or when to end a bracket, why is it that these elements are perceptually difficult to find? It seems that if function words are so important in locating brackets, they should be perceptually prominent. To the contrary, they do not receive stress. In fact, many function words are optional under certain conditions. How do we find a relative clause if the relative pronoun isn't there (e.g., The man I like is sitting over there)? The model leaves us with too many unanswered questions.

While these are problems that can be dealt with by incorporating a more adequate linguistic description into the model, a more serious criticism is that semantic and pragmatic information is not taken advantage of until very late in the process. In this model, everything is bracketed before turning to identification of content word meanings. This seems counter-intuitive at best.

Semantic Processing

An alternative method of understanding utterances is the semantic model (Table 3), adapted, again, from Clark and Clark (1977).

The semantic approach assumes that we begin with the content words and try to construct propositions that seem logical, given our understanding of the real world and the immediate context. The order of mention helps us to determine the role of the content words—that is, in English at least, the first N is likely to be the subject.

Psychological data to support the semantic processing model comes from a number of experiments. For example, if you give children toy animals to play with and ask them to show you:

> The horse kissed the cow.
> The cow is kissed by the horse.

they will pick up the first mentioned toy and make it kiss the second (see Sinclair-de Zwart, 1973). In making such responses they seem to be using strategy 4 in Table 3. Many experiments have also shown how we will disregard word order (strategy 4) and use content words to build propositions that make

Table 3 Semantic Approach

---

1. Use content words alone, build propositions that make sense and parse the sentence into constitutents accordingly.
2. Look for constituents that fit the semantic requirements of the propositional function that underlies the content words.
3. Look for definite noun phrases that refer to entities you know and replace the interpretation of each NP by a reference to that entity directly.
4. Expect the first N-V-N sequence to be agent, action, and object unless it's marked otherwise.
5. Look for the first of two clauses to describe the first of two events and the second clause the second event, unless they are otherwise marked.
6. Look for given information to precede new information unless the sentence is marked otherwise.

---

sense (strategy 1). Thus, we will hear what we expect to hear in such sentences as "The man bit the dog" (heard as "The dog bit the man") and "John ironed and washed his shirt" (heard as "John washed and ironed his shirt"). Many slips of the tongue go unnoticed because they are converted, by "slips of the ear," back to what the speaker really intended to say.

The semantic strategies model is intuitively appealing to those of us who are second language learners and language teachers, for it helps us understand how we can comprehend so much of a new foreign language. If we know enough content words, have good background information, and our knowledge of the world is adequate, we can arrive at proposition meaning even though we cannot easily process the syntax. Such comprehension, however, is liable to error. We do not comprehend languages just by working from word recognition. We supplement it with whatever syntactic and world knowledge we possess.

Just as word recognition alone will lead us to make comprehension errors, Levinson and Liberman found that their word recognizing machine (mentioned in Chapter 2) had problems working with words alone in order to arrive at sentence meaning. As the number of word templates was increased, it became more and more difficult for the computer to discriminate among words. The probability of error in word recognition increases with the number of words in an utterance. That is, in a three-word utterance, if the probability of recognizing single words is .8, the probability of recognition of all three words would be .8 × .8 × .8, or about one-half. While people find it easier to recognize words in a syntactic context, for a machine working from word-recognition templates, the error increases with the number of words.

However, by adding a simple finite state grammar (similar probably to that in Table 2, since it is a linear rather than a transformational grammar), we can dramatically decrease the number of errors. With a syntactic component, the computer could work much faster. Instead of matching all possible templates, we only need to check those templates that can occur in the syntactic slots described. Since only a small subset of the vocabulary can appear in a given syntactic position, word recognition increases in accuracy with fewer matches required.

Computer Comprehension Model

Levinson and Liberman's computer at Bell Labs has also been supplied with a rudimentary semantic processor. In one program, the semantic information has to do with airline information. The acoustic and syntactic processors work together for input recognition. A memory system consisting of facts (airline schedules, conversions for time zones, conversions for days of the week, etc.) was added. The rest of the communication system is devoted to semantic processing.

The constant checking back and forth between word templates, syntactic structure, and the semantic component allows the computer to work fairly well.

However, at this point Levinson and Liberman suggest that the limited vocabulary of their machine (127 words) and the syntactic component leave much to be desired. Nevertheless, the machine, working within these limits, is able to carry on the following telephone conversation:

Machine: This is the Bell Laboratories flight information system. May I help you?

User: I want one first-class seat on flight number 31 to Denver on Sunday.

Machine: I am sorry the flight is not available on Sunday.

User: I would like to leave on Saturday.

Machine: Flight number 31 leaves New York at 9:45 a.m., arrives in Denver at 1:10 p.m.

User: What is the flight time?

Machine: The flight time is five hours and twenty-five minutes. . . .

To comprehend the sentences, the computer counts the number of words in each sentence to be recognized and also divides the utterance into a series of "frames" every fifteen milliseconds. This is illustrated below. The word "NFRAM" is the number of frames per sentence. The computer then matches each word to its stored word templates according to the position of the word in the sentence. Possible matches (those that are similar in phonetic shape and are possible according to the sentence grammar) are listed. The numbers given after the possible word are measures of the distance between the word and the template. The shorter the distance, the closer the match to the template. A "metric" is given for the distance measures for all the words in the sentence string. The smaller the metric, the closer the match. If the smallest metric results in a sentence which is not allowed by the grammar, then the next smallest metric is chosen as the correct analysis. For example, in the utterance "What is the flight time?," Levinson and Liberman list the outcome as follows: (It is not clear, in the following example, why "What is one flight time?" would not be acceptable and have a smaller metric.)

NFRAM=396
No. of words=5
Candidates for word no. 1   20 frames
What   1   .180
Candidates for word no. 2   29 frames
is   1   .270
Candidates for word no. 3   24 frames
nine   1   .343
one   1   .278
six   1   .370
seven   1   .242
the (alt)   1   .314

Candidates for word no. 4   24 frames
some   1   .296
flight   1   .341
one   1   .414
three   1   .390
Candidates for word no. 5   28 frames
nine   1   .378
oh   1   .390
time   1   .291
one   1   .411
seven   1   .396
times   1   .315
What is seven some time
metric=.1279442E 01
What is the flight time
metric=.1396801E 01
The flight time is five hours and twenty-five minutes.

This computer comprehension model has characteristics of both the syntactic and the semantic sentence processing models. The computer model is very rudimentary at this time. However, it gives us some clues as to the effectiveness of each sentence processing model described by Clark and Clark. No one claims that either of these two processing models is without fault. Since neither model is satisfactory, perhaps it is some other combination of the two, with checks back and forth between them in ever-shifting combinations, that allows us to understand utterances.

One other point should be mentioned regarding the models and the importance assigned to syntax in each one. Neither the computer comprehension nor the syntactic processing models would work for natural, unplanned oral language. In natural conversations much of the talk does not conform to the grammar descriptions based on planned text. The question is whether talk is to be analyzed as showing slightly defective syntax, or whether it is different in kind, and therefore deserving of linguistic description. Do we comprehend utterances in talk by analogy to the syntax of citation sentences? (Note that the computer telephone is not natural conversation. Rather it consists of highly planned, syntactically organized sentences. This will be considered in more detail in Chapter 8.)

Procedural Grammar

Kempen and Hoenkamp's (1981) procedural grammar attempts to rectify this gap. In their model, sentences are not built in a single sentence-producing center consisting of sequential phrase structure and transformation rules. Rather, the work is parceled out to a team of workers, so to speak, each responsible for a small part of the sentence. Kempen and Hoenkamp's model has three parts. The *conceptualizer* which presents conceptual fragments, the meanings that are to be expressed in the utterance; a *formulator* which takes the conceptual fragments, lexicalizes them, and builds a syntactic structure for them; and an *articulator* which is responsible for the saying of the utterance.

The conceptualizer has no special syntactic knowledge; it presents semantic fragments to the formulator team which is charged with building the syntactic structure. To do this, first a team of specialists must look up meanings in a dictionary to select the best match for the conceptual fragments (and, perhaps, some of the next-best matches as well). When a close match cannot be found, modifiers may be selected to fill out the meaning. For example, if the fragment covers the meaning of roller skate (as a verb) but also sidewalk, roller skate might be chosen and the leftovers shunted to a modifying prepositional phrase (PP sidewalk). The formulator team will then begin to build a syntactic structure organization which respects the syntactic properties of the lexical items (word class, restriction rules, etc.). It may even work out possible syntactic organization for several synonyms which are held in abeyance pending success/failure outcomes of the favored lexical choices. The formulator team is made up of procedure "experts" who specialize in one type of assembly:

For example, procedure NP knows how to build noun phrases; procedure PP can deliver prepositional phrases; procedure SUBJECT is responsible for the shape of subject phrases in main and subordinate clauses. Like the procedures or routines of ordinary computer programs, syntactic procedures are permitted to call on each other as subprocedures ("subroutines"). Procedure S, for instance, may decide to delegate portions of its sentence formation job to SUBJECT and OBJECT as subprocedures. OBJECT need not necessarily wait for SUBJECT to finish: they can get started simultaneously and run in parallel. They, too, are free to call further subprocedures, a typical candidate being NP. Thus, a hierarchy of procedure calls arises which is conveniently depicted as a tree. (Kempen and Hoenkamp, 1981, p. 11)

The category procedures build syntactic shapes such as NP, PP, and S, while the functional procedures take care of the relationships among the structures (subject, object, modifier, etc.). The formulation teams (the noun experts, the subject experts, the verb experts) work simultaneously on the different segments and the entire team is *lexically driven.* This is in keeping with recent linguistic theory which has shifted many syntactic rules to the lexicon. Bresnan (1978), for example, argues that all rules are essentially lexical (except those that cross variables). Aranoff (1976) and Roeper and Siegel (1978) give further examples of syntactic rules which may be more precisely handled as lexical rules. The flow chart, then, would be:

$$\text{conceptual} \longrightarrow \text{lexical} \longrightarrow \text{syntactic}$$

rather than:

$$\text{conceptual} \longrightarrow \text{syntactic} \longrightarrow \text{lexical}$$

or

$$\text{conceptual} \begin{cases} \longrightarrow \text{syntactic} \\ \longrightarrow \text{lexical.} \end{cases}$$

Each conceptual fragment is handled piecemeal: the NP experts may work simultaneously with the S experts on some conceptual fragments. At the same time, other conceptual fragments are being set up by other specialists. The formulator grows a syntactic tree for the fragments. As each new conceptual fragment comes down, the tree will be supplied with more branches. The formulator may be forced to modify the tree as new material comes down, or it may have to discard it if a new conceptual fragment is lexicalized with material that cannot be attached to the developing tree. The formulator, then, is seen as growing branches of the tree in parallel.

The output, each formulated fragment package, is queued in the order received. Decisions are made on ordering according to the properties of the package, its destination markers, source, and contents. The output of fragments may not match that needed in the final utterance. The formulator tries to move each fragment as far to the left as possible. Ordering, however, relies at least in part on what the speaker wishes to emphasize and, so, the order may be closer to that given by the fragments than we might guess it would be. That is, we could get a variety of acceptable utterances depending on the conceptual fragment orders (e.g., "Yesterday, at the park, we roller skated on the sidewalk," "On the sidewalk at the park, we roller skated yesterday," "We roller skated on the sidewalk at the park yesterday.") Ordering of the fragments intuitively should be a late decision. For example, there is nothing special about direct and indirect objects that select one NP before the other.

There are clear advantages to such a piecemeal assembly model. Kempen and Hoenkamp point out that there is an obvious work advantage. If you think in terms of computers, there aren't any wait periods with the motor idling followed by hectic bursts of work when everything must be changed to a syntactic form. The concept of piecemeal work also helps us understand the slip of the tongue literature mentioned in Chapters 2 and 3. You will remember that Fromkin showed that words are frequently interchanged in utterances and that inflectional morphemes sometimes get stranded as well. Kempen and Hoenkamp point out similar examples from Garrett (1975, 1980) with word exchanges such as "She donated the LIBRARY to the BOOK" and stranding errors such as "She's already trunkED two packs." If the formulator is working on several conceptual fragments simultaneously, and ordering rules are fairly low-level, it is easier to see why words that may be far apart in the surface tree suddenly appear in the wrong place. When the formulator is working on several NP's simultaneously and morphological functors are being assigned to them simultaneously, it is easy to see how stranding slips can occur.

In addition, when we run into serious trouble during an utterance, we don't recast the complete sentence (as one would expect if the utterance were produced by a single, central agency). We frequently backtrack to the beginning of the last constituent, repairing it as a unit rather than repairing the entire utterance. Hesitation also would occur only at the beginning of sentences if there were a single central agency. Instead, we find hesitations in many places within utterances as failures occur in the procedures or as word searches have to be reinitiated. This model, then, has several advantages over the syntactic or the semantic processing models, and yet uses the strengths of each.

The models, however, differ in that the models from Clark and Clark are for sentence comprehension while the description of procedural grammar looks like a production model. Kempen and Hoenkamp argue, however, that procedural grammar can also work as a comprehension grammar. Syntactic parsing, they believe, is similar to syntactic formulation—that is, both are seen as lexically driven. They operate on the basis of syntactic information stored with individual words in the lexicon. The words, though, come from a different source—word recognition in the case of sentence comprehension and from lexicalization in the production model.

Procedural grammar is an appealing model particularly because it does try to account for natural language data (including hesitations, false starts, lexical repair, and syntactic repair). Whether it will be adequate to the task is yet to be seen. Considering this model when two languages, rather than one, are to be used raises some interesting questions. First, think of the task of a simultaneous translator. As the translator listens to one language, she or he utters the message immediately in the second language. Do the "experts" who are working on the comprehension, listening team (wearing the team colors of L1) race about disassembling L1 packages while the "experts" on the production, speaking team (wearing the team colors of L2) begin building them for the output? Since procedural grammar is lexically driven, this takes us back to all the questions raised earlier regarding the representation of lexical items in a bilingual mental dictionary. Assuming that we have separate data cards for lexical entries according to language, and that different lexical-syntactic rules are punched, depending on language as well as other factors (rather than one card with two language punches for the form and rules of each language), do we also have separate NP experts for each team, and separate Object experts for each team to do the syntactic development? If so, then the simultaneous translation task does seem to require one to be a "split person" in a rather amazing sense. That is, the languages must be completely separated and running simultaneously. Equally amazing are the reports of simultaneous translators who claim never to truly "hear" the messages they translate. After having spent a half-hour translating a speech, these translators often claim they have no idea what the content of the speech might have been, as though it were all done "on automatic." (Typists who work from tape recordings often report the same kind of phenomenon, typing out a draft of what they've heard—ear to hand messages—without processing anything of the message.) One might want to rethink the procedural grammar model, considering both the simultaneous translation research (e.g., Barik, 1974) and the research involving shadowing in a second language, in terms of what the model has to say that is relevant to bilingual lexical storage.

A second area to think of when considering the procedural grammar model is the research on language mixing. *Language switching* at major boundaries or in tags (e.g., Atashi suki da yo, *y'know*; Time to get started, *¿no?*) should pose no real problems for the model. Repetition of statements in the L2 are also common in language switching (e.g., sa skal vi spise, time to eat; Maleesh, maleesh, cherie, never mind, never mind; Nakanai no, nakanai no, nobody cry). Do such examples show that teams of experts are simultaneously preparing the same output in both languages and that both get out either by mistake or intent?

However, how would the model handle *language mixing*? In some cases it would appear that one lexical item is thrown into the processing without any special adjustments being made. Uyekubo (1972) has shown that English words can be inserted into Japanese utterances with little fuss. In some cases, rules that are already in existence in Japanese may be used to accomplish the mix. For example, Japanese has a set of verbs which are constructed from a noun + *suru* (to do)—benkyoo (studying) + suru = to study; ryokoo (travels) + suru = to travel. When English verbs are mixed as single words into Japanese utterances, they follow this pattern: Ta da moo *memorize suru* bakkai dakara. Similarly, when an English adjective is inserted into a Japanese utterance, the *na* marker is placed between it and the Japanese noun: *intellectual na* benkyoo; *cool na* nominomo. Does this mean that, for Japanese-English bilinguals, the English verb entries have a special "mixing rule," or that adjectives have a special "mixing rule" in case they get put into Japanese utterances?

Let's consider a trickier case which might argue against such interpretations. Cornejo (1973) gives examples of five-year-old children mixing English lexical items into Spanish. Remarkably, the English lexicon is produced with Spanish articles appropriate for the Spanish equivalent: *una* bike (una bicicleta), *el* dress (el vestido), *al* shopping center (al centro). Is this, then, to be taken as evidence that there is only one basic representation in a bilingual lexicon with two separate forms attached and tagged for language? That is, did the language "experts" select the Spanish noun on the first quick run through, give it to the Spanish NP specialists to build its structure, and then, at the last moment, provide the wrong phonological form? Or did the experts select the English word, give it to the Spanish noun team, only to have it run into problems and check back for the gender mark on the original Spanish noun? Again, the possibilities are fascinating. We may want to look back through the extensive literature on language mixing and switching, checking for the problems we would have to deal with if we wished to use procedural grammar as a model for the data.

Humans are, of course, extremely successful in comprehending language. We are less successful perhaps in constructing models of that process. For an excellent critical review of a full range of comprehension models, see DeBeaugrande, 1981. The models (whether grammar models or computer models) make comprehension appear to be an almost impossible task. But since we are so successful at it, we should be able to discover *how* we manage to comprehend and produce language. Those who study child language, both first and second language learning, investigate these same questions from a different perspective. The topic of the next chapter is the literature on child first and second language acquisition which speaks to the questions related to sentence syntax.

6 Syntax and Language Acquisition

In the 1960s there was a lot of interest among linguists in using child language data to test linguistic descriptions of syntax. That interest has recently been revived (cf., Tavakolian, 1981), and child language is once again seen as the testing ground for linguistic theory. In the 1960s Brown, Bellugi, and others began writing formal linguistic rules to describe the language production of three children (Adam, Eve, and Sarah) studied by the Harvard group. Such rules could then be compared to those of theoretical linguists, and claims on the ease of acquiring basic syntactic structures versus the difficulty of acquiring complex structures could be validated. That is, descriptively difficult syntax should not appear early in child language. Rather, it should evolve after basic sentence forms have been acquired.

As you might imagine, child language researcher wrestled with many complex issues as they wrote their formal rule descriptions. If a learner produced a WH-question (e.g., "What's that?"), was it really a question formed by rules, or was it rather a one-unit utterance learned as a chunk? If "What's that?" questions had been highly frequent in the input, could we be sure that the child wasn't imitating it as a chunk? Even when they discovered rules, researchers were still not clear about how much of the data could be accounted for by the rules. In addition, since there was variation from child to child, at what point could researchers claim that rules were valid and that there was indeed an order of acquisition for the various syntactic structures?

After rules had been written and acquisition stages described, it wasn't clear whether growth in syntactic systems reflected development of a truly independent language system or whether it was tied to (and thus perhaps reflective of) general cognitive growth. Psychologists strongly supported the latter. Linguists, on the other hand, accumulated evidence on the independence of the two systems. For example, persons with low cognitive ability can acquire complex syntactic structures (Yamada, 1981). Furthermore, cognitive maturity is a less attractive explanation for late acquisition of certain parts of the system, since second language learners (cognitively mature adults) also acquire these same structures later than others. Yet the link between cognitive development and linguistic development remains strong.

Second language research is clearly relevant to these important issues. Although first and second language research look superficially very similar (see Table 1), the questions asked in second language research have been broader in scope. For example, both first and second language researchers have studied the growth of grammatical morphemes in learner language as well as a variety of other syntactic areas, but the focus has been different.

Second language researchers came to psycholinguistics with a very different history of research. In the heyday of contrastive analysis (the late fifties and early sixties), we believed that second language acquisition was governed

Table 1 Acquisition of Syntax—First and Second Languages

	Representative Research Reports		
Structure	L1	L2 Child	L2 Adult
Gr. Morphemes	Brown, Cazden, Bellugi et al. deVilliers & deVilliers Berko	Dulay & Burt Fathman Swain et al. Adams	Bailey et al. Larsen-Freeman Fuller Andersen
Negs	Bellugi & Klima Lord McNeill	Adams Milon Young Gerbault	Cancino, Rosansky, & Schumann Shapira
Q-formation	Bellugi & Klima Brown	Ravem Huang Gough	Cancino, Rosansky, & Schumann
Passives	Slobin Harwood Turner & Rommetveit	–none–	–none–
Conjunctions (time)	Hatch Clark & Clark Katz & Brent	–none–	–none–
Logical Connectors	Hatch Olds	–none–	–none–
Comparatives	Kennedy	–none–	–none–
Rel. Clauses	Brown Hatch Sheldon	Hakuta	Schumann Ioup & Kruse Schachter Chiang
Min. Distance Experiments*	Chomsky Cromer d'Asaro	Syngle	Syngle Cook d'Anglejan & Tucker

*This set of experiments tests the hypothesis that language learners assign "subject" functions to the preceding NP closest to the verb.

almost totally by the influence of the first language. We felt then (as some researchers do now) that second language acquisition is a matter of using first language syntax along with second language vocabulary—a relexification process. We thought we could contrast syntactic structures in the native, source language with the second, target language to see where transfer would work and where it would not work. Thus, we could predict the errors students would make. Then in the late sixties and early seventies those of us also working in first language acquisition began to comment on the similarity of the data between second language learners and child first language learners. At the same time there was a great upsurge of interest in language universals, and proposals were made that the phrase structure rules of transformational grammar might be universal to all languages. If that proved correct, then perhaps the similarity among child first language data, second language acquisition data, and pidgins might be accounted for as reflecting this basic language core which was seen as part of our genetic inheritance. The universal language component and universal acquisition process should result in such similarities in learner data.

Interlanguage

About this time Selinker coined the word *Interlanguage.* In the spirit of the times, Interlanguage was thought of as a universal series of interim grammars which all learners would systematically work through as they acquired the new language. The universal process of Interlanguage would be modified by such things as first language syntax, instruction, communication strategies, and so on. These factors could be used to explain differences found among learners, and also differences in the data from that of first language learners, while still preserving the notion of a universal learning process underlying both first and second language learning.

Researchers set out to document Interlanguage in a number of ways. The first hypothesis they tested was "Does L2 learning = L1 learning?" Would data analysis support their observations of similarities in the two? Table 1 is a sample of the researchers whose goal was to compare second language acquisition data with first language acquisition data.

The Aux System

The major area of initial research was the development of the Aux system. This includes negation, yes/no questions, WH-questions, and the acquisition of *do* as a tense carrier in negatives and questions. The data has been presented in three ways: formal rule descriptions comparing first and second language learners; descriptions of stages of acquisition; and implicational scales and variable rules.

Let's begin with *formal rule descriptions.* Following the work in first language acquisition research, Huang (1970) described the acquisition of questions and negation for a five-year-old Taiwanese child learning English. Brown had established the average length of a child's utterance in morphemes, the Mean Length of Utterance (MLU), as a measure of stages of language development. Using the MLU, Brown divided acquisition into a series of MLU stages. First language learners' acquisition of questions and negatives was described by writing formal phrase structure and transformational rules to cover the data of each MLU stage. Huang hoped to follow this method but immediately found that the MLU could not be used to set periods of development for his second language learner. His learner was able to produce very long utterances (e.g., "It's time to eat and drink") almost immediately. Huang's solution was to divide the data into months of exposure to English and to write formal rules to describe negatives and questions within these time periods.

Ravem (1974), studying his two Norwegian children Reidun and Rune (ages: 6:6 and 3:9) as they learned English, also used formal rules to show the development of negation and questions. Different sets of rules would have to be generated for the two languages. Comparing his rules for negation in English and Norwegian:

English

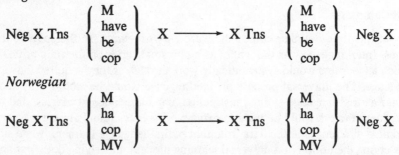

Norwegian

Ravem predicted that the children would produce correct negatives except in the case of main verb negation. Based on the Norwegian rules, they should produce forms like "He like not the house" or "He like it not." However, he found that his learners instead used negatives similar to those of first language learners of English (e.g., "He not like the house" and "He don't like it").

Similarly, the development of question structures could not be traced to Norwegian. The rules of Norwegian would predict WH-questions like "Where live Tom?" Instead, the children produced questions similar to those of first language learners: "Where Tom live?"

In copula yes/no questions, Reidun and Rune typically used inversion in the early stages. Only occasionally (and optionally) did Reidun make use of intonation alone as a question signal. Ravem attributes this to transfer from Norwegian which also requires inversion. Learners favor two possible patterns of yes/no questions which require *do*-support: either intonation as the question signal (e.g., "You like ice cream?") or transfer of the Norwegian rule (e.g., "Like you ice cream?") Reidun typically chose intonation, while Rune chose the Norwegian inversion pattern.

Although the patterns in the development of questions and negatives found by Ravem were similar to those found by Brown and Bellugi, there were enough differences between L1 and L2 and also between the two learners to lead Ravem to state that neither the L2 = L1 learning hypothesis nor the contrastive analysis hypothesis of interference/transfer in their extreme formulations were strictly supported in his data. Huang, on the other hand, found strong similarities between his Taiwanese learner's acquisition of negatives and questions and those of first language learners.

Other researchers preferred to look for regular changes in Interlanguage in terms of *stages of acquisition* rather than formal rules. M. Adams (1972) studied ten Spanish-speaking children (kindergarten children) as they learned English, and charted their acquisition of questions and negatives. Pooling the data from her subjects (collected in observational sessions, and in translation and story-retelling tasks), she developed the notion of stages. While she acknowledged a good deal of overlap between the stages, she found sequential development of negatives and of questions in the data.

Her learners followed this sequence for negation: Although there were some examples of *no* placed either immediately before or immediately after an utterance (e.g., "No dis one no"), these were not as numerous as those found in the early data of first language learners. Instead, the negative element appeared within the sentence—*no* directly before the main verb (e.g., "I no sing it") and *not* before predicates where a copula would be required in adult speech. The copula was frequently omitted by the children (e.g., "It not hot"). One of the ten learners, however, had a more general rule, which was to place *no* immediately before main verbs, modals, and even forms of *be* (e.g., "I no wanna play"; "We no can go on the bars"; "He no was there"). In this early stage, *don't* appeared only in a few utterances learned as chunks, such as "I don't know." In the next stage, *don't* + main verb began to take over as *no* + main verb subsided. *Don't* was overgeneralized and used in place of other forms (*doesn't, won't, can't,* etc.). *Not* was still used with auxiliary *be* and the copula. Next, the scope of *don't* became more limited as the modal auxiliaries *can't* and *won't* began to emerge. Then *do* began to appear as a true tense carrier, with the distinction among *don't, doesn't,* and *didn't* gradually being worked out. Double marking of tense was common (e.g., "didn't found"; "doesn't wants"). At this stage the indeterminates also began to appear, again with frequent double marking (e.g., "don't want nothing"; "ain't gonna never"; "nobody won't"; "doesn't want no crayons"; etc.).

At the end of two years of observation, most of Adams's learners still hadn't produced sentences with the Aux element *have + en*. Two learners were beginning to acquire the structure, making errors such as "haven't do" for "haven't done."

The yes/no question data could be divided into three stages. In the first stage, the children used rising intonation as the only signal for a question (e.g., "Is good?"; "Play blocks?"; "Wanna see something?"). In the second stage, rising intonation was still the common question form for yes/no questions, but there were also a few chunk-learned questions using *do* ("Do you got X?"; "Do you know?"). *Can* questions with inversion ("Can I go?") also appeared at Stage 2. The use of *be* in yes/no questions was variable. Sometimes the copula was omitted (e.g., "You the teacher?"); sometimes it was present but placed after the noun phrase (e.g., "He is de monster?"); other times it was inverted (e.g., "Is he right?"). By the third stage, *be* inversion stabilized for all learners and more modals began to appear inverted in question forms (*will, could, should*).

WH-questions also fell into three stages of development. In the first stage, the WH-word appeared at the beginning of the question followed by declarative word order (e.g., "What you want?"). This was the most common form in Stage 2 as well; however, *be* was now frequently inverted. This inversion of *be* was then overgeneralized to embedded questions as well (e.g., "I don't know where is mines."). There were a few examples of verb inversion (e.g., "What say that?"), perhaps testing out transfer of a Spanish rule. By the third stage, *be* was used correctly in WH-questions. *Do*-support appeared in yes/no questions first. Shortly thereafter, it began to emerge in WH-questions as well. Again, tense was often doubly marked ("Where did he found it?"; "Where's this one belongs?").

Much of the data in the Adams second language acquisition study looked similar to that of child first language acquisition. While Brown's MLU system could not be used to equate them precisely, and while some evidence of transfer of Spanish was found, the data appeared to support the notion of similarity in first and second language learning processes.

The Cazden, Cancino, Rosansky, and Schumann study (1975) also discussed the developmental patterns of negatives, interrogatives, and Aux *do*. For negatives, they found that their six Spanish-speaking learners began with *no* + verb ("I no can see"; "But no is mine"; "I no use television"). Simultaneously, or shortly thereafter, the learners started to use *don't* + verb. Here, *don't* was considered simply an allomorph of *no* (rather than *do* + *not*). The subjects produced sentences such as: "I don't hear"; "He don't like it"; "I don't can explain." In the third stage, auxiliary + negative, the subjects learned to place the negative after the auxiliary. In general, the first auxiliaries to be negated in this way were *is* (*isn't*) and *can* (*can't*). In the final stage, the learners acquired the analyzed forms of *don't—do not, doesn't, does not, didn't, did not* (e.g., "Because you didn't bring"; "He doesn't laugh like us"). At this point, *don't* was no longer considered a negative chunk, but as *do* + negative.

Like Adams's child learners, these learners, two children, two adolescents, and two adults, showed some variable behavior within the stages. In order not to lose the individual variation in the acquisition process, line drawings were used to display the data for each subject. Figure 1 shows one adult's variable use of *no* + V and *don't* + V.

WH-questions in the Cazden et al. study were described as follows:

Stage I — Undifferentiation: Learner did not distinguish between simple and embedded WH-questions.
a. Uninverted: Both simple and embedded WH-questions were uninverted.
b. Variable inversion. Simple WH-questions were sometimes inverted, sometimes not.
c. Generalization: Increasing inversion in WH-questions with inversion extended to embedded questions.
Stage II — Differentiation: Learner distinguished between simple and embedded WH-questions.
    (Cazden, Cancino, Rosansky, and Schumann, 1975, p. 38)

As you can see, the findings of the Cazden et al. study are similar to those for Adams's Spanish speakers. Both studies in broad outline show similarities with first language data, but differences as well. Their findings are supported by other observational studies of Spanish speakers (cf., Butterworth, 1978; Young, 1974). Nevertheless, it was impossible for researchers to generalize the notion of stages of Interlanguage on the basis of so few studies, particularly since most of the learners were from the same first language background.

To check the systematicity of Interlanguage of learners from language groups other than Spanish, Schumann (1979) reviewed case studies for negation development of second language learners whose first languages were Japanese, French, Greek, Norwegian, Taiwanese, and Italian. Looking only at the appearance of pre-verb negation (e.g., "I no want"; "He no is busy"), he found that the position of the negative in the first language did influence how long this stage persisted in their English. For example, Spanish speakers used *no* + V extensively and persistently; for subjects from first languages with post-verb negation (e.g., Japanese), *no* + V was only a fleeting phenomenon. Though the survey covers only a few subjects, it involves hundreds of negative utterances in the samples, so one should feel some optimism about the generalizability of the findings. That is, the stages remained constant; but learners passed through the

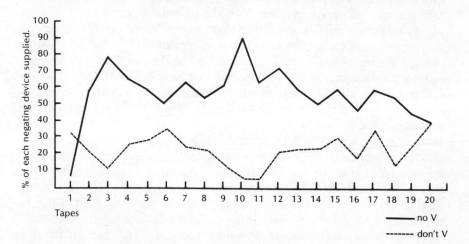

Figure 6.1   Development of Negation in Alberto Showing Proportion of Each Negating Device to Total Negatives in Each Sample

stages more or less rapidly, depending on the similarity/difference of negative placement in English and in the learner's first language.

Other researchers have preferred to solve the problem of generalizability by turning to an experimental approach. Hyltenstam (1977), using a modified cloze procedure, tested 160 adult students learning Swedish as a second language. The test was administered twice. Time 1 refers to the first test given three weeks after instruction began; Time 2 refers to the second test given after eight weeks of instruction.

Swedish rules require that the negative particle be placed after the main verb in main clauses (e.g., Kalle *kommer inte* idag = "Charlie comes not today"), and before the verb in subordinate clauses (e.g., Det ar skont att Kalle *inte kommer* idag = "It's fine that Charlie not comes today"). When an Aux is present, the negative particle follows it in main clauses and precedes it in subordinate clauses. (Deviations from the rule are possible, but all test items concurred with this rule.) In looking for overall patterns, Hyltenstam found that two ranks could be constructed for accurate negative placement in main clauses and subordinate clauses. (1) In main clauses, all Aux verbs were negated according to the rules, but main verbs were not. (2) In subordinate clauses, just the opposite was the case. There, negatives were placed appropriately for main verbs while negatives used with Aux were incorrect. In other words, the two ranks were almost exactly reversed. This order remained the pattern at Time 2, though many more learners gave correct responses at Time 2 than at Time 1. Apparently what happened was that the learners put the negative in front of all verbs, whether in main clauses or subordinate clauses and whether an Aux preceded the verb or not. This gave them correct responses to sentences with Aux in main clauses and incorrect responses with Aux in subordinate clauses. It gave them incorrect responses to sentences with main verbs in main clauses and correct responses to negatives with verbs in subordinate clauses.

Hyltenstam, realizing that this overall picture might be due to certain learners following the pattern and other learners exhibiting variable behavior, checked for individual variable behavior in the data. To do this he used *implicational scaling techniques.* Test items are listed in columns across the top of Figure 2, and subjects' responses are coded as correct (+) or incorrect (−) for each item. The pattern of +'s and −'s is then scanned for regularity of response, not only across all subjects but also within each subject's data. Separate scales were set up for the main and subordinate clause data. Placement of those learners of Swedish who were native speakers of English are illustrated in Figure 2. Notice, first of all, that there is a pattern to the data. There are always more pluses to the left of the scales than to the right. The line drawn separates Aux verbs from main verbs. Subjects, particularly at Time 1, responded more accurately on negatives for Aux verbs in main clauses. However, individual learners do show other patterns of response. Subject 47, for example, got all main clause negation right and all subordinate clause negation wrong at Time 1—he did not differentiate clause types but placed the negative *inte* after (rather than before) the verb. At Time 2, he had learned to make this distinction. Learner 193 usually put the negative before main verbs and after Aux verbs, though there was some variability in his responses. By Time 2, he had learned the rule correctly. None of the learners showed absolutely random performance. The learners can be identified along the continuum according to the parts of the negative rule they had acquired. Their progress on the continuum can be shown in line drawings. Learners who had only acquired the negative after the Aux in main clauses would appear at the lower left in Figure 2. The learners who had acquired both Aux + negative and MV + negative placement, would be on the second step of the continuum. Learners who had acquired all the rules would appear at the top right-hand corner of the continuum chart. Once the learners are placed on the continuum, we can check to see whether first language of the learner makes a difference. We find this is not the case, since *S*s of each language group spread over the continuum rather than group together in one place on it.

On the basis of the scales, Hyltenstam concluded that these 160 learners used a very regular route in acquiring negatives in the second language (a route undifferentiated by source language, length of education, knowledge of foreign languages, etc.). Unfortunately, statistical analyses to support these claims are not given in the summary article, so it is impossible to determine the scalability of the continuum and how strong the support was for the other claims as well.

Hyltenstam's description of acquisition of Swedish negation is very similar to descriptions by Adams and by Cazden et al.: First the negative marker is placed before the verb—similar to the *no* + V stage described by Adams and by Cazden et al. Soon learners realize that *no* + V is not the way native speakers of either Swedish or English form negatives. So learners of English change their *no* + V to *don't* + V. Learners of Swedish begin by putting negatives after Aux verbs, and then, somewhat later, put them after main verbs. However, these solutions are not quite the same as those of native speakers. Swedish learners have to differentiate main clause negation from subordinate clause negation, and so begin to sort out this distinction. For English learners, *don't* has to become an analyzed form of *do* plus negative *(do not, doesn't, does not, didn't, did not)*.

There is, of course, variation among learners at various times along the road to acquisition of the negative. Some backsliding may be expected, since many parts of the language are being learned simultaneously. As new forms come in, the learner's attention may be diverted from newly acquired rules and variability in performance should be expected.

The claims of studies on the acquisition of the Aux system (that is, negatives and question formation) are somewhat less sweeping than those made in the morphology studies. The search is for a regularity in the learning process that would allow us to believe in the systematicity of Interlanguage. The findings, since they look at the process rather than at the end product, are not radically different from the approach used by Slobin in his search for universals in first

Time 1

Main clauses

S/C[1]	kan	vill	vill	får	ska	hinner	stannar	arbetar	kommer	börjar	bor	sover
	1	2	3	4	5	6	7	8	9	10	11	12
284	+	+	+	+	+	−	−	−	−	−	−	−
28	+	+	+	−	+	+	−	−	−	−	−	−
34	+	+	+	+	+	+	−	−	−	−	−	−
193	+	+	+	−	+	+	−	+	−	−	−	−
264	+	+	+	+	+	−	−	+	−	−	−	−
50	+	+	+	+	+	−	+	−	+	+	−	−
22	+	+	+	+	+	+	+	+	+	−	+	−
215	+	+	+	+	+	+	+	+	+	+	+	−
33	+	+	+	+	+	+	+	+	+	+	+	+
37	+	+	+	+	+	+	+	+	+	+	+	+
47	+	+	+	+	+	+	+	+	+	+	+	+
56	+	+	+	+	+	+	+	+	+	+	+	+
69	+	+	+	+	+	+	+	+	+	+	+	+
86	+	+	+	+	+	+	+	+	+	+	+	+
301	+	+	+	+	+	+	+	+	+	+	+	+
79	+	+	+	+	+	+	+	+	+	+	+	+
202	+	+	+	+	+	+	+	+	+	+	+	+
247	+	+	+	+	+	+	+	+	+	+	+	+
257	+	+	+	+	+	+	+	+	+	+	+	+

Time 1 (continued)

Subordinate clauses

S/C	sover	kommer	stannar	arbetar	bor	börjar	hinner	ska	får	vill	vill	kan
	1	2	3	4	5	6	7	8	9	10	11	12
257	−	−	−	−	−	−	−	−	−	−	−	−
247	−	−	−	−	−	−	−	−	−	−	−	−
79	−	−	−	−	−	−	−	−	−	−	−	−
301	−	−	−	−	−	−	−	−	−	−	−	−
86	−	−	−	−	−	−	−	−	−	−	−	−
69	−	−	−	−	−	−	−	−	−	−	−	−
56	−	−	−	−	−	−	−	−	−	−	−	−
47	−	−	−	−	−	−	−	−	−	−	−	−
37	−	−	−	−	−	−	−	−	−	−	−	−
215	−	−	−	−	−	−	−	−	−	−	−	−
33	−	−	−	+	−	−	−	−	−	−	−	−
202	+	+	−	−	−	−	−	−	−	−	−	−
22	+	−	−	+	+	−	−	−	−	−	−	−
193	+	+	+	−	−	−	−	+	−	−	−	−
264	+	+	−	−	+	+	−	−	−	−	−	−
50	+	+	−	+	+	+	−	−	−	−	−	−
28	+	+	+	+	+	+	−	−	−	−	−	−
34	+	+	+	+	+	+	−	−	−	−	−	−
284	+	+	+	+	+	+	+	−	−	−	−	−

Figure 6.2   Scales 1-4. Native Speakers of English

Time 2

Main clauses

S/C	1	2	3	4	5	6	7	8	9	10	11	12
50	+	+	+	−	+	−	+	−	+	−	−	−
28	+	+	+	+	+	+	+	+	−	+	+	−
22	+	+	+	+	+	+	+	+	+	+	+	+
33	+	+	+	+	+	+	+	+	+	+	+	+
34	+	+	+	+	+	+	+	+	+	+	+	+
37	+	+	+	+	+	+	+	+	+	+	+	+
47	+	+	+	+	+	+	+	+	+	+	+	+
56	+	+	+	+	+	+	+	+	+	+	+	+
69	+	+	+	+	+	+	+	+	+	+	+	+
86	+	+	+	+	+	+	+	+	+	+	+	+
79	+	+	+	+	+	+	+	+	+	+	+	+
193	+	+	+	+	+	+	+	+	+	+	+	+
202	+	+	+	+	+	+	+	+	+	+	+	+
215	+	+	+	+	+	+	+	+	+	+	+	+
247	+	+	+	+	+	+	+	+	+	+	+	+
257	+	+	+	+	+	+	+	+	+	+	+	+
264	+	+	+	+	+	+	+	+	+	+	+	+
284	+	+	+	+	+	+	+	+	+	+	+	+
301	+	+	+	+	+	+	+	+	+	+	+	+

Time 2 (continued)

Subordinate clauses

S/C	1	2	3	4	5	6	7	8	9	10	11	12
37	−	−	−	−	−	−	−	−	−	−	−	−
56	−	−	−	−	−	−	−	−	−	−	−	−
69	−	−	−	−	−	−	−	−	−	−	−	−
28	+	+	+	−	−	−	+	−	−	−	−	−
50	−	+	+	+	+	+	+	−	−	−	−	−
33	+	+	+	+	+	+	+	−	−	−	−	−
86	+	+	+	+	+	−	+	+	−	−	−	−
202	+	+	+	+	+	+	−	+	−	−	−	−
34	+	+	+	+	+	+	+	+	+	+	+	+
47	+	+	+	+	+	+	+	+	+	+	+	+
301	+	+	+	+	+	+	+	+	+	+	+	+
79	+	+	+	+	+	+	+	+	+	+	+	+
193	+	+	+	+	+	+	+	+	+	+	+	+
215	+	+	+	+	+	+	+	+	+	+	+	+
247	+	+	+	+	+	+	+	+	+	+	+	+
257	+	+	+	+	+	+	+	+	+	+	+	+
264	+	+	+	+	+	+	+	+	+	+	+	+
284	+	+	+	+	+	+	+	+	+	+	+	+
22	+	+	+	+	+	+	+	+	+	+	+	+

[1] S = subject, C = context

Figure 6.2 *continued*

language acquisition. They all describe a set of operating principles which learners appear to use as they gradually differentiate the rules for the system.

One reason that language acquisition research is so difficult lies in the variation in the data—that is, the degree of variation from subject to subject and even in the performance of one subject during the process. In observational data, the learner may produce lots of "I don't know" utterances at an early stage. Or, he or she may produce lost of "whatcha" questions. Are these to be counted as forerunners of *do* in negatives and questions? The problem of acquired chunks (also called "prefabs" by Hakuta and "formula utterances" by Wong-Fillmore) and how they are to be dealt with in tracing acquisition has not been solved to anyone's real satisfaction. We can look for *do* elsewhere in the data and decide to throw out chunk-learned utterances as being outside the "real" data. But, some learners also learn "I don't want," "I don't like," and other *don't* + verb chunks in addition to "I don't know." How many of these do we need to find before we decide that they may have an effect and should be counted and described as part of the learning process?

The variability in early stages between correct and incorrect forms is complicated by the large number of chunk-learned utterances. The degree of variability from learner to learner has led to some speculation on how much variation is allowed before the claim of systematicity has to be discarded. Taylor (1975), finding that adult ESL learners showed great variability in producing correct/incorrect verb forms on a written translation task, argued that Interlanguage is a suspect concept indeed when variation is found not only among learners but within each learner's performance as well. Nevertheless, Hyltenstam, Andersen, and others believe that implicational scales and variable rules can deal with variable data and can reveal the Interlanguage continuum for second language structures. Others argue that the rather small amount of variation found in Hyltenstam's data may be due to the cloze procedure task which does not allow for much variation in choice. If we agree that Hyltenstam's continuum is a real scale, the question still to be answered is whether such a continuum can be found for other syntactic structures as well.

Minimal Distance and Relative Clauses

Aside from the Aux system, two other favorite areas of first language research are relative clauses and a set of four structures which are associated with the minimal distance principle. Second language researchers wondered whether tests of these structures would reveal similar patterns for first and second language learners.

C. Chomsky (1969) tested the minimal distance principle to see whether or not children acquiring English as a first language would attend to surface proximity of nouns and verbs in processing sentences, or whether or not they would use underlying syntax in processing. She assumed that children might interpret the noun closest to the verb as the subject of the verb in such sentences as:

1. The doll is easy/eager to see.   (Predicted error: doll does all the seeing)
2. Bozo asked/promised Mickey to sing.   (Predicted error: Mickey does all the singing)
3. Ask/tell Bozo what to eat.   (Predicted error: Bozo does all the eating)

The fourth sentence type Chomsky looked at involved pronoun reference. Would children, for example, identify the correct pronoun referent in such sentences as "After *he* got the candy, Mickey left" and "Pluto thinks *he* knows everything." And, if so, would they recognize the nonidentity of the pronoun in such sentences as "*He* found that Mickey won the race"? Her findings showed a progression with age—older children completed the tasks much more accurately than younger children. The youngest children used "nextness" as a way of assigning noun-verb connections, and were not as accurate in locating pronoun referents.

Van Mettre (1972) tested thirty-two Spanish-English bilingual children on these minimal distance structures and found "an orderly sequence of the structures" which paralleled that of first language learners. Cook (1973) tested twenty adult ESL learners on the easy/eager distinction and found stages similar to those described for first language learners. d'Anglejan and Tucker (1975) found adult ESL learners, particularly beginners, relied on surface proximity rather than sentence syntax in processing such sentences. Syngle (1973) tested 198 adult learners from various source languages and sixteen child second language learners and found essential similiarities in adult's and children's comprehension of these sentences. He also found no differences that could be attributed to the learner's source language.

The relative clause studies, on the other hand, do not mirror first language data quite so exactly. First, as Schachter pointed out in her now-famous "Error in Error Analysis" paper (1974), ESL learners vary not only in how accurately they produce relative clauses but also in how frequently they use relative clauses according to their native language. Students whose first languages have relative clause structures similar to English in most details (e.g., Persian or Arabic) use as many relative clauses in writing as do native speakers of English, but they make a large number of errors on the finer details of English relative clauses. Students whose source languages differ radically from English in their relative clause structures (e.g., Chinese or Japanese) produce few relative clauses when writing English, but those they do produce contain very few errors. First language does make a difference here.

Bertkau's work (1974)—on comprehension and production of relative clauses by adult ESL learners—further substantiates the claim for differences. She found Japanese students scored lower on comprehension of relative clauses than did Spanish ESL learners, and that Japanese students had special problems in comprehension of relative clauses that follow subject noun phrases. She concluded from the production data that individual learners vary greatly on relative clause production. Individual idiolects, she claims, rather than one discernible Interlanguage continuum, determine relative clause use.

Other researchers currently working on relative clause data use scaling techniques. However, at this point, their findings show that it is still not clear whether or not patterns can be discerned for all learners, regardless of their source language.

Proficiency Tests and Error Analyses

Proficiency tests could be a valuable source of information on acquisition of sentence syntax. If first language has no real effect on the Interlanguage sequence (as is so often claimed in the literature), then proficiency tests should give us some ideas about what is learned first, second, and so on, for all learners. In addition, many tests (e.g., *Ilyin Oral Interview*, 1979) allow the examiner to terminate testing once learners are unable to respond to several test items in a row. This must assume an order of acquisition for the items on the test. Such information might tell us a good deal about the Interlanguage system and shed light on the nature of the psychological difficulty of various types of syntactic structures.

Fathman, the developer of the SLOPE test, reported an accuracy order on the test items for 200 ESL children (ages six to fifteen). Older children received higher scores on morphology and syntax subtests, but the accuracy *order* for the structures remained the same across the age range. She subsequently tested sixty ESL learners (six to fourteen years) and found no differences in the accuracy order for language background (Spanish or Korean), age, or instruction method used in teaching the children English. The subtests for the SLOPE cover most of the areas mentioned in the morphology and Aux studies discussed above, not a full range of syntactic structures.

To really discover the sequence of Interlanguage we need proficiency tests that have a very broad range of syntactic structures. The problem is that proficiency tests are usually constructed so that the smallest possible number of test items are used to discover what the learner does or does not know. Furthermore, most test designers feel that global measures (such as cloze and dictation tests) can place students more accurately than can discrete item grammar tests. Global measures won't help us discover sequence. While cloze passages and dictation are popular test measures, many entrance exams also include a sample of syntactic structures. These should be useful for our purposes.

The few studies that look at proficiency data are not very encouraging if we want to discover one Interlanguage continuum which is *not* influenced by the first language of the learner. These studies, unlike those reported by Fathman, involve adult students. Kemp (1975) took data from the entrance exams

(Michigan Test of English Language Proficiency) of 425 foreign students. Fifty-five error types were identified and cross-tabulated for students' native language and proficiency levels. Significant differences were found among language groups on nine error types, while fifteen error types differed according to the students' proficiency levels. In other words, an Interlanguage continuum for fifteen error types could be set up and nine error types would have to be specified as affected by the first language of the learner. Farhady (1980) has shown that first language does make a difference in the types of items missed; as well as in how well learners do on integrative, discrete-point, and communicative competence tests. Data from entrance exams that test grammatical items could be coded to test Kemp's and Farhady's findings. Comparison of test results ought to be especially valuable; so many students of many different source languages take proficiency tests at major universities each year. Meanwhile, we might look at error analysis to validate differences due to first language interference/transfer and/or the psychological difficulty of specific language structures.

Linguists such as George (1972) and Richards (1974) have discussed learner errors in terms of their universal characteristics—errors shared by all language learners. Neumann (1977), in her attempt to contrast the shared errors of intermediate learners with those of beginning learners, analyzed errors made in compositions of 158 students. Her classification system, which includes the errors made in each category, is much too lengthy to display here; however, the most frequent errors of the intermediate students may be of interest. Raw scores are as follows:

885 Noun modification errors (including 262 omissions of definite article; 206 omissions of indefinite article; 226 articles used where not needed)
501 Verb errors (including 260 tense substitutions, largely present for past; 95 voice errors showing confusion of passive/active)
493 Preposition errors (240 substitutions, especially of locatives; 172 omissions, again especially of locatives; 81 supplied were not needed)
404 Lexical errors (including 251 semantic errors, especially in verbs; 132 morphology word class errors)
281 Sentence structure errors (including 146 fragments; 100 word order errors)
234 Complex syntax errors (including 114 for gerund/infinitive forms; 17 relative clauses)
172 Number agreement (including 114 in determiner-noun agreement)
145 Noun errors (including 113 singular/plural errors, especially generic nouns)
 65 Logical clause relationships (including 39 in conjunction choice)
 30 Adverb of time/place not requiring preposition errors
 18 Negation errors

Error figures were adjusted for length of composition, and means were compared to check for differences among the different intermediate classes and among the beginning, intermediate, and advanced learner classes. The part of the study that concerns us here is whether or not errors on structures would differ according to the first language of the learner, and whether or not the scores would vary according to the proficiency level of the student. In order to check this, eight error type groups were identified and compared across beginning, intermediate, and advanced class levels. Surprisingly, the mean number of errors in each of the categories failed to show significant change across levels with one exception—word order errors. In this, beginning and advanced students made more errors than the intermediate group. (Does this show that beginners and advanced students are more adventurous in experimenting with word order?) It is surprising to see so little evidence of progress from level to level (and therefore no continuum). Unfortunately, standard deviations are not given, so we do not know the extent of variability within groups. Either the students show a great deal of variability in errors (and therefore no continuum), or else there is a plateau in the progress made on these syntactic structures.

Neumann also found that the native language of the learner did make a difference on two error types. Japanese and Korean students made more article omission errors than other learners; students from Germanic/Slavic and from Japanese and Korean language backgrounds differed from other language groups on preposition omissions. While mean scores seemed to show that students from certain language groups made more errors overall than students from other groups, when scores were adjusted for length of composition, the differences were not significant.

Neumann's study, like most error analyses, is based on written data. In contrast, Linde (1971) worked with oral data, tabulating errors made by Japanese speakers during conversations. He found that each of his Japanese learners made the same error many times in the speech sample. This may be evidence (contrary to Taylor's findings, 1975) that each learner's Interlanguage is consistent and reliable. However, error ranks across subjects did not agree. That is, not all subjects made the same errors, despite their common first language—evidence for the variability of and lack of influence from the source language. Linde also claims that frequency counts in error analyses are misleading. As teachers, we are aware that Japanese students have problems with English articles. We would expect the accuracy sequence to change for Japanese students, then, since they acquire articles late. At least, articles would be out of line in the learning sequence compared to the data of other learner groups. Linde found extremely high error counts on articles for his learners. However, articles are high frequency words in English; they occur everywhere. If scores are adjusted for frequency of article appearance in English, then the errors on articles for Japanese speakers are no more common than their verb tense errors.

While Linde urges that scores be converted for frequency (which might help to reveal the Interlanguage continuum), one could argue that corrected scores are also misleading. Nevertheless, that is precisely what we do on proficiency exams. We control for frequency of possible error. There may be two multiple-choice items on articles in a complete test, and one of these may do double duty in testing for mass/count noun distinctions. Given this control on frequency of error types, we should not expect first language to be a major factor in proficiency exams. Again, variation among learner groups as well as individual variation is being lost, both because of our test instruments and because of our data analysis procedure.

Obviously, proficiency exams alone cannot answer the question of systematicity in the learning process, nor are they designed for that purpose. Error analysis studies can help remedy this, but they too must be carefully thought out if they are to answer the questions we pose. The main purpose of both proficiency exams and error analyses has been a very practical one—getting information to teachers about the common errors and the specific errors of second language learners:

While approximative systems of language learners may be studied as entities worthy of attention in and of themselves, the results of such study should also provide feedback to language teaching practice and to general linguistic theory. (Richards, 1974, p. 15)

A combination of observation and experimental research, error analysis, and proficiency testing does, however, give us some provisional answers to questions posed about Interlanguage:

1. While there is a good deal of argument about the degree of systematicity in Interlanguage, many researchers and teachers believe that the move from the beginning stages of language learning to later fluency follows a sequence which is not random.

2. While each learner's Interlanguage may show systematic change, that system is not an invariant one for all learners. There is a good deal of overlap within the data of even one learner moving from one stage to the next. Untutored learners may, for example, begin by using *me* as the first person pronoun, then use *me* and *I* interchangeably for some period of time, and finally arrive at *I* as the correct form. While all this can be systematically described, the correct/incorrect forms may shift back and forth several times as the learner sorts out the rules for each part of the system. In addition, there is variation among learners. Part of this may be due to the source language of the learner (unpopular as that notion may still be). In other words, the invariant sequence is not all that invariant. Despite the variability found within the data of one subject and in the data between subjects, most researchers still believe there is enough similarity to allow us to talk about Interlanguage as systematic.

3. There is much difference of opinion about the influence of transfer/interference from the first language on the order (or speed) of acquisition of syntactic structures. Given a list of pronunciation errors, most teachers could identify the learner's first language. Given a list of syntactic errors (excluding frequency of article errors), it is less likely that the first language of the learner could be deduced.

4. The Interlanguage sequence is thought to show the same systematicity and the same variability in data whether the learners are adults or children.

5. Both claims and counterclaims regarding the similarity of second language data and first language learning data have been made. Similarities are there, but differences have also been found. Differences have been attributed to a number of causes, but especially to the greater cognitive development of the second language learner and to the effect of the first language on second language learning. On the other hand, forms acquired late by both first and second language learners must make us question cognitive explanations for late acquisition of these forms by first language learners. If these forms are also acquired late by second language learners (with much more advanced cognitive development), perhaps other factors such as markedness theory may provide better explanations for both.

T-Units and the Syntactic Index

Another way of looking at Interlanguage is to take a more global approach. As mentioned earlier, most placement examinations use what are called "global measures," such as cloze or dictation, in measuring students' English abilities. Rather than examining the development of specific syntactic structures, we might want to look for an overall growth index. A number of researchers have been searching for a measure that would show us, in some sort of reasonable way, the overall progress that students do make in syntactic development. Hunt (1965) suggested that we could judge syntactic maturity of first language learners by counting the length of T-units in their compositions. The T-unit is a single independent clause together with all its modifying subordinate clauses. As the student matures, his or her T-units become longer, especially if embedding is used. That is, "The fence is painted" is a four-word T-unit. This may appear to be just a measure of sentence length, but not quite. "The fence is painted and the house needs paint" is two T-units, each four words in length, since there are two independent clauses in the sentence.

Scott and Tucker (1974) modified the T-unit for use with second language learners. Since students, even in the early stages of their language development, could produce fairly long T-units by translating from the first language, Scott and Tucker's measure looks at the percentage of error-free T-units in composition. Larsen-Freeman and Strom (1977) further modified the T-unit method by calculating the average length of the T-unit, but, unlike Hunt, included only those T-units that were error-free. Their purpose, however, was different, for they believed we need an index, a Syntactic Index, against which we can plot acquisition of structures. In first language acquisition the mean length of utterance (MLU) was proposed as a better index of development than age. When children are at Stage 2 (MLU = 2.0 to 2.5), we expect that their syntax will be of a certain type (e.g., their negatives can be described in a certain way; their interrogatives will be of a certain type, and so on). In second language acquisition we talk rather loosely about "stages" in Aux development, but we have no outside measure (e.g., age or MLU) that will tell us which syntactic structures the learner should have acquired at any point. The Syntactic Index, then, could serve the same function for second language research that the MLU has for first language research.

Arthur (1979) further modified the T-unit measure to include other writing abilities, as follows:

Measurement	Ability Tested
Average words per minute of writing time	Fluency; articulateness
Average length of T-units	Grammatical sophistication
% of error-free T-units	Grammatical sophistication
Type-Token ratio	Size of active vocabulary
Average grammar errors/100 words	Ability to correct/avoid errors
Average misspelled words/100 words	Ability to spell correctly
% T-units ending with punctuation mark	Ability to punctuate
Semantic errors as % of total errors	Seriousness of grammar errors

Using these measures, he charted the progress made by fourteen lower-intermediate ESL students (university students) who produced a total of 152 compositions during the school term. The comparisons were made between six compositions produced during the first half of the course by each *S* and six produced during the second half. The students did improve over time, but the most interesting findings were not the differences in improvement according to first language groups nor the differences among the three T-unit measures; rather, it was the finding of total variability over time on each of the measures that was so astonishing. For example, a student might produce eight words per minute in week 10, five in week 11, and eight in week 12. Also, the T-unit measures for each *S* were not stable over time. Yet, despite this variation, the teacher's sense that students had improved was substantiated in the analysis. The charts of individual students show an "up and down" scoring for individual measures. Yet, even with the highs and lows on errors in each half of the data, the lows became lower as time went on. The students did improve overall. This is important, for it's a word of warning to both researchers and teachers regarding reliability of T-unit scores. Students' final examination compositions should not be expected to mirror their growth during a semester, since scores on each part rose and fell dramatically from composition to composition during the term. A fairer analysis of progress can only be seen by comparing the gradual drop in errors over time.

The Heidelberg group (1978a; b) has also searched for an Index of Syntactic Development. Rather than look for a global measure to identify Interlanguage stages, they use the Index as an achievement measure similar to a proficiency test. They collected data from tape-recorded interviews between learners and native speakers, rather than from test measures. After the data had been transcribed, phrase structure rules were written for all structures that occurred more frequently than fifty times. Then they described each *S*'s data via these rules. The Index weighs some of the rules more heavily than others and uses those rules that show variability among learners. Compared to the T-unit analysis, the method is very complex and a number of points regarding it are not clear. It is difficult to determine whether it is the presence or the accuracy of the form that is being considered. Second, supposedly no transformations were included; that must mean questions, negatives, and so forth would not be included in the analysis, though the examples show this is clearly not the case. If we examine those rules that are most highly correlated with the total Index number, they are verbal group, complete NP-VP sentences, pronouns, and determiner. Aux development, adverbs, and relative clauses rate further down the list. Ss who are rated as having acquired a good deal of syntax (i.e., have a high Syntactic Index figure) are those who used complete sentences, included a V in the sentences, and elaborated the NP by including determiners. Such ratings seem to reflect sentence length even more than the T-unit analysis does. Short answers, so typical and appropriate to interviews, do not give one a high rating. If this description is accurate, it shows again how easy and misleading it is to look at form outside context. If an interviewer asks "Where do you work?" or "How many children do you have?" (and example data suggest that these are the kinds of questions asked during interviews), one can quite acceptably use an incomplete sentence and even a simple one-word response. Interviews are supposed to elicit information rather than conversation. It is probably true, however, that the learner who is best able to change an interview into a conversation—a learning opportunity—probably *is* the best learner and deserves the higher Index figure.

In this chapter I have talked about a number of areas of syntactic research, beginning with some of the research on syntax acquisition by first and second language learners. There are a variety of ways to codify and present information on syntactic development: rule writing, stages, implicational scales, experimental research on comprehension, proficiency tests, error analyses, and syntactic indices. Each method gives us part of the picture of the developmental sequence of sentence structures. Continuing research using this multiple-method approach should give us more information, not only on the order in which structures are learned, but also on the developmental process itself. Such research is crucial if we wish to develop teaching materials that take advantage of both the proposed natural order and the influence of first language on second language learning. It is also crucial if we wish to use second language data as a testing ground for new proposals on syntax, rules, and rule ordering (see Tavakolian, 1981).

To understand the developmental process, however, we need to know more than just what syntactic structures are acquired; we need to know whether they are or are not used appropriately. In order to talk about appropriateness of syntactic choice, we have to move on to the next level, discourse. Just as it is clear that lexicon puts constraints on syntax (and vice versa), so it is also clear that discourse puts constraints on syntactic choice as well. The next two chapters address this topic.

7 *Discourse and Sentence Syntax*

For psycholinguists, simply describing the sentences learners can produce or comprehend is not enough. We need to know in addition if learners choose sentence forms that are *appropriate* for a particular discourse function. To do that, we need to know the linguistic *functions* of syntactic forms, a problem linguists and psycholinguists are now beginning to investigate in depth.

Syntax gives us a variety of ways to express our thoughts. Yet, we seldom organize our thoughts into single one-sentence utterances. Instead, information may be spread out over many sentences, many paragraphs, or many conversational exchanges. We need some sort of discourse plan to allow us to organize how we will present information (or, in the case of conversation, how it will be negotiated among the participants), and the syntactic forms that will make the organization clear.

A Functional Approach

Context analysis, Celce-Murcia (1980) says, "begins with a (linguistic) form or forms and seeks to describe the meaning function and restrictions on the form(s) as used in context" (p. 41). A stronger way of saying this is that discourse uses syntax to promote understanding.

Let's consider a few examples for a better understanding of the functional approach to syntax. The narrative is, perhaps, the most discussed discourse genre. If I want to tell you about something that happened, there are parts of the story that I will want to emphasize as being in the "foreground" of the happening. There will be other parts that will give you a fairly precise orientation to the story—"background" information about setting, time, and characters. There may be previous information that I need to fill in for you, and there may be some sidelights I need to mention as well. I also may make comments to help you evaluate the story, so you know why I'm telling it or what the point is. The question is how to make some of these stand out as important and let others slip into the background. Longacre (1978) talks about three syntactic devices most languages of the world seem to use in order to give prominence to parts of narratives: (1) verb tense/aspect, (2) word order, and (3) special particles. So context analysis helps us understand not only that languages use devices like tense/aspect in discourse but also *why* such mechanisms have been created in the first place.

In English we use *verb tense/aspect* to highlight parts of narratives. For example, we use the copula in simple past tense to set the scene and to describe the list of characters. The narrative itself consists of a set of actions which build to a climax point in the story. Simple tense is used, usually simple past tense, for the major actions of the story, to separate them from the rest of the narrative. Other actions paralleling the major story line are presented in progressive aspect, and flashbacks to events that happened before the story began are usually in the pluperfect. Descriptive states, feelings, or prolonged activities are usually in the past progressive. Explanations, motives, alternative courses open but not taken may be in various aspect forms. Let's look at the following text narrative sample taken from *Donald Copey of Harvard.*

As a small boy, Charles had often been attracted by some bright red berries which grew beside the fence outside the house of an old lady "with corkscrew curls," he remembered, who lived down the street from the Copeland home. One day as the boy came by, the blinds were drawn, and the opportunity to indulge his longing seemed at hand. He plucked a berry and ate it, but its taste was bitter, and he took no more. As he was about to turn away, the blinds of a window flew open, the old lady leaned out and cried, "Now, you naughty boy, you have found your reward. Those berries are deadly poison, which I keep especially for naughty boys. Tomorrow you will be dead!" Charles' heart leaped in his breast. Reflecting on how sad a fate it was to die when his life had scarcely begun, he hurried, panic-stricken, to his home. There he found his brother Lowell in the hall, and poured out the dreadful story, begging his brother's forgiveness for all the injuries he had done him, exacting a promise that he would attend the funeral, and telling him of certain prized possessions he would leave to him. Charles then kissed his brother, who was by that time in tears, told him he would see him once more, and went out of the house. In the garden he found his father, and told him all that happened. His father smiled, took him by the hand, and led him back to the scene of his crime. Quivering before the old lady, Charles implored her forgiveness and begged her to give him something which would forestall his imminent end. She exacted his eager promise that never again would he bother her property, whereupon she produced a gumdrop and plopped it in his mouth. Thus comforted, he took his father's hand and left for home. (J. Adams, 1960, p. 54)

In this narrative, the backbone event verbs are marked with simple past tense: "came by, plucked, ate. flew, leaned, cried," etc. If we abstracted these clauses from the story, we would have a reasonable précis of the action line. Pluperfect is used to show events that occurred earlier: "had been attracted." The progressive is used for descriptive states and feelings: "reflecting on, begging forgiveness, exacting a promise." Thus, simple past tense is used for the foregrounded major story line, while aspect (perfect and progressive) is used for the background. However, this distinction between simple completive and durative or perfective is not used consistently for this function. Rather, the foregrounded story will have a high proportion (but not 100 percent) of simple tenses and background will contain a high proportion of progressive and perfect verb forms.

Longacre has pointed out that this tense/aspect distribution works much better in Romance and Slavic languages than in English. In the following example (taken from Longacre's article), the tense distinction is much closer to a one-to-one correspondence, clearly separating the foregrounded story from additional embroidery information.

Walter Schnaffs demeura d'abord immobile, tellement supris, et éperdu qu'il ne pensait même pas à fluir. Puis un désir fou de détaler le saisit; mais il songea aussitôt qu'il courait comme une tortue en comparaison des maigres Français qui arrivaient en bondissant comme un troupeau de chèvre. Alors, apercevant à six pas devant lui un large fossé plein de broussailles couvertes de feuilles sèches, il y sauta à pieds joints sans même songer a la profondeur, comme on saute d'un pont dans une rivière. . . . Soudain quelque chose remua contre lui. Il eut us sursaut épouvantable. C'était un petit oiseau qui, s'étant pose sur une branche, agitait des feuilles mortes. Pendant près d'une heure, le coeur de Walter Schnaffs en battit à grands coups presses.

The verbs that tell the story line are in the passé simple: *demeura, saisit, songea, sauta,* etc. The background material is given in the imparfait: *pensait, courait, arrivaient,* etc. At the end of the excerpt we find that Walter's heart beat in great, hurried strokes for nearly an hour. Yet *battit* is in the passé simple. Even though it's "continued action in the past," the passé simple is used to show that it is part of the main story line, not part of the background material.

As mentioned earlier, Longacre suggested that one function of the tense/aspect system is to separate foreground and background information in narratives. Hopper suggests that it is only from the discourse viewpoint that tense/aspect at the sentence level becomes intelligible:

One finds typically an aspect marker specialized for foregrounding, or one specialized for backgrounding or both functions marked. Superimposed upon these markers there may be quite precise indicators of tense properly speaking, i.e., the location of an action on the temporal-deictic axis. Most of these tense-markers can be expected to function in background only, e.g., pluperfect, remote-past, future-perfect, future, etc. Their purpose is to gather in information and other detail scattered at arbitrary points on the axis. Because background tense markers signal happenings and states which are not "in sequence" and which by their very temporal inconsistency cannot and do not move the discourse forward, they have access to a much wider spectrum of temporal deixis. . . . Background is less constrained in tense than foreground because details which are of indirect relevance to the narrative do not have to be contemporaneous with the narrative, but may be part of the pre-history of the narrated event (pluperfect), or may provide a preview for a total perspective of the event (future or future-perfect), or may even suggest contingent but unrealized events (irrealis forms such as conditionals and optatives). In foreground, by contrast, the only tense-indication needed is a conventional location of the successive events of the narrative in a . . . framework. In many languages this tense is known as a "preterite" or "simple past." (1978, pp. 30–31)

If we as speakers or writers wish to make certain parts of a story stand out dramatically, we may suddenly *shift tense* (from past to present) as a way of spotlighting that section. We often use a direct quote, rather than an indirect report of what someone has said, as a way of making that segment stand out more. As will be described later on, bilinguals also switch languages as another way to spotlight parts of narratives. This is especially true when we tell stories in the "performance mode." That is, if we wish not only to tell a story but to dramatize it as well, we use a number of devices to make the story entertaining for our listeners or readers. If we want to simply give information, our narrative may be factual and brief: "I heard the explosion. At the time, I was just getting in the shower. So I got dressed, ran outside, and saw a cloud of smoke in the air." The story line is in simple past and the parallel action is in continuous aspect. However, given a few minutes and a desire to convey the drama of the scene, we can heighten emotional impact by using gestures, sound effects, repetition, asides, direct speech, and tense switching. We often switch tense to the *historical present.* It's true that we often caution students against using the historical present, because we associate it with sports broadcasting ("Bibby tosses up a prayer, and it's answered, 78–80, and Dr. J. takes it on a quick outlet pass . . .") or travelogues ("We come over the top of the pass and see spread out below us the charming village of . . ."). Nevertheless, it is an effective device which heightens the dramatic impact of conversational narratives:

> Yeh, well I—I heard th— this exPLOsion, POOWUMMM. It took—the whole place shook. The whole HOUse was shaking an' I stood there thinkin' "should I?"—I wuz jus gonna take a shower—"Should I?" I play tennis, yknow, and my tennis shorts—I just got home and was changin. I wuz gonna take a shower when I HEARD it. GOD, it wuz loud. So I quick jump into my clothes and run outside. 's my neighbor's place down the block. I can't beLIEVE it. The smoke—the smoke wuz like a—a tower. An I run over and I'm wavin my arms like this lookin for Ida and there she was crying. She looks at me and she says, "My God, my God". . . . (excerpt from radio report, KNXT, June 1979)

Wolfson (1978) looked at the use of the historical present in 150 tape-recorded stories and claimed that it is not the tense which is crucial (though it does, I think, put the listener in the shoes of the narrator for the moment), but the switch itself. She argued that if the narrator wants the listener to relive certain events and so consistently uses the historical present, we should be able to predict which verbs would be in the past and which in the historical present. Since her data did not allow such predictions, Wolfson claimed that it is not the choice of tense—past or present—but the switch back and forth from one to the other that creates a theatrical effect.

Schiffrin (1981), however, suggests that the variation of historical present and past can be explained (if not predicted). Looking at seventy-three narratives, she found that the historical present occurs only in the temporally ordered section of the narrative, not in the orientation, evaluation, or coda sections. Since narrative events are understood as having an event time (because of their order in the discourse), tense is, she says, freed from its main job of providing reference time. Time is already provided by the sequential nature of the events. Therefore, switching can occur. The switching from past to historical present within the narrative is also predictable to some extent. Schiffrin found that narrative sections most typically begin and end with simple past. The use of historical present is most common in environments where present tense has a "present" (a single moment in time), rather than "habitual," understanding (for example, with certain action verbs, with verbs of "saying," etc.). She found restrictions on the use of the historical present where time reference is not clear (e.g., between main and subordinate *when*-clauses). She also showed that the use of the historical present is more frequent where temporal conjunctions show a break in the event line. Contrary to Wolfson, Schiffrin claims that the direction of the shift is not random; only the switch from historical present to past separates the events in the narrative.

Beyond this, Schiffrin claims that the historical present can be an evaluative device. It is a way of making an action that occurred in the past sound as if it were occurring at the moment of speaking; a way of making it more vivid or dramatic. The historical present can also highlight very subtle points. For example, Schiffrin discusses three stories told by one speaker, a woman concerned about her role as a mother. The three stories are very similar. In each, the problem is the same—the mother discovers that her child is in need of help—and the resolution of the problem is the same—the mother takes a dramatic action to avert catastrophe. One would expect, then, that the historical present would be used in the same way in all three stories. This is not the case. In two, the historical present is used at the climax of the story and at the resolution point. In the third it is not. Rather, it is used in a series of external evaluation clauses. Schiffrin showed that in the first two stories the historical present is used to highlight the speaker's competence as a mother. In the third story it is used by the mother to evaluate her own competence in the role. If the researcher were to count the number of times the historical present occurs at the most dramatic point in stories, such subtle distinctions (where the historical present serves as an evaluative device) would be lost.

In discourse, then, we use the tense/aspect portion of sentence syntax for a variety of narrative functions. As Longacre suggests, *word order changes* also serve many such functions. Consider the so-called *root transformations* which change word order:

The lead marathoners paced up Heartbreak Hill.
Up Heartbreak Hill paced the lead marathoners.

The chairman of the department was talking on the telephone.
Talking on the telephone was the chairman of the department.

Some graduate students were lined up at the Placement Office.
Lined up at the Placement Office were some graduate students.

Sgt. Begay stood on the ledge overlooking the mesa.
On the ledge overlooking the mesa stood Sgt. Begay.

Gary (1974) investigated root transformations, looking for discourse cues to explain when such transformations are grammatical and when they are not. Compare the acceptability of the transformations in the following examples from his paper:

Keith Sebastian had given me detailed instructions on how to find his house; he was to meet me there with the money. I drove up the driveway and got out of my car. Just as the door closed, I heard the main door to the house open.

Out of the house stepped { *Keith Sebastian.
Dan Carlyle.
the Sheriff.

In the first case the transformation is not acceptable since it serves to spotlight something unexpected. There is no need to spotlight Keith Sebastian, for he is the person the reader expects, according to the previous discourse, to be at the door. The same is true of other root transformations:

First I made sure that Arnie parked the Cadillac we were going to use for the getaway car safely on a side street, where we could pick it up easily. Then I drove the armoured car to the prearranged storage garage. I slowly edged the cumbersome armoured car against the back wall and locked up the place. I then made a run downtown to see if the robbery had been reported yet. It hadn't so I felt safe returning to the garage. I slid open the massive door and stepped inside.

Sitting against the back wall was { *the armoured car.
the getaway Cadillac.

Here again, Gary showed that the armoured car is unacceptable because it is expected from the previous discourse (since the narrator parked it there, it should still be there). The Cadillac is acceptable in the sentence because it is unexpected and should, therefore, be highlighted. New information is usually placed in final position (where it should be easier to hold in memory). Since the information is not new, it should not be placed in final position. These transformations, then, have a functional basis which can be clarified by an examination of discourse.

In her thesis, Sher (1975) showed that word order is important in explaining what have been called "symmetric predicates." It may appear that "X is like Y" is synonymous with "Y is like X." Sher put such forms into context to show how this assumption is faulty:

In describing to an Easterner the relationship between Daly City and San Francisco, how would you be more apt to put it?

A. Daly City is near San Francisco.
B. San Francisco is near Daly City.
C. No preference.

Because Rolls Royces and Volkswagens are both cars, you can see that they resemble each other more than an ink bottle and a chicken resemble each other, so you might say:

A. Volkswagens are similar to Rolls Royces.
B. Rolls Royces are similar to Volkswagens.
C. No preference.

With many such items in a questionnaire, it would be easy to see that we do have strong preferences (guided by size, age, social importance, or other "standards") and use word order to show those preferences. Again, the syntactic change serves a discourse function.

Many word order studies have been done (active versus passive, separated and unseparated two-word verbs, reversed *if/then* clauses, etc.). While the findings may not always be clear, what is clear is that, not only do changes in word order make a difference in sentence meaning, but also the choice of one over the other depends on the discourse context. Bolinger (1977) claims there are no truly synonymous syntactic forms. Each change gives a slightly different shade of meaning to the discourse.

As Longacre suggested, then, we do use word order changes and tense/aspect for various discourse functions in English. However, we do not seem to use Longacre's third possibility, particles. Instead, we use a number of devices to distinguish between known and unknown information in discourse. For example, after we have identified the hero or heroine of a story, we usually want to *fade out* this known information—that is, relegate it to the background—and concentrate on his or her actions—the verb parts of the narrative. One way to do this is first to describe and name the person and then move to a pronoun place-holder thereafter.

Some ESL texts leave much to be desired regarding pronoun information. In *Rapid Review of English Grammar* (1959), for example, Praninskas explains our use of subject pronouns: "Never use a third person pronoun without first mentioning the person or thing to which it refers. . . . Repeat the pronoun each time when making statements about the same person or thing." The first part of the rule is clear: we don't use a pronoun immediately because we need to be sure the listener or reader knows who the hero (person/thing) is. Once this is known, we fade it out by using pronouns. The second part of the rule, however, is misleading. Consider the following passage about a potato expert.

Our speaker today is Dr. Sheryl M. Strick. _____ is a professor in the Department of Vegetarian Diet at the College of Agriculture and Environment at UCLA. _____ graduated from Florida State University, and after a summer as an assistant seed breeder for the Burpee Company in Texas, _____ went on to do graduate work in plant genetics at UC San Diego. After receiving _____ 's Ph.D., _____ joined the Pennsylvania State University faculty where _____ remained except for trips to the Himalayas and Outer Mongolia to collect potato varieties and do research on potatoes. _____ wrote that _____ was bitten by the potato bug in _____ 's grade school days and never completely recovered. _____ remembers all the excitement _____ felt when _____ placed _____ 's first mail order for seed and how _____ did everything wrong in sowing the seeds. Later, while still at home, _____ spent every available hour working on the farm that _____ 's mother managed. It was clear even then in _____ 's life _____ would deal with plants. It is a pleasure to introduce to you _____ who will speak to us on "The Potato." _____ . Sherry.

Once we know the potato expert's name, can we automatically change all the other references to she/her? What are your discourse reasons for changing to full reference or partial name reference in the places where she/her seems inappropriate to you? Is it a matter of time (the name hasn't been mentioned for a while and you may have lost track of which person is being referred to)? Is it related to possible confusion with other characters in the story who have intervened since she was last mentioned by name? Is there a need to spotlight Sheryl again rather than her accomplishments or actions?

ESL teachers are quick to notice that such fading out of proper names is not universal in all languages. Some languages do not allow you to fade out the hero or heroine (even if it's yourself) as much as English does. She or he has to stay there as a proper name; not to do so would be considered rude. In English, our decision to repeat a noun or change to the pronoun depends, in part, on how necessary it is to reidentify the referent. We repeat the noun when it seems necessary to give a gentle reminder. Other reidentifications, Bolinger (1979) says, respond to a variety of implied or underlying assertions about the referent.

Another way to spotlight nouns in the foreground, or to shift them out of focus in the background, is the use of *articles*. Indefinite articles mark the following noun as something new (foreground), while definite articles show it is not new (background): "I wanted *a* class in science fiction but *the* class was closed." "I bought *a* book but *the* book wasn't the one I wanted." Sometimes nouns which are new in the discourse are marked with *the* rather than *a*, even on first mention, but this is based on expectation of "shared world knowledge." For example, we might say "Just give it to *the* principal" since we all know that schools have principals. We might say "Would you put this in *the* kitchen" since we assume most homes have kitchens. Linde and Labov (1975) showed this is true in interviews where *S*s, talking about their apartments, used *the* hall, *the* bath, and *the* kitchen on first mention. Nevertheless, most count nouns are marked with indefinite articles on first mention. Once the noun is accepted as shared information for speaker and hearer, not only is that noun now definite, but parts or characteristics of it are also definite:

As I walked into the kitchen, I saw *a* refrigerator against the wall. *The* door was smeared with streaks of red paint. The red splotches continued below it forming a pool along the floor. *That* puzzled me but only for a moment.

Thus *door* is definite even though it hasn't been mentioned before. Following definite marking, the noun can then become a pronoun and all aspects of it can also become pronouns. The complete picture can then be faded into *that,* which covers the entire scene—the refrigerator, the door, the splotches, the pool, the puzzlement. It is this last step—taking the whole happening and fading it out with a pronoun—that frequently confuses ESL students (though I have no data to substantiate this claim). Does this mean that fading out large parts of the discourse is not universal? For further discussion on how discourse organization influences the use of pronouns such as *it* and *that,* see Linde, 1979.

Some languages—for example, Semitic—not only fade mentioned nouns into the background but let them disappear entirely. Arabic and Hebrew allow sentences of this sort. Verb-initial sentences stress the on-line story, highlighting action with a disappeared subject. When the subject is present, the assertion seems to be more about the noun than the action.

It seems, too, that English speakers highlight new material by placing it near the ends of sentences. New information should be placed in a position where it is most easily retrieved, and, as the previous chapter demonstrated, it's easier to retain new information when it is presented at the end of the utterance. Once topics have been introduced at the ends of utterances, we can assume they are in focus for the listener and can then be moved to the beginnings of other utterances as "known" topics. In introducing a topic we'd more likely say, for example, "By the way, the guy that hit the homer? That was Ron Cey," rather than "Ron Cey was the guy that hit the homer, by the way."

Other languages also place information in various parts of utterances, and this placement may differ from English. Schachter and Rutherford (1978) have looked at *topic-comment* languages—languages where the topic is usually mentioned first, followed by a comment. In English this would be something like "Salt, I like it on my food" or "As for baseball, the Dodgers deserve the pennant." Schachter and Rutherford looked at English errors made by foreign students who have first languages in which topic-comment is the major sentence type. They found English errors like the following:

Most of the food which is served in such restaurants have cooked already.

Irrational emotions are bad but rational emotions must use for judging.

Chiang's food must make in the kitchen of the restaurant but Marty's food could make in his house.

If I have finished these four jobs, I am confident that my company can list in the biggest 100 companies in the world.

Language teachers unanimously diagnosed these errors as active/passive problems. That is, the first one should be "Most of the food which is served in such restaurants has been cooked already." Bilingual English-Chinese and English-Japanese speakers, however, felt that such sentences had nothing to do with active/passive. Rather, they suggested that the sentences should read:

(As for) most of the food which is served in such restaurants, (they) have cooked it already.

Irrational emotions are bad, but rational emotions, (one) must use (them) for judging.

(As for) Chiang's food, (he) must make (it) in the kitchen of the restaurant, but Marty's food, (he) could make (it) in his house.

If I have finished these four jobs, I am confident that (as for) my company, (someone) can list (it) in the biggest 100 companies in the world.

From these judgments, Schachter and Rutherford were able to show that the learner may be making predictions that, in written English, the left-most noun phrases are reserved for topics and new information (the comment) will not occur in sentence-initial position. Their study of such presentatives should revive interest in contrastive analysis—a contrastive analysis of how, in various discourse genres, syntactic structures are used in first and second languages.

Natural Discourse

Linguists have been primarily concerned with understanding the function various syntactic structures serve in discourse; in so doing they have raised other interesting questions as well. That is, the study of discourse functions helps us understand why certain syntactic markings, such as tense/aspect and pronominalization, have evolved in language. In addition, it helps us consider the following questions: (1) Do certain syntactic structures occur more frequently in certain discourse genres than in others? (2) By looking at discourse, can we explain the use of cohesion markers and of such expressions as *perhaps, just, uh, ah, well, oh,* etc.? (3) Are performance utterances in natural discourse to be analyzed as slightly defective citation sentences? That is, are they semi-sentences to be understood by analogy to the syntax of sentence grammar, or are they different in kind?

Since all three questions depend to some extent on the answer to the last one, let's begin with *natural discourse.* Theoretical linguists, having chosen the sentence as the unit of linguistic analysis, have been faced with the task of writing descriptions of that unit. In order to limit the task, sentences are defined as those which educated, native speakers would agree are acceptable sentences. (The grammar describes all and only the grammatically correct sentences of the language.) Such sentences turn out to be those of written text or of highly planned oral language. The task of the linguist, then, is to describe the underlying syntax, the learner's language competence, which generates such sentences. On the other hand, ordinary utterances in conversations may be fragments, may contain false starts and hesitations, or may show vocabulary choice repair and other marks of unacceptable sentences. These utterances, while riddled with performance "errors," are still thought of as produced (and understood) in terms of the underlying competence. Once sanitized of performance factors, natural data should, then, conform to that described by theoretical syntacticians.

Many psycholinguists, child language and second language researchers, conversational analysts, and functional linguists question this assumption. For some of them, natural utterances are *different in kind,* not faulty versions of sentences described in sentence grammars. In face-to-face communication (whether the participants are child first language learners, adult second language learners, or adult native speakers of English), the amount of syntacticization differs markedly from that of a lecture or written text. The performance "errrors" fulfill important discourse functions. Such researchers argue that conversations would not be improved by changing the amount of syntactic organization or by removing performance "errors." Therefore, the utterances are not faulty versions of more highly syntacticized sentences. They are different in kind.

While it is difficult to show that the grammar of such natural data is different in kind, it is not difficult to show that it is different. Ochs (1977, 1979), for example, has outlined some of the differences between the two extremes of the continuum from unplanned to planned discourse. Unplanned discourse is that which the speaker utters without having had a chance, or taken the time, to plan what is to be said. Highly planned discourse might be thought of as revised and polished written text.

In unplanned discourse, the context itself can be used to express propositions which would otherwise be expressed syntactically. Ochs gives four examples to clarify this point. First, referents may be deleted in much the same way child first language learners point, reach, or move their gaze to the referent of their speech. In natural conversations among adults, pointing or eye gaze may also set the referent, but the discourse itself can serve this function:

B: Y'have any cla—y'have a class with Billy this term/
A: Yeah he's in my Abnormal class.
B: Oh yeah//how
A: Abnormal Psych.
B: Still not married.
A: Oh no definitely not// (no)

(Schegloff, "Two Girls")

The referent for the person still not married must be retrieved from the discourse as being Billy.

Second, Ochs shows that the relationship between the referent and the proposition may also be clear only from the discourse:

A: Ohh I g'ta tell ya one course
B: (Incred-)
A: The mo- the modern art the 20th Century Art, there's about eight books.

(Schegloff, "Two Girls")

Here, the relationship between the course and the number of books is not stated syntactically (i.e., eight books are required for my 20th Century Art course). Rather, the context of the discourse and the "next-ness" of clauses is used to make the relationship clear.

Third, Ochs claims, there is heavier use of left dislocation (e.g., "Uh this guy, you could yell "Hey John, Hey John" . . .) in unplanned discourse. Focus is obtained by presenting the NP in the left-most topic position.

Finally, rather than being linked syntactically, propositions may simply be placed next to each other. For example, "I'm so . . . tired ( ) I played basketball today the first time since I was a freshman" was used rather than "I am so tired *because* I played basketball . . ." It is clear from the discourse that the sentences are linked, but the relationship need not be specified when the context of the discourse can supply the link. In written discourse, on the other hand, such markers are crucial to maintain cohesion.

Ochs found that, in addition to allowing the context to express propositions or the relationships between them, unplanned natural discourse also uses a simpler morphology than planned discourse. To show this, Ochs compared unprepared spoken versions of narratives with their written versions. She draws comparisons in seven areas. First, deictic modifiers were frequently used in place of the definite article in unplanned discourse. Such modifiers give a stronger verbal pointing than does the definite article (e.g., ". . . edge of *this* platform and *this* group of people . . ."). Relative clauses were used much less in unplanned discourse. Simple determiner + noun ("this man, this guy" rather than "a man to whom she'd been talking") was used. Prepositional phrases were also used frequently in unplanned discourse where relative clauses were used in planned (e.g., "girl with the prom" in spoken discourse and "the girl that I met at the prom" in written). Finally, compounding seems to be used in preference to relative clause formation (e.g., ". . . the Indian class and they stuck it in this crazy building and they're, they're not finished yet" rather than "the Indian class which they stuck in a crazy building that's not finished yet"). Ochs also found less use of passive voice in unplanned discourse. Verb tense morphology was simpler, and, in narratives, simple present was frequently used for simple past once the time was set in the story.

Lexical choice also differs in planned and unplanned discourse. Ochs found high use of repetition, hesitation, repair of vocabulary choice, and the use of words with similar sounds. When editing written text, we catch most of our repetitions and plug in synonyms in order to make our writing agree with conventions of written text. Sound touch-offs may be cultivated as a literary style, or we may try to vary sounds as well in revision of text. However, in checking through taped transcripts of unplanned discourse, it isn't difficult to trace the use of similar sound patterns over a stretch of discourse.

The differences that Ochs has found between planned and unplanned discourse are similar to those outlined by Givon (1979). Both show us how we can alter or loosen syntax, given time and space for expansion in conversation. They show us how context and word knowledge fill in the gaps, allowing us to identify referents and the relationships between sentence propositions. While these papers show us that utterances in natural discourse are different from that described in sentence grammars, they do not show us that they are totally different in kind. It is clear, though, that one is not just a faulty version of the other.

Concerning our second question above on the use of cohesion markers, linguists have discarded from their sentence grammars *particles* like *uh, oh, ah,* and *well* on the basis that they are performance, rather than syntactic, phenomena. The performance wastebasket, however, holds many interesting phenomena which may be looked at from a discourse perspective. Furthermore, linguists have given us less than satisfactory descriptions of the use of such words as *just, perhaps,* and various cohesion markers. James (1974), however, showed that there are semantic and syntactic constraints on where interjection particles (*oh, ah, uh, say, well*) can be used. For example, certain particles will be acceptable only when there are possible alternatives to the thing to which the particle refers. That is, the speaker could have said something else and therefore there is reason to stop and consider alternatives (e.g., "I'll have one of the *uh* chocolate ones"). *Uh* seems to be used when the speaker is searching for the best or most accurate alternative; *oh* is more often used when none of the alternatives seems especially more accurate or better than the rest.

Sentence-initial *oh, ah,* on the other hand, show that the speaker has just become aware of something. This awareness may be of a fact or piece of information (e.g., "Ah, that's the way to do it"), a strong emotion (e.g., "Oh, why did you do this?"), or something the speaker should do (e.g., "Oh (say), let's go"). However, sentence-initial *oh* and *ah* differ in their usage. *Ah* indicates pleasure at the new information while *oh* need not express any emotion, or it conveys a negative emotion of anger or exasperation. In addition, James outlined the syntactic placement of particles and how they relate to a variety of syntactic facts (neg. raising, neg. polarity, presupposed *if*-clauses, sentence adverbials, etc.). Her work shows that the parts of language that had been excluded from syntactic analysis on the basis of being performance (and therefore not interesting) could be given syntactic and semantic descriptions and thus incorporated into sentence syntax.

However, James did not investigate the use of such particles in natural discourse. Conversational analysts, working with natural data, claim that only a description that differs in kind can describe such particles accurately. The use of *uh* to signal that the coming message will differ from what the hearer might want it to be (a "dispreferred response marker"), and the use of *well* as a sign that one is ready to end a conversation, are but two examples. In this case we can see that semantic and syntactic analyses may be a good beginning, but they do not adequately describe the function of such particles in oral discourse.

The final question has to do with the *frequencies* of syntactic structures in various discourse genres. For example, narratives have been described as having temporally ordered clauses. The participants are usually first or third person. The time is past (accomplished), and it is the agent, the hero or heroine, and what she or he does that is important. The setting or orientation to the narrative will include many copula structures, and the story line will contain many clauses in simple past or present tense. Procedural discourse (how to do X) will usually have clauses arranged in sequential order. The participants are nonspecific or 2nd person you. The time is projected or general, and the thing being done is of primary importance in the discourse. Hortatory discourse (sermons, pep talks) will have clauses in logical order; the participants are 2nd person you; the time is future projected time (usually with high use of modal "ought" and of *if/then* conditionals); and primary importance is given to the addressee.

Frequency counts of tense/aspect, pronominalization, ellipses, modals, conditionals, etc., have been conducted across genre types. This may seem like dull work, but the results should be interesting to teachers and to developers of materials who must know the kinds of syntactic structures students need in order to write or to orally produce each discourse genre. The question here, though, is whether frequency tells us much about the function of particular syntactic devices, for while it seems possible to do frequency counts of structures in planned monologues or text, no one has tried to describe conversations in this way. That is, we do not normally think of face-to-face communication (except for the occasional narrative, joke, recipe, or recitation which can be abstracted from the conversation) as having a series of utterances that could sensibly be categorized via frequency counts. The description of natural face-to-face discourse may require an analysis which is different in kind (rather than one that treats it as a series of error-prone versions of sentence syntax).

In summary, linguists have looked at a variety of questions that relate discourse to sentence syntax. By taking a functional approach to the use of syntactic structures in discourse, they have come to understand how, in the narrative, for example, the listener/reader identifies old and new information, topics, main story lines, and events which are expected or novel. In English, this is accomplished mainly through pronominalization, tense/aspect, and word order changes. An examination of discourse has made it easier for us to understand why particular syntactic structures have evolved in language. While this research has been accepted as reasonable work for linguists and researchers, others are urging that another step be taken. That is, we must be willing to test the limits of syntactic and semantic analyses to see how far they can be stretched to accommodate information from the discourse level. When they cannot accommodate the data, then an analysis which is different in kind may need to be considered. This does not mean that syntactic and semantic analyses are unimportant. They are crucial, for without syntactic markers most of our writing (if not our conversations) would be unintelligible. Those syntactic markers have evolved, in part, to serve discourse needs. However, the discourse context itself may determine how crucial syntax is for comprehension. When setting and context help make meanings clear, we can afford less syntactic organization. When the context does not clarify meaning, then syntactic organization becomes a major means of making meanings clear.

8 *Discourse and Communication*

Just as linguists long concentrated on phonology and morphology because they were easier to describe than syntax, we now tend to cling to the sentence syntax level because it is easier to describe than the discourse level. Another look at the discussion of discourse in Chapter 1 and that presented in Chapter 6 will show you that the discourse level can include some very divergent things. In this chapter I want to categorize the spoken discourse level, describe the variety of research that has been done as spoken discourse analysis, and show how the discourse work in applied linguistics fits in with that of other fields.

One way to structure the discourse level is to divide it into three sublevels: speech act, speech event, and speech situation. Hymes (1972) suggested we might think of this as a matter of magnitude. Imagine a party (speech situation), a conversation during the party (speech event), and a directive within the conversation (speech act). The same speech act could occur in other speech events (e.g., a lecture). And a speech event could take place in different speech situations (e.g., the conversation could take place while jogging with a friend instead of at a party). The task is to define each level (if they *are* mutually exclusive) and show how they interlock or overlap.

Speech act is a term taken from the work of philosophers of language, J. R. Searle and J. L. Austin in particular. Just as we can utter an infinite number of sentences using a finite number of syntactic structures, there is an infinite number of utterances, all of which can be classified as "doing" a finite set of things. What we "do" with sentences are speech acts. For example, consider:

Is Sybil there? I see someone chewing gum! What's that on the floor? Clean-up time! You'd make a better door than a window. Where do these shoes belong? Could we have the garbage can over here, Susie? Chris, let's get this list run off before the faculty meeting starts. Doncha know what time it is? Were you born in a barn?

While the syntactic forms of these sentences may differ, they all "do" the same thing. All the forms represent *directives* from one person to another to do or to stop doing something. When a doctor says "Let's give him one tablet before bedtime for the next three days and see how that works," it's highly unlikely that the doctor plans to show up at the child's bedside for the next three days around 9:00 p.m. Whatever the form of these utterances, the function is directive; someone else is or is not to do something.

Depending on what source you consult, the number of speech acts may vary, but there are at least five generally accepted acts. We've talked about one of them already—the directive. The five speech acts in Searle's system are: representative, directive, commissive, expressive, and declaration. Each of these has, in turn, several subcategories. For example, in uttering a *representative* (e.g., John stole my bike), the speaker declares a belief in the truth or falsity of something. But the statement may be softened, made less direct—this is called "mitigation." Or, it may be extremely strong and direct—and that is called "aggravated." Using a representative, the speaker can suggest, hint, deny, swear, and so on. The choice reflects the scale from true to false on which the speaker places the statement; the choice between suggesting and hinting is not a choice between separate speech acts but rather the speaker's natural response to social and psychological factors which require that the speech act be mitigated.

Commissives, such as promises or pledges, commit the speaker to act in a certain way at some future time (e.g., "I'll do that tomorrow"). *Expressives* (e.g., "Sorry I'm late") express the speaker's feelings about something. This includes thanks, apologies, condolences, congratulations, or expressions of how good or terrible the speaker feels about something.

Declarations are acts expressed in statement form, such as "I christen this ship the Sloop Susie Simms" or "I hereby appoint you TA for today." These declarations ("I now pronounce you man and wife") are supposed to bring about a new state when they are uttered.

Directives, as mentioned earlier, are used by speakers to try to get the listener(s) to do, or not do, something. But the speech act directive is broader than the imperative-type directive mentioned earlier. The speech act directive includes questions. Questions (both yes/no and WH-questions) are seen as trying to get the listener to do something—in this case, to offer information.

The range of linguistic forms available for each speech act varies, but for each the forms range from aggravated to mitigated. Frequently, foreign students do learn the neutral forms, but lack the softened or strengthened forms that smooth over social interactions. Johnston, in her diary study of learning and using French in a summer immersion experience in France, frequently comments on her inability to use indirect forms:

> For example, when all the buckets disappeared from the second floor bathrooms, I didn't know if the woman in charge of the house needed to know it or not. In English I would have dropped this information in passing, in a dependent clause, when I was talking about something else, and expected her to pick up on it if it were important and otherwise to ignore it. But in French I had no option but to do nothing, or to tell her explicitly: "the buckets have disappeared—is it important?"

To tell her all the small things like this seemed like bothering her with a lot of trivial (in most cases, but I never knew just which ones weren't) details. In this particular case, her attitude was "what are you telling me for?" And I resolved never to tell her anything again. But the point is that my language limitations drastically interfered with the flow of casual, incidental information, because the categories of "casual" and "incidental" did not exist in my language competence. (1973)

It is clear that lack of language proficiency is at the bottom of Johnston's comment that her directness hurt others, that she needed less direct (more mitigated) ways of speaking with people. However, it may be the case that *when* one uses a softener, *when* one hedges, is different in different cultures. Tannen (1976), in her papers on Greeks, Greek-Americans, and Americans, talks about how her own most indirect statements were taken as directives. For example, when living with a Greek family in Crete she mentioned to the mother that Americans have another way of fixing eggs—mixing them all up. Another time, trying to make polite conversation, she asked why she hadn't seen many grapes around since she connected Greece with grapes. From then on every morning, no matter how early she got up, she was faced with scrambled eggs and grapes. Actually, she didn't like scrambled eggs, and grapes were not her favorite food either. She believes that her most indirect forms were not indirect enough, especially when the family was responding to her comments as custom may require of a good host.

At this point it may be evident that there is some overlap between speech *act* and speech *event*. For example, an apology is an expressive speech act. We could set up an experiment to find out how people do apologies. We might find that apologies are not single-utterance speech acts; they might extend over several exchanges. Or we could set up an experiment to see how people do complaints. The complaints might occur within a conversation speech event, yet take up most of the time/space of the speech event. All the utterances in the apology research might not be expressives, and all the utterances in the complaint research might not be expressives or directives. Rather, the apology and complaint would have evolved into *small structured speech events*. I shall return to speech acts and small structured speech events later in this chapter.

Since the boundary line between speech act and speech event is not entirely clear, we could argue that if a speech act has a structure beyond the single-utterance level, then it is a *speech event*. For example, one may make a directive, a speech act utterance. The directive may be turned back on the original speaker by the other person as a new directive. As these directives fly back and forth, an argument is constructed. The argument, since it has internal structure, can be called a speech *event*. And that argument might, in fact, take place within a larger speech event, the conversation. Or, one may "express" one's feelings of unhappiness about some state of affairs—an expressive speech *act*. As one continues to explain the unhappiness, a complaint evolves. The complaint, since it has internal structure, is a speech *event*. Yet, it too takes place within a larger speech event, the conversation. The overlap is a problem. As a heuristic, for this chapter, we will say that if speech acts are strung together to form some higher unit and that higher unit has a describable structure, then the higher unit is a speech event. Thus, complaints, apologies, compliments, etc., which have structure beyond the sentence level, would be classified as speech events. And, speech events of this sort can fit into larger speech events such as conversations, lectures, and interviews.

The dividing line between speech event and speech situation seems at first glance to be more sharply defined. Speech acts occur within speech events and speech events occur within speech situations. You may do a directive (speech act) during an argument (speech event) during a class (speech situation). Or you may do a commissive (speech act promise) during a conversation (speech event) during a party (speech situation). A judge does a question (speech act directive) during an interview (speech event) during a trial in court (speech situation). The speech situation, then, appears to be the total setting, including all the sociolinguistic information about speakers and hearers, their status relationships and responsibilities or roles. It includes the environment, and it includes the time.

Clearly, the *speech situation* influences the form of the speech event in many ways. For example, complaint structures become more elaborate when the complainer is an employee, the addressee the boss, and the location the board room. In fact, many people will be so threatened by such speech situations that they will "let off steam" by griping outside the board room instead (gripes are complaints voiced to persons not responsible). Mary Richards (personal communication) has contrasted the forthrightness of complaints dropped anonymously into "complaint boxes" with the self-justification given in gripes to friends; and contrasted again this forthright complaint with the elaborately indirect nature of complaints to responsible others with whom one has close ongoing relationships. The real complaint to responsible others is difficult to negotiate because we want to end the speech event with both sides still valuing each other and with the relationship still intact. The outcome after the complaint has to be that each person is still "OK." That's why complaints are so difficult to negotiate properly for most people, even in a first language.

In our three-level paradigm, a setting like a classroom should be a speech situation. Yet, what goes on in that setting has a special structure which can be described. Classroom discourse has been described in some detail. While the classroom and participants are the speech situation, the classroom discourse is a speech event writ large, just as conversations are speech events writ large, or court trials or doctor-patient interviews are speech events in this larger sense. Within classroom discourse, many small speech events will occur—narratives, jokes, how-to discourse (recipes, how to assemble a bicycle, how to construct a triangle), hortatory discourse (teacher sermons or pep talks), for example. And single speech acts (e.g., a directive such as "turn in your papers") can be identified as well.

The three-way classification of speech situation, speech event, and speech act is simple on the surface and intuitively appealing. It is perhaps less formal than we would like and the overlap of the levels is confusing.

ESL teachers are familiar with a body of literature which divides discourse in other ways. Those who work with *notional-functional* syllabi have probably become used to the van Ek (1976) system. The subcategorization is also built on the work of Austin and Searle in speech act theory. However, it is presented somewhat differently.

The discourse functions are again divided into a finite number of things that we do with language. In a sense they are similar to speech acts:

1. Exchange factual information
2. Exchange intellectual attitudes
3. Exchange emotional attitudes
4. Exchange moral attitudes
5. Suasion
6. Socializing

Function 1 seems similar to representatives; 5 seems to be similar to directives; 2, 3, and 4 seem to relate to expressives. These are only surface similarities, however, as will be seen once we examine the subcategories of each function. Each subcategory can contain both questions and statements. That is, questions do not *only* fall under "suasion," as they do under directives. Each function has a number of subcategories, some more than others. For example, 3 (exchange emotional attitudes) includes (dis)likes, (non)preference, (dis)satisfaction, worry/confidence, fear/optimism, surprise/boredom, hope, sympathy, and so on.

The functions are divided into subfunctions. The model also includes notions, the things we talk about. These are either general or specific. The general notions are what psychologists usually call "concepts"; e.g., categories of *time, space, qualitative, evaluative, mental, relational, deixis, existence.* The specific notions seem somewhat similar to speech situations since they identify people, objects, and environment. But they also include such categories as *pets, hobbies,* and *medical.* The third level of the notional-functional system is the lexicon which is cross-referenced to the notions and functions listed at the top two levels.

The notional/functional model is a discourse model directed toward syllabus planning for language classes rather than toward eventual description of discourse levels in language. The goals are different, so it is not surprising that the categorization is also somewhat different.

A number of other suggestions have been made for dividing up the world of discourse. For example, Halliday (1973) uses seven functions: Instrumental (= Austin's declaration?); Regulatory (= Austin's directive?); Representational (= Austin's representative?); Interactional, a category which promotes successful social exchange; Personal (= Austin's expressive?); Heuristic, which allows us to learn the why's of our environment; and Imaginative. These seven major functions are then broken down again into lists (e.g., bragging, complaining, interrupting, requesting) which are not specifically tied to any one of the functions. The seven functions fit into Halliday and Hassan's (1976) three major categories: Ideational, which has to do with content which may be either experiential or logical; Interpersonal, the social and expressive parts; and Textual, the linguistic structure and cohesion. The Textual category seems more in line with the research on discovery of structure of speech events and the ways that discourse uses syntax to make that structure clear.

These three systems for categorizing levels of discourse are presented in Table 1. Each system maps the range of research that could be done on oral discourse. Once we include speech setting in the discourse plan, however, we incorporate much of sociolinguistic research into our psycholinguistic perspective. And once we look at the structure of conversational interactions as speech events, we also encompass the research of sociologists. As you will see, once we examine inferencing in such discourse, we also become involved in the philosophy of language and in psychiatry as well. The legitimacy of such forays into the territory of other fields will be discussed at the end of this chapter.

Perhaps the easiest way to understand the work of researchers in spoken discourse is to look at one of the large speech events, conversation. Clearly conversations can take place in many speech settings, and the conversation itself will vary according to the setting. However, the double question of psycholinguistics is, once again, can the linguistic structure of conversations be described? and what evidence is there that speakers use the described system in doing conversations?

Conversational Analysis

Goffman (1976) has laid out a series of prerequisites for communication. For conversation to take place, whatever the language and whatever the culture, there must be:

1. Two-way acoustically adequate and interpretable messages. That is, we have to be able to hear the message and it must not be so garbled that it cannot be understood nor in a language that we have never heard before.
2. Back-channel feedback. We need some feedback to inform us that reception is occurring. This can be in the forms of mmhmm's or headshakes or eye contact from the listener.
3. Contact signals. There has to be some way to show that we want to talk, some way to show that talk can begin, and some way to close off the channel at the end.
4. Turnover signals. There have to be ways of indicating the end of messages, and there have to be ways of signaling next speaker selection.
5. Preempt signals. There have to be ways to interrupt a talker in midstream to get a rerun of what was said or to capture the channel.
6. Framing capabilities. There have to be cues to distinguish "bracketed" communication. The speaker has to somehow mark ironic asides, quotes, jokes, etc. And the hearer must signal that this bracketing is followed.

Table 1   A Comparison of Three Discourse Models

Three-level Analysis
---

1. Speech situation (town meeting, court trial, classroom, etc.)
2. Speech event (narrative, conversation, service encounters, etc.)
3. Speech act
   Directive (to get someone to do/not to do something)
   Commissive (promise, oath, etc.)
   Declaration (change state on uttering; e.g., "The court finds you guilty.")
   Expressive (feelings, emotions)
   Representative (statements of facts, etc.)
   Shopping lists—with a range from mitigated to aggravated forms for each act; and hedges re speaker responsibility/ accountability for the speech act (e.g., directive includes asking, suggesting, demanding, begging, ordering, etc.)
   "Function" used as "These linguistic forms all have the same function—they are all directives."

Notional-Functional
---

1. Functions
   Exchange factual information
   Exchange intellectual attitudes
   Exchange emotional attitudes
   Exchange moral attitudes
   Suasion
   Socializing
   Shopping lists—within each function; e.g., emotional includes (dis)likes, (non)-preference, (dis)satisfaction, worry, confidence, fear, optimism, surprise, boredom, hope, sympathy, etc.
2. Notions
   General—categories of time, space, qualitative, evaluative, mental, relational, deixis, existence, etc.
   Specific—identification of people, objects, environment, pets, hobbies, medical, etc.
3. Lexicon—cross-referenced to Functions and Notions

Halliday

Functions
1. Instrumental (brings about a change of state)
2. Regulatory (approval, disapproval, behavior regulators)
3. Representational (states facts)
4. Interactional (allows for successful social exchange)
5. Personal (expressives)
6. Heuristic (allows you to learn the why's of your environment)
7. Imaginative
   Shopping lists—(e.g., interrupting, complaining, requesting, etc.) not tied specifically to above functions

Halliday & Hassan
Ideational—logic and experiential content
Interpersonal—social and expressive
Textual—structure and cohesion

---

7. There have to be norms (see Grice, 1975) that the respondent will reply honestly with whatever is relevant to ongoing conversation and no more.
8. Nonparticipant constraints. Competing noise, contact with others outside the conversation must be blocked or, if others are meant to be included, eye contact and the outside "noise" must be admitted to the channel.

Much of the work in conversational analysis has described these system constraints in conversations. For example, much work has been done on how we open and close conversations, the turn-taking system within the conversation, and the rerun system (how speakers fix up "trouble spots" to make their messages clear to the hearer and/or to themselves).

Schegloff and Sach's work on conversation closers (1973) is especially interesting to those of us who are not skillful in ending conversations. When the phone rings and the person says, "Hi, I'm Greg," we try to match the voice with any Greg's we know, only to hear him go on about the wonderful deal Village Carpet Cleaners has this week. Then it is easy to violate all politeness rules for conversation and close off the channel by hanging up. But face-to-face conversations require much more delicacy.

In a conversation, once we have raised and discussed all the points we hoped to cover, we may finish with a "pass"—that is, we need to pass on the turn. We don't say *pass,* of course, as in cards, but we do say things like *OK, yeah, well,* or *so* with falling intonation. According to Schegloff, this pass says that the speaker is willing at this point to consider closing the conversation. It can also serve as a marker that *now* is the time to bring up any other topics if the partner hasn't finished his hand. If the pass is accepted, the other speaker may also pass. With two empty turns, the closing can then take place:

B: Why? B'cause they hg— b'cause they have—. hh they asked you first.
J: Yeah.
B: Yeah.
J: So.
B: Well, just—I'll talk to you tomorrow, okay?
J: Yeah okay.
B: Okay, bye bye.
J: Yeah, bye.

(Daden, 1974)

If we want to stop the closing after we've agreed to close by using passes, we have to use some sort of special marker, something like "oh, by the way—," "Oh, I *did* mean to tell you—," or "Wait a min—":

B: . . . . Okay an then my—I'll ask my mom if she'll pick us up from there.
J: Okay.
B: (0.5) Okay. Wait a mn—(0.6) hh what's the street you turn on to get to your place?

(Daden, 1974)

As everyone who has ever tried to cut off a conversation knows, it's not always so easy. We do not want to appear rude. Picking up our belongings and edging out the door doesn't work when we're at home. And it's hard to cut off all the "by the way's" that prevent closing off the channel. "I gotta go, the cookies are burning," and the secretary's buzz that the next appointment is in two minutes, seem to be invented for people who have problems with closing. More common are statements such as "I'll let you get back to your work" where one voices concern for the other while bowing out of the conversation. These frequently frame back to the opening:

A: Ya busy?
B: Nope, just looking for a paper.
      .
      .
      .
B: So.
A: Yeh. Well, letcha get back to looking for that paper.
B: Yeh. Okay. See ya later.
A: Yeh, bye.
B: Bye.

Openings for conversations have also been studied in detail. More interesting, perhaps, for the applied linguist is the work that has been done on entering conversations in bilingual or lingua franca situations. Jordan and Fuller (1975) studied lingua franca talk and described the devices used when two parties speak two different native languages and communicate via a third of which neither is a fluent speaker. One of their questions was how, when the ongoing conversation is in a language we don't know, do we signal that we want to enter the conversation (Goffman's point 8 above).

If you think about how we, as native speakers, signal that we want into a conversation, you may recall throat-clearing, body movements, and other ways to clear the way into the communication channel. We may begin to speak by repeating part of the overheard conversation, or we may state the topic of the conversation and then say why we are specifically entitled to have overheard the conversation in the first place. (E.g., "Were you talking about morpheme acquisition? I just happen to be on my way home from the Morpheme Acquisition Institute in Helsinki" or "Excuse me, I couldn't help overhearing you—I shop at Alpha Beta too.")

In lingua franca conversation, merely overhearing a common language expression embedded in other-language talk constitutes grounds enough for entrance, and also gives the person who wants in the resources for constructing an entrance request: (g and n are English speakers; J and M are Mayan speakers. All speak Spanish as a lingua franca. Examples are all drawn from Jordan and Fuller, 1975.)

J & M:	(Maya talk)
J:	(Maya) Estados Unidos (Maya)
g:	Hey, we're getting talked about over there. ¿Hablan de nosotros, uh?
J:	Eso oigo.
All:	(laughter)
g:	Estados Unidos.
J:	Yo entiendo Estados Unidos. El nombre que tienes estados. Realmente el carácter que tienen las es personas. Entonces por eso . . .

As in monolingual talk, a laughter segment can also be played on for an entrance request (e.g., "What's so funny?"):

J, M:	(Maya talk) (laughter)
g:	¿Qué es, qué es broma?
J:	Mira, doña Gitti (showing *g* an apparently blood-stained cloth).
g:	Ah, bueno.
J:	Piensa, piensa que es sangre. ¿Hm?
g:	¿Qué es sangre? No es sangre.
J:	No, no es que está aquí, nosotros digamos.

Mimicking unfamiliar sounds in the unknown language provides a way of getting into the talk, and often provides a new topic for the conversation:

J, M:	(Maya talk)
g:	The contractions are pretty slow. Not slow but short.
J:	Not slow but short. (mimics words she does not understand)
n, g:	(laughter)
J:	(laughs)
g:	(laughing) Bueno.
J:	(laughing) Bueno, debo de aprender . . .
g:	aprender hablar . . .
J:	debo de aprender que has dicho por no sé que dice.

In fact, just noting that the others are speaking an incomprehensible language provides a way of getting into the conversation:

J, M:	(Maya talk)
g:	¿Es Maya, uh?
J:	Hah.
g, J:	(laughter)
J:	Eso es Maya.
g, J, M:	(laughter)
J:	¿Eso es Maya entonces, eh?
g:	Si.
J:	Pues, así está las cosas. Bueno, pero la Maya siempre entiendes algo.

g: No, no comprendo Maya.
H: Ay, pues eso lo que da trabajo.

Entrance requests can be foreseen and forestalled as well. Jordan and Fuller note:

> An interesting obverse to "You are speaking Maya, aren't you?" is "We are speaking Maya."
> It happened to us more than once that when listening to, for us, incomprehensible Maya talk, one of the speakers would turn to us and say "Nosotros hablamos Maya," whereupon he would resume doing just that. We see this as preventing inclusion trouble from coming up. (1975, p. 15)

Conversational discourse has been described in the formal system of openings, closings, and the turn-taking system within conversations (see Sachs et al., 1974). While the turn-taking system (as to who selects the next speaker, etc.) may well be universal, it seems clear that pause length which frequently marks the place for turn-taking does vary across language groups. Gaskill (1980) has mentioned that his data (ESL learners conversing with native speakers of English) are filled with pauses when one would expect the learner to respond. When the pause is not filled quickly ("quickly" meaning in the normal pause limits for an English speaker), the native speaker of English will be driven to pick up the speaker role again. It isn't clear that an unfilled pause means that the learner is unable to reply. Perhaps the length of pause acceptability varies across languages and the native speaker simply doesn't wait long enough to allow the learner to reply. Phillips has pointed out that, for Warm Springs Indians,

> The pauses between two different speakers' turns at talk are frequently longer than is the case in Anglo interactions. There is tolerance for silences—silences that Anglos rush into and fill. Indian speakers rarely, if ever, begin to speak at the same time and rarely interrupt one another. (1974)

Both Weeks (1976) and Phillips have noted not only that pause length is much longer for Yakima and Warm Springs Indians, but also that back-shadowing is quite different as well. Even within our turn at talk, we watch our listeners for signs that they are following along. We expect "mmhmm's" to fill the pauses in our stories; we expect the listener to nod, to smile, or to laugh. If the listener disagrees, we expect to see a frown, a shift forward in the chair (as though to jump into the conversation with an objection). As a teacher, I have looked for typical Anglo back-shadowing (Goffman's point ?) from my foreign students, only to be much misled. For example, some of my Japanese students would nod at every pause point during lectures. The nods, however, did not signal comprehension of the lecture point; rather, they were signs that the person was paying attention. That is, they meant "I'm listening," not "I'm following." Conversely, other students would look blank while I desperately tried to think of new and more enlightening ways to make my point clear; but, in fact, they understood me all along. If our listeners continue to give us no back-shadowing, we frequently feel that what we are saying is not only incomprehensible but also just plain stupid or somehow morally wrong. Lack of back-shadowing from our listeners is, to say the least, disconcerting. A good deal of work has been done by anthropologists on the matching of kinesics within and across cultures. However, little if any work (beyond that of Phillips and Weeks) has been done to show how the mismatch of back-shadowing might change the nature of conversations among learners or between learners and native speakers.

Back-shadowing sometimes takes on formal characteristics when the communication itself is somewhat ritualized. The chiming in of audiences, the "amen's" in sermons, the *gritos* in Mexican songs, and recitation are all examples of formalized back-shadowing. In such cases, there must be formal rules as to who may perform the back-shadowing and when it may occur.

While conversing or lecturing, this back-shadowing may cause us to insert asides into our turn at talk. These must be bracketed in some way (Goffman's point 6). Such asides may include jokes, an illustrative story, or a simple departure from what we had been saying. Bracketing may be signaled by physical movements:

> *LF:* (reading from a paper) . . . to the tota:1—(looks up and directly at audience) I'm reading this as fast as I can because I bet you're as hungry as I am. I didn't eat any breakfast this morning. (audience laughter, looks back down and continues reading)
>
> *EH:* (talking in classroom . . . the next night I'd—(.2) (head moves from right to left looking at students) and this isn't going to be a thousand and one nights, in case you wondered (students smile and all shift slightly in chairs) I'd think . . .

Though hand and body motions are the most salient features of bracketing in the above examples, intonation is also used. In the first example, the second syllable of "total" is held and the intonation is rising rather than falling. In the second example, there is a short pause prior to the head and hand movements in bracketing the aside. L. McCleary (personal communication) has suggested that a study of the phonological phenomena signaling prepared asides written into papers and unplanned asides might be even more interesting than the physical motions accompanying them.

Applied linguists are interested in all of Goffman's prerequisites for communication, but they have directed their research primarily to Goffman's rerun system and the "two-way, acoustically adequate and interpretable messages" (point 1). To make messages interpretable, native speakers talking with language learners must make many adjustments, and both learner and native speaker must work very hard on reruns (repairs in conversations) as well.

As we speak, we reformulate, restate, or repair our messages (Goffman's point 1). Using examples from Schwartz (1980), we can see that sometimes the repairs make the message more precise. For example, in talking to her study partner, Ming says, "But the test will be on that too, I mean (.2) today's quiz." *Quiz* is more accurate than *test* and may improve the message. In some cases, it appears that repairs allow the speaker more planning time: Natasha says, "Becuz I—I wanna take like (.4) you know I want take something to—to make ya know just (.2) to have fun." In other cases, repairs allow time for a vocabulary search (without having to give up the turn at talk). For example, Hamid says, ".h that uh i—i— that was a (1.2) uhh it has a bar."

Goffman, in point 5, says that the system must permit requests for reruns and repairs. Schegloff, Jefferson, and Sachs (1977) have pointed out that, in natural conversations, we allow people to repair their own mistakes as much as possible. When we offer corrections, those corrections are usually preceded by a pause. In fact, a pause alone may cause speakers to repair the utterance or to back down on the certainty of their claims:

> B: ... an' that's not an awful lotta fruitcake.
> →   (1.0) Course it is. A little piece goes a long way.
> A: W'll that's right.

                                                      (Pomerantz, 1978)

Pauses and noncommital responses may lead to a quick shift in topic as well:

> J: Whaddiyuh think of a picnic thishyir. (1.0)
> A: This th' firs'time I've been tuh one.
> J: Oh is it?
> A: Yea:h. (1.0) It's pretty diffrent I: mean y'know it's jist (.7)
> →J: Art g'nna bow:l this yir?
> A: ga:mes 'n stuff.

                                                      (Pomerantz, 1978)

When the speaker does not repair the trouble spot, corrections are made by the hearer, but the corrections are usually mitigated or softened by expressions like "y'mean" or "I think."

> Ben: Lissena pigeons. (.7)
> Ellen: Coo—coo:::: coo:::
> →Bill: Quail, I think.
> Ben: Oh yeh? (1.5) No, that's not quail, that's a pigeon.
> Lori: But y'know single beds'r awfully thin tuh sleep on.
> Sam: What?
> Lori: Single beds. //they're
> →Ellen: Y'mean narrow?
> Lori: They're awfully narrow, yeah.

                                    (Schegloff, Jefferson, and Sachs, 1977)

Speakers do invite their listeners to offer corrections. Second language learners frequently do this as one way to be sure their meaning is clear.

The work that native speakers do to help make their messages comprehensible to learners has been studied and reported under the cover term "foreigner talk." When native speakers get back-shadowing cues that their speech is not understood, they repair and restructure speech in ways to either make it more intelligible or to make it easier for the learner to take turns at talk.

In phone conversations between service personnel and adult learners, we find native speakers use all sorts of devices to be sure they are understood. Words are repeated many times, but when repetition does not clarify meaning, restatements are often made with several repairs of troublesome vocabulary items:

(The native speaker, NS, is a typist who wants to know whether the thesis is in final draft form.)
NS: Is this the final?
M: Uhh, it's un mmm pardon?
NS: Is this your final?
M: Fine ... ?
NS: Are you filing or is this the rough draft ... or the final?
M: Oh, I see. Final you mean last one?
NS: Right. Is it the last one?
M: Yessss (sounds unsure)
NS: Yeah, last copy?
M: Mmhmm (still sounds uncertain)
NS: Right ... is it all typed now?

Even with all these checks on comprehension, the native speaker and learner frequently end up talking about entirely different topics without even being aware of the fact, as can be seen in the example on page 174 in Chapter 9. In a different example, involving a language therapist and a bilingual aphasic patient, we also see two people working on different word searches. The therapist is trying to elicit names of professions from the client and the word is "chef." The client is searching for "chips," but repairs never lead to a comprehensible message:

(T=therapist; C=client)
T: (shows picture of chef)
C: Food uhhh, any food that we eat.
T: mmhmm
C: Ah, and chief.
T: That's /šef/. Chef?
C: Chief.
T: mmhmm
C: Is the potato uh I think what is this chief, the potato?
T: Potato?
C: p-p-potato (4.0) chief.
T: What does a *chef* do? He's—?
C: It's this, the thin potato? Made out of potato?
T: I'm not sure I know what you're talking about?
C: /po/ the /kamoti/ /kəmoti/ I mean (laughs) make very thin very thin slice?
T: Thin slice potatoes?

C: Yeah.

T: I don't know what they are called. Are those chef potatoes? Maybe they are.

C: For uh—

T: I never knew that, but it's possible. What about, what about the *per*son?

C: The person?

T: Yeah. What does a person who's a chef do?

C: She works in the restaurant, or in the restaurant.

T: mmhmm

C: See, he many of those food, those food that is potatoes and potato chief and (4.2) and (5.0)

T: (softly) Okay, a chef, a lot of time, is a person who cooks or=

C: Yeah.

T: =or who tells the cooks=

C: Yeah.

T: =what to do.

C: Yeah, I do the one he uh different sizes very thick and (3.1) uh ahh (1.0) different kinds for po— cutting.

T: Okay. Mmmm, you're talking about a machine? Yeah? That makes different size stuff?

C: Yeah, a machine, the machine, it's the machine.

T: (softly) I see, I see. Okay, I was saying that a chef is also the name of a *per*son, is what we call a *per*son who cooks in a restaurant.

C: Yeah, the chief he.

T: Yeah.

There are, of course, enormous differences between language learner and language disorder data. In conversations with native speakers, learners can get around the vocabulary problem by inviting repairs from the native speaker. Sometimes they are highly successful in this "other repair" work, and sometimes their attempts fail. But, in listening to some of the learner and native speaker conversations, one is struck with its charade-like quality ("guess the word I'm trying to say"): The second example below shows how successful the charade strategy can be, but the first ends in a complete disaster.

R: Brother of my, how do you say, my my uncle woman, you know?

NS: Your uncle's wife.

R: Yah... woman is my uncle.

NS: Oh, your aunt. Aunt.

R: My aunt husband.

R: Patinas. How do you say (mimics ice skating)

NS: Skating.

R: Yeh. They're skating.

(Butterworth, 1978)

Learner-learner data also abounds with repairs as the speakers negotiate the meanings of words, and that negotiation includes an immense variety of extralinguistic features as well. In the following example, Mari and Hamid are talking about an amusement park, and Mari seems to be searching for the word "ferris wheel":

Mari: . . . for junior high school?   or adults because
                                            ⌜ claps hands
           that's uh many kind   ⌞ of
     ⌜ looks up and flutters eyelids, purses lips,
     ⌞ uhh (1.0) mmmmm
     ⌜ closes eyes, grits teeth,   ⌜ opens hands, looks at H.
     ⌞ (1.5)   ⌞ example "Jet Corso"?
     ⌜ looks away, hands in lap ⌜ hands up
     ⌞ and uh mmmm   ⌞ Water Shoot?
     ⌜ looks back at H,   ⌜ closes eyes, fingers moving
     ⌞ very, very mmmm ⌞ (1.) ve:ry

Hamid: inter ⌜ esting ⌝
Mari: ⌞ yeah ⌟ interesting and
     ⌜ fingers in circle motion ⌜ iconic gestures
     ⌞ huh huh huh   ⌞ Jet Corso is uh
     very fast.
Hamid: Yeah like merry-go-round.
Mari: Not—not merry-go-round because (.2)
     ⌜ gestures over shoulder
     ⌞ we are— we are (.2) opposite.

                                         (Schwartz, 1980)

As you can imagine, the discourse of learners, whether with other learners or with native speakers, requires much work in order to make messages clear. In native speaker conversations, stranger-stranger discourse requires more negotiation than that of intimate friends. What is a "clear message" between intimate friends or among family members is likely to be much less clear to outsiders. The differences, however, are not in the structure of conversation itself (i.e., not in the structure of openings, closings, etc.) nor in the syntactic structures used, but in the amount of *inferencing* that can be taken for granted in any topic area. If you recorded a conversation between yourself and a friend and tried to trace out the inferences, you would be amazed at how much you would have to tell a computer to make it possible for *it* to truly understand the conversation.

In point 7, Goffman set requisites for norms of conversation. In trying to formalize the logic of conversations, Grice drew up a series of maxims which must be followed if conversations are to make sense. That is, we do not expect our conversational partner to say "My daddy says so, that's why" when we ask "Where's the catsup?" A cooperative conversationalist is, among other things, one who will make a relevant reply. We assume that replies *are* relevant. The search for relevance can require a great deal of inferencing. Consider the following service encounters:

A: Do you have orange juice?
B: Large or small?
A: Small.
B: That'll be 45 cents.

A: Do you do buttonholes?
B: She'll be back in an hour.

In the first example A can infer that they do, indeed, have orange juice and that the question response of B is not to be interpreted as querying the original question (whether they *have* large or small glasses of juice). The response in the second example is assumed to be a relevant response and the inference is that the person who makes buttonholes will return in an hour. It would be difficult to see how such a response could be any more relevant than "My daddy says so, that's why" if we could not *assume* that such responses *are* relevant.

Hildyard and Olson (1978) separate inferences into three types: *propositional, enabling,* and *pragmatic. Propositional inferences* follow logically and necessarily from a given statement. They include (1) transitive relations or syllogisms (A is bigger than B. B is bigger than C. Propositional inference: A is bigger than C); (2) Implicature verbs (John forgot to shut the door. Propositional inference: John didn't shut the door); (3) Comparatives (John has more than Mary. Propositional inference: Mary has less than John); and (4) Class inclusion (A is a B. B is a C. Propositional inference: A is a C.). *Enabling inferences* are those that provide causal relationships between concepts or events (John threw the ball through the window. Mr. Jones came running out of the house. Enabling inference: John broke the window. *versus* John threw the baby through the window. Mr. Jones came running out of the house. Enabling inference: The house is on fire.). The third type, *pragmatic inference,* is based on implicit world knowledge which is not essential for the processing of the sentences. Rather, it gives information which elaborates the meaning (e.g., The old lady stepped into the chauffeur-driven Cadillac. Pragmatic inference: The old lady is rich.).

In sum, enabling inferences are important in discourse because they make the discourse cohesive. Pragmatic inferences are, however, probably a greater source of learner error. A learner may be quite able to guess that a medical operation is being described as soon as he reads "Chief Resident Jones adjusted his surgical mask..." If he reads "The professor was eating lunch," he can quite likely infer that the professor was hungry. However, a great deal more inferencing is involved in analyzing most conversations among friends. And those inferences are not only culture-bound but may also be based on a lifetime of shared experience.

A mother talking with her adult children can assume much shared "old" information. By Grice's conventions, she won't insult them by reporting old information (unless she still regards them as babies who have to be given this information). However, if she is talking with a new acquaintance, much more background must be given. Many people believe that the "egocentric" quality of child speech has to do with their lack of awareness that others don't already share all their experiences. Bye (1976) in his dissertation looked at how young children gave directions on how to get to school. The range of ability (or inability) of children to consider the addressee and background information is remarkable. The child narrative in Chapter 1 is similar to the following in that neither appears to consider the amount of shared information available to the listener:

(S is an adult female and R is a 7-year-old boy)

S: Y'ever been fishing?

R: Nnnn my my cousins always goin fishin cuz they're /loki/ (lucky) for me. I cu'n go cuz I didn't know how t'fish. They're lucky go—they go with my mom with my mommy and my—her sister's father named Russell Magurry. Russell Magurariy. We call him Magurburry.

S: Uh-huh.

R: That's what we call him. But his real name is Russell.

S: Just like yours, huh?

R: Yeh, an y'know what?

S: What?

R: My fa—grandfather Russell, he lets us in the boat Saturday and Sunday, y'know what would we do? I'm not—when we taking a day off, me and my mom and dad and Jess go to see my cousin and then sometimes we stay there longer and sometimes we don't cuz y'see we can—we went there before and first time when we's gonna come to here but we hadda stay over there and we came we went a LOT of places=

S: Uh-huh

R: =slipped (slept) at night. And we hadda we—we hadda go at night and mornings until we finally got to Las Vegas, Nevada. And then took a shortcut to here and then we shorted cut that way to this rest area and he telled us go this way and then we went to Los Angeles and came this kwa—this lady. And then I we found Burbank and and then we slipped in this hotel room and then we found an apartment and we moved out here.

S: Okay, let's let Peter tell a story.

Children often do misjudge the amount of information they share with others, but adults misjudge this amount of shared information as well. Inference reconstruction may be a difficult task for both the listener and the linguist who hopes to show how conversational exchanges are understood. Labov and Fanshel, in their book *Therapeutic Discourse* (1977), have worked out a model for inference reconstruction. The following example is to encourage you to read their book, since it is impossible to summarize their method here. The patient, Rhoda, suffers from anorexia nervosa, a classic psychosomatic disease where the patient may eventually die of starvation. Such patients are often in family situations where there is a conflict in role relationships, and noneating can be seen as a way of arguing a point that such patients are not in a position to make overtly. Rhoda reports a phone conversation with her mother to the therapist:

1.8 Rhoda: An–nd so—when—I called her to'day, I said, "Well, when
                 do you plan t'come *home*?"
1.9 Rhoda: So she said, "Oh, why?"

The expansions which are arrived at in carefully detailed methods (please see the text) show us how much has been deleted and must be inferred by the therapist:

Expansion

R: <N When I called my mother today (Thursday), I actually said <F "Well, in regard to the subject which we both know is important and is worrying me, when are you leaving my sister's house where   2   : your obligations have already been fulfilled and   4   returning as I am asking you to a home where   3   : your primary obligations are being neglected, since you should do this as *HEAD-MO* head of our household?" F> N>

R: <N So my mother said to me, <F "Oh, I'm surprised; why are you asking me when I plan to come home, and do you have a right to do that? There's more to this than meets the eye: Isn't it that AD-R you can't take care of the household or yourself, as I've told you before, and I shouldn't have gone away in the first place?" F> N> (1977, p. 50)

In fact, we can make even more inferences about these two utterances, for Rhoda is simultaneously implying that the therapist is at fault since she stressed how important it was for Rhoda to state her feelings. Since stating her feelings in this case didn't work to her advantage (Rhoda's mother being very good at turning role accusations back to the assertion that Rhoda is not adult and can't take on an adult role), then the therapist is incompetent, or at least wrong in making such suggestions.

Inferencing is a very important part of discourse analysis, whether text and literary analysis or conversational analysis is being done. Inferencing in a second language must be difficult at both the propositional and enabling levels to some extent, yet intuition says that it is at the pragmatic level that the fluent second language learner encounters the most uncertainty. This must be difficult at both the processing and the production levels: How much can we leave up to the listener and still make our messages clear? and what inferences can we draw beyond the bare bones of messages that are directed to us? And, more important yet, from a psycholinguistic perspective, what are the mechanisms which allow us to draw inferences?

Again, even in this area, there may be language or cultural differences that determine the amount of inferencing one should leave up to the listener. For example, Lilith Haynes (personal communication) comments on the desirability of leaving as much inferencing as possible up to the listener in Guayanese discourse. We probably all know someone who gives us more detailed information than we ever wanted to know about anything, every time they hold the floor. For others, it's a game to see how little information they can give, how obtuse their references can be, before they lose their listeners. There may be considerable individual variation. Certainly there is variation according to our audience and the amount of inferencing we can expect them to do. However, for the culture/language group as well, there must be norms as to the amount of inferencing one can leave up to the listener.

It seems unfair in every sense to include this brief section on the research on requisites of communication without also including a complete review of the researchers in sociology who are the leaders in conversational analysis: Schegloff, Sachs, Jefferson, Pomerantz, Moerman, and their colleagues. It is their work on conversations, openings, closings, turn-taking, repair, and topic nominations that has given us the framework from which to study conversations of second language learners. However, even from this brief review of conversation as a speech event, it is clear that such researchers have shown that conversation does have an abstract system which can be described. It is also clear that the abstract system can be used to predict the form of new conversations. It therefore meets the test of linguistic description. The natural data from which the system has been drawn can, in turn, provide a test of the abstract system description. People do appear to use the system in order to do conversations.

Inferencing is not part of this described system. Rather, it looks at the processes that allow a speaker/listener to turn utterances into cohesively related conversation. Hildyard and Olson (1978) and others have begun to work out inference models which may show us how we search for relevance—that is, what allows us to discover the relevance of responses when complex, or even simple, inferences must be drawn.

Speech Acts

Research has also been done on utterance-level speech acts; that in philosophy and in linguistics has been primarily either in terms of categorization of citation sentences or in tests of successful execution of a speech act, rather than related to conversational data. This research also considers the role of presupposition in assigning speech act function to the data. Sociolinguists, on the other hand, have tried to categorize the form of the speech act in social settings. Ervin-Tripp (1977) has looked at the forms of directives in a variety of speech settings. D'Amico-Reisner (1981) has looked at disapproval statements. Manes and Wolfson (1981) have looked at compliments, a subcategory of the expressive speech act. These descriptions capture the stereotypic nature of the protocols.

Manes and Wolfson, for example, found the linguistic forms used for expressing compliments extremely limited. Over half of the 686 compliments they collected were in the NP-(is, looks)-(really)-ADJ structure (e.g., "Your hair looks nice. That shirt is so nice."). Adding two other syntactic forms—I-(really)-(like, love)-NP (e.g., "I really like those shoes."), and PRO-(is)-(really)-(a)-ADJ-NP (e.g., "This was really a great meal.")—cover 85 percent of the data. Only nine syntactic patterns were needed to cover the data (see Figure 8.1).

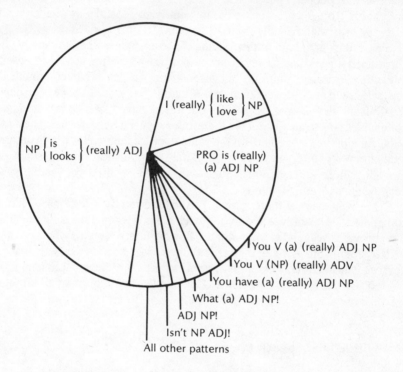

Figure 8.1   Distribution of Compliment Patterns

Rintell (1979), Walters (1979), and Scarcella (1979*a*) have conducted similar research with ESL students. They asked how foreign students perform speech acts in English (and in their native language) and how they mitigate (or behave politely). It may seem difficult to set up situations that would elicit the data one would need to answer such questions, but procedures have been worked out. Walters, for example, set up four settings for data on doing requests:

1. Supermarket
       a. requesting to be shown rice
       b. requesting to get ahead in the checkout line
2. Lunch money
       a. requesting lunch money in the cafeteria
       b. requesting lunch money in the school office

3. Outside at play   a. requesting to play in addressee's yard
                             b. requesting a ball to play with
4. Outside, selling cookies a. requesting that addressee buy cookies
                             b. requesting addressee to sign form

Unfortunately, it would be impossible to take the thirty-two child learners he used (ages: 7–9.5) to each of these places and have them really do the task. The next best procedure appeared to be role play. The children role-played the requests with puppets (puppets that varied in age, sex, and race) in English and in Spanish. Role play has proved to be a fairly successful way of eliciting data from adults as well. Rintell (1979), Scarcella (1979a), and Cook (1981b) have also used this technique in their studies. Those studies where data have been videotaped suggest that we may want to look, not just at linguistic forms used for mitigation in doing requests, but also at the various other communication strategies used in the task. (Some "real situation" encounters have been devised by Galván and Campbell, 1979, but these have been to elicit data on communication strategies rather than to test speech acts/events. They asked bilingual children to come to the school office and act as translators or facilitators for interviews between Anglo administrators and supposedly monolingual Spanish parents. Such data could be used for testing speech acts/events as well.)

However, each of these speech acts is followed by a response. That is, a compliment is usually answered by an acknowledgment. A statement of disapproval is responded to, and the following interaction may become a full-fledged complaint. A request requires a response. If no response is made, its absence is noticeable. Therefore, a response is *part* of the compliment, *part* of the request, *part* of the complaint. This has led to study of small structured speech events.

Small Structured Speech Events

Now, let's turn to a brief example of research on smaller speech events. Research has been done in several areas (e.g., jokes, compliments, apologies, invitations, complaints). Again, the double question for psycholinguistics is whether or not such events have a structure which can be described (whether the descriptions can predict new instances of the speech event), and whether or not people use the structure in producing or comprehending the speech event.

Claims have been made that speech acts are universal. We can, I think, safely assume that all languages have ways of issuing directives, giving apologies, and so on. But we cannot assume that the range of ways to, for example, request or complain are the same across language groups. Nor can we assume that shifts in range that go with social variables in the setting (for example, status, sex, age correspondences between speaker and listener) will necessarily be similar.

For example, Olshtain and Cohen (in press) investigated the structure of *apologies* in several languages. They describe the apology as consisting of one or more of the following five parts:

1. An expression of apology
   a) an expression of regret, e.g., "I'm sorry"
   b) an offer of apology, e.g., "I apologize"
   c) a request for forgiveness, e.g., "Excuse me," "Please forgive me," or "Pardon me."
2. An explanation or account of the situation, e.g., "The bus was delayed."
3. An acknowledgment of responsibility
   a) accepting the blame, e.g., "It was my fault."
   b) expressing self-deficiency, e.g., "I was confused," "I wasn't thinking," "I didn't see you."
   c) recognizing the other person as deserving apology, e.g., "You are right."
   d) expressing lack of intent, e.g., "I didn't mean to."
4. An offer of repair, e.g., "Let me help you get up."
5. A promise of forbearance, e.g., "It won't happen again."

In those cases where the offender did not recognize the need to apologize, two basic types of denial occurred:

1. A denial of the need to apologize, e.g., "There was no need for you to get insulted."
2. A denial of responsibility
   a) not accepting the blame, e.g., "It wasn't my fault."
   b) blaming the other participant for bringing the offense upon himself/ herself, e.g., "It was your own fault."

The first study reported by Olshtain and Cohen was conducted at Hebrew University where forty-four college students were given a role-play task where they reacted to written situations with apologies. Twelve Ss were native speakers of English and responded to English situations. Twelve Ss provided Hebrew apologies to the same situations, and twenty students provided English responses while Hebrew was their native language.

The written situations included four which were designed to elicit different degrees of intensity in apologizing: hitting a car, bumping into a lady and (a) hurting her, (b) just shaking her up, and (c) because she was in the way. Four additional situations were designed to test the effect of status of the addressee on the form of the apology: (1) insulting someone at a meeting, and (2) forgetting a meeting with (a) a boss, (b) a friend, (c) your son. The Ss read the situation and then the investigator role-played the person to whom the apology was to be addressed.

Olshtain and Cohen conducted a second study using this same procedure but involving Russian and English native speakers learning Hebrew. Twelve Russian speakers responded to the situations in Russian. Thirteen speakers of

English and fourteen speakers of Russian, all intermediate learners of Hebrew, were asked to react to the situation in Hebrew.

Finally, Olshtain and Cohen discuss data from four student projects where data were collected using the same procedures from speakers of English, Spanish, Korean, and Chinese. While the number of Ss in these four studies was limited, they add more information on cross-cultural use and form of the apology.

The data showed that native speakers within a language group perform apologies in similar ways. Further, it appears that second language learners, even at the intermediate stage, may lack the linguistic ability to adequately perform apologies. Finally, the data showed that second language learners do transfer apology behavior acceptable in their first language to the target language situation. For example, Hebrew learners of English in the English role-play situations did not express an apology as often as did the native speakers of English when insulting someone at a meeting and when forgetting to take their son shopping. Nor did they offer a repair as frequently as did native speakers of English when forgetting a meeting with their boss and when forgetting to take their son shopping. There were, however, some situations where Hebrew speakers used nativelike apologies rather than Hebrew patterns in English apologies. For example, they expressed an apology for bumping into a lady, though Hebrew native speakers in the parallel Hebrew situation did not. In addition, while Hebrew speakers performing in English often did give an apology, the intensity of regret (e.g., "I'm *very* sorry") did not match that of native speakers.

Evidence of transfer of first language patterns to the target language is found in natural data as well. Among many examples, Wolfson (1981*a,b*) cites *compliments* and compliment responses which are direct translations from the first language. For example, two Iranian friends said:

S: Your shoes are very nice.
A: It is your eyes which can see them which are nice.

and an Iranian boy said to his mother:

S: It was delicious, Mom. I hope your hands never have pain.
A: I'm glad you like it.

Following Wolfson, students in one of my classes collected compliment responses from foreign students and from native speakers. The task was for students to compliment five native speakers of American English and five foreign students on an article of apparel ("That's a nice NP"). While native speakers most frequently acknowledged the compliment with "thanks," they also followed with a bridge to a new topic (e.g., "I got it at Robinsons. I can't believe how expensive they are."). Japanese students were most likely to deny the positive evaluation (e.g., "Ohh no, it's nothing.") which resulted in the native speaker reinforcing the compliment ("No, really, I like it a lot."). The need to reoffer the compliment and the lack of bridge led to uneasy continuation of these small speech events for complimenting.

Yet, ESL learners do not always find small speech events difficult. For example, Cook (1981*b*) gave students a task of asking direction or requesting the time. Their data did not differ much from that of native speakers. They requested and thanked their informants for the information. The heavy use of modals did make the foreign speech seem more formal and polite than native speech. They also used idiosyncratic expressions such as "Thank you I very gratitude you" or "Be so kind of saying the shortest way to the bus station." Nevertheless, the overall structure of the information-seeking task was appropriately done, and the responses to sex and age differences in informants were similar to those of native speakers.

Researchers have also investigated the structure of *complaints*. Rader (1977) defined the complaint as an utterance, or set of utterances, that identify a problem or trouble source and seek remediation, either from the person responsible for the trouble or from a third party who has the power to affect the situation. Complaints are implicitly comparative since they compare what happened with what should have happened. Clearly, complaints should be problematic for second language learners since it is assumed that there are shared cultural presuppositions between speaker and hearer about what is good (what should be) and what is bad (what actually happened). Both Rader and Sharrock and Turner (1978) have discussed data on complaints to third persons (letters to Ralph Nader in the Rader study and phone calls to the police in the Sharrock and Turner study).

In their research, Giddens (1981), Inoue (in preparation), and Schaefer (1982) further delimited complaints, classifying complaints made to third persons as gripes (where the third party had no power to remedy the situation) and as trials (where the complainer tries to convince the third party to take action against the responsible party).

Giddens, Inoue, and Schaefer elicited complaints to responsible others from Spanish, Japanese, and English native speakers in order to obtain data that would allow them to describe the syntactic and discourse components of complaints. They also hoped to show how the sex of the complainer and that of the person to whom the complaint was directed influenced the complaint structure. To obtain the data, they constructed twenty role-play situations (e.g., noisy stereo at 2:00 a.m., cutting in line, cold food, borrowed money, faulty merchandise, etc.). These situations were tape-recorded with a "lead-in" statement or question which signaled the S to respond with a complaint. (On Tape A, ten situations were narrated by a male and ten by a female; on Tape B, the situations were reversed.) The tapes were played to forty native speakers, twenty female and twenty male (ten of each receiving Tape A and ten, Tape B). This gave a corpus of 800 complaints from each language group.

In all three language groups, the same discourse components appeared. These included:

1. *Opener* An utterance made by the complainer that initiates the speech event and does not provide information about what has gone wrong, why the wrong merits a complaint, or how to remedy the wrong (e.g., "hi," "hola," "oye").

2. *Orientation* An utterance that provides information about the speaker's identity and/or intentions in initiating the speech event (e.g., "I'm your nextdoor neighbor," "Vengo a quejarme").

3. *Act Statement* An utterance that states the problem (e.g., "You charged me too much," "Me han desconectado el teléfono").

4. *Justification*
   a. *Justification of the Speaker* An utterance by the complainer that explains why he personally is making the complaint (e.g., "Yo ha pagado todos los recibos puntualmente." "De mi zona, soy la única persona que no tiene servicio telefónico").
   b. *Justification of the Addressee* An utterance that gives a reason for the addressee's having committed the wrong (e.g., "I know you enjoy listening to music, but . . . ," "Yo creo que cualquier persona que se suba en avión se pone un poco nerviosa, pero . . .")

5. *Remedy* An utterance that calls for an action to rectify the wrong (e.g., "Get back in line," "Sería tan amable de cambiarme los zapatos").
   a. *Threat* A type of remedy in which the complainer states an action he will execute contingent upon an action made by the addressee (e.g., "Le suplico, por favor, o que me da bien una pizza caliente sabrosa o simplemente me retiro sin pagar y no volver nunca más").

6. *Closing* An utterance that concludes the turn at speaking.
   a. expressions of appreciation (e.g., "thanks")
   b. expressions of apology (e.g., "sorry")
   c. goodbyes (e.g., "adiós," "goodbye")

7. *Valuation* An utterance made by the complainer to express her feelings about either the addressee or the wrong committed.

While the data analysis (and the comparisons across the three language groups) has not yet been completed, it is safe to say that strong differences have been found as to the effect of sex of addressee and of speaker across the three language groups. Secondly, the syntactic forms and the formality of lexical choice also appear to differ across the three groups.

Final reports on this project should support the findings of Loos (1981) in his study of foreign students' abilities to recognize socially appropriate complaints (socially appropriate for English). Using a multiple-choice test, Loos found that nationality, native language, major field of study, and university status all significantly influenced the test performance of his 278 Ss. While overall language ability (particularly reading skills) influenced their performance, different language groups recognized appropriateness of complaints better than other language groups.

These studies have revealed problems of methodology (Can role play elicit data that show what *S*s would do in natural complaint situations or when making apologies in the real world?). However, there are many problems in interpreting natural data as well. For example, foreign students often complain to our office staff about not being able to get into classes and/or about their entrance exam scores. Some students are accusatory in voicing complaints, some seem hardly to know how to express their unhappiness, others ask about procedures for making legal complaints. Few seem to do complaining in an "appropriate" manner ("appropriate" = the way I would do it). How are we to categorize their successes or failures as complainers? Is it that they have only learned the strongest or weakest of all the possible ways of "doing" that function—that is, is the problem in the aggravated to mitigated scale? Is it cultural—that is, are you supposed to yell at secretaries or are you supposed to stand looking unhappy and saying little? If so, does failure signal inability to perform the speech *act* or failure to recognize the speech *situation* in which the complaint should be made? Is it a failure in using a variety of speech acts in constructing a complaint speech *event*? Or is failure due to the grammatical structures used in complaining in the new language?

All of these issues deserve further research, particularly those which might relate to markedness theory. As mentioned earlier, Cook and others have suggested that foreign students seem to learn (or at least use) the most polite forms. While formal, polite forms may not necessarily be the least marked, they seem to be the forms learned first (perhaps because these are the forms that are presented in EFL textbooks). Learners also know they must choose language appropriate to a wide range of sociolinguistic variables. By choosing only the form they judge to be most polite, learners may feel that they won't make any great social blunders. However, they may be wrong in this judgment, for the rules for addressing speakers of equivalent or different status (i.e., age, sex, role, and power) are likely to vary across languages. Polite formality may easily be misinterpreted as hostility or distancing, where this is not the learner's intent. In cases where such politeness may seem offensive, where sociolinguistic rules are imperfectly learned, Ervin-Tripp (1972) suggests the utility of retaining an accent. If mistakes are made, it is, she says, better to be designated as a foreigner than to risk insulting or offending the listener.

When foreign students come to this country, the frequency weight of informal, colloquial forms begins to break through this politeness register. When this happens, collocations of extremely polite and friendly, informal forms occur. What could be a more inappropriate combination than Scarcella's (1979*a*) examples of "Hello, my teacher" or "Hi, sir," or Ervin-Tripp's (1972) hypothetical example, "How's it going, Your Eminence?"

The intent of all these examples is to show that, while speech acts and small speech events may be universal, the range of ways of expressing each differs from language to language and is sensitive to sociolinguistic variables. While second language learners may have directives, commissives, representatives, expressives, and declaratives, while they may have compliments, invitations, complaints, jokes, and information-giving exchanges in their first languages, it is unlikely that speech acts or speech events are carried out in exactly the same way in the second language.

I began this chapter with the hope that I could outline the areas of spoken discourse analysis. To do that entirely would move this chapter far beyond the confines of psycholinguistic research. Psycholinguists and sociolinguists are involved in experimentation which might show how the speech situation influences speech events. Psycholinguists' interest is mainly in terms of how it relates to the comprehension and production of language within speech events. Sociologists are involved with describing individual and group interactions in conversation. Psycholinguists are interested in such research, again, in terms of what it has to say about human language comprehension and production. Philosophers are working on relevance and inferencing. Psycholinguists are vitally interested in this research too, for it has the potential of contributing a great deal to our understanding of language comprehension and production. Thus, what may seem like forays into territories outside that of psycholinguistics are not forays at all. Rather, psycholinguists hope that information from these fields will help in our search for answers to the questions of human language processing and production.

In this chapter we have looked at only a few examples of spoken discourse. However, we can also chart some of the other areas of discourse analysis and the questions posed (see Table 2).

At this stage much of the work in discourse analysis is descriptive. Experimentation is just beginning to be done, testing many of the claims that have been made in these descriptions. Hopper and Thompson (1980), for example, have begun to test some of the claims that have been made about tense/aspect and transitivity in narrative text. Wiggins (1977) has tested some of the claims made about the organization of scientific text related to tense/aspect. Walters (1979) and others have begun to test for differences in the ways speech act/events are carried out when social/language group is varied. Schmidt and Richards (in press) and others are trying to manipulate variables to see how input to learners might change under a number of exposure settings. Celce-Murcia (1980) and her students have run numerous experiments on the effect of discourse context on selection of syntactic structures. It is this experimentation that will bridge the work of researchers in discourse with that of researchers in sociolinguistics and psycholinguistics.

Table 2 Types of Discourse Research

1. *Conversational Analysis*
    What is the structure of natural conversations?
        English: Sachs, Schegloff, Goffman, Jefferson, et al.
        Other languages: Moerman, Daden
        ESL: Gaskill, Schwartz
    What is the structure of service encounters? Merritt
    What is the nature of relevance and inferencing? Hilyard & Olson
2. *Unequal Power Discourse*
    What is the structure of trials? Labov, Blount, Shuy
    What is the structure of doctor-patient interviews? Labov & Fanshel, Cicourel
    What is the structure of classroom discourse?
        Elementary school: Sinclair & Coulthard
        ESL classes: Allwright, Bailey, Fanselow, Chaudron
        American Indian classes: Phillips, Weeks
3. *Text Analysis*
    What is the structure of spoken narrative?
        English: Labov & Waletzky, Bowditch, Linde
        ESL: Godfrey
    How does discourse differ in unplanned to planned versions?
        English: Ochs, Givon, Bennett
        ESL: Krashen, Schlue
    What is the structure of other genres?
        Text: Longacre
        ESP: Selinker, Trimble, Montford, Wiggins
4. *Smaller Speech Events/Acts*
    What is the structure of requesting, arguing, apologizing, complaining, etc.?
    How does the structure differ over social/language groups?
    Gumperz, Hymes, Fraser, Walters, Rintell, Scarcella, Carrell, Wolfson, Giddens, Inoue
    & Schaefer, Cohen & Olshtain
5. *Contextual Analysis*
    What form is chosen in context a, b . . . n? Fraser, Celce-Murcia
    What is implied by choice X in context a, b . . . n? Labov & Fanshel, Gary, Celce-Murcia,
    etc.
6. *Language Acquisition Discourse* (see Chapter 9)
    How is input to a learner structured in discourse?
        Input focus—first and second language learning
        Interaction focus—first and second language learning

9 Input/Interaction and Language Development

In the mid and late '60s a grand polemic raged between behaviorists and linguists over whether or not imitation and analogy could explain child language acquisition. A strong argument against such an explanation was that child language seldom matches language used by adults. Children's utterances such as "no want cooky" could not be found in adult speech. While adult speech production *is* replete with error, false starts, and digressions, child language matches neither these performance errors nor linguists' descriptions of grammatically correct sentences. Adult language "performance" is quite different from what was called "competence," and it is competence in the language—the underlying language system—that linguists believe the child must be acquiring. How could the child acquire this competence, given all the performance errors in most adult speech, if language were acquired by imitation and analogy?

Since language is extremely complex, and since performance errors appeared to be ubiquitous, it was assumed that the child learner must have some special Language Acquisition Device (LAD), some sort of template of language universals, which does most of the acquiring for the learner. That is, the child really has some innate "black box" labeled Language (capital L) and needs only to let it operate to find the special rules of language (small l). It was popular at that time to talk about "imprinting," a term borrowed from animal behavior studies. For example, since ducklings newly hatched must identify their mothers, at some point in biological maturation they "look up" and whatever they see is "imprinted" as mother. Someone passing by, a motor boat, or a cat or dog may become the duckling's mother. And it will follow the mother everywhere. By analogy, then, at some point in the infant's biological maturation it suddenly "looks up" and says "ah, English" and begins to follow it everywhere, adapting its wired-in language component to the special rules of English. Only by positing an inherent Language Acquisition Device could developmental psycholinguists account for the rapid (i.e., five-year) acquisition of the basic language system. Much language is acquired later than this, but in the '60s most researchers believed that all language is acquired by age five. The five-year mark also made the "black box" claim more valid, since learning then appeared to be a magic, all-at-once phenomenon rather than a difficult drawn-out process.

Motherese and Foreigner Talk

Snow was among the first to seriously question whether the language of adults in adult-adult conversation really matched that of adult-child communication. Her research was followed by an avalanche of studies on what was first called "baby talk" and later "motherese" (though fathers also speak it). It soon became clear that language used in communicating with young children (and others with less verbal ability or less facility with a particular language) is modified in specific ways. None of the following could appear in normal adult conversations:

    Mother: What else have you got in your face?
                 Where's your nose?
                 Where's you nose?
                 Ann's nose?

                                                   (Snow, 1977, p. 19)

    Teacher: explaining "bath" and "bathe" to an ESL class:
                 In your house . . . you . . . house . . . a tub . . . you (gesture) wash.

                                       (Hatch et al., 1978, p. 1)

    Clinician: using PICA therapy:
                 Mr. Mottl? . . . *show* me (gesture) how you use it (gesture) *show* me. No, don't tell me, *show* me.

                                               (Simms, 1978)

Roger Brown (1977) suggested that modifications in register, of which motherese is just one example, serve two functions: to promote communication and to express affective characteristics. The second function includes the register of language between lovers, language to pets, language to plants, and so on, as well as to babies. Such modifications may give a special affective boost to language acquisition. A third claim might also be made—that the simplification of input is either an explicit or an implicit teaching mode.

In this chapter I hope to demonstrate that (1) certain modifications occur in speech when the language is addressed to those who are learners or relearners; (2) despite many differences, there are strong similarities in speech modifications regardless whether the addressee is a first or second language learner or a language relearner; (3) these modifications may occur as implicit or explicit teaching activities, as expressions of empathy or affection, and, most importantly, they do facilitate communication; and (4) the modifications are a natural outcome of the negotiation of communication.

This topic is relevant to psycholinguistics for several reasons. First, in order to better understand how children, foreigners, or persons with language disorders learn or relearn a language, it is helpful to know the characteristics of the language they are exposed to. Second, we may be able to estimate roughly where an individual is at, linguistically and cognitively, by studying how the individual is addressed. Third, as teachers, parents, psycholinguists, or speech pathologists, we are interested in how some input facilitates speech and language while other input does not. And, finally, it provides us with the opportunity to discuss the connection between social interaction and language development.

Characteristics of Language Addressed to Learners

Table 1 compares characteristics of language addressed to learners. In no sense should it be taken as complete coverage of the research. Unfilled cells are not to be considered as showing differences among groups, rather they are cells to be filled in following a more complete survey of the voluminous research on the topic. For useful reviews of the literature on motherese, see Clark and Clark (1977), deVilliers and deVilliers (1978), Farwell (1973), Landes (1975), Snow (1977), Vorster (1975), and Long (1980). For an excellent review and evaluation of research on language addressed to second language learners, see Long (1980). In addition, studies listed do not necessarily claim that statistically significant differences were found. Rather, many simply give examples of the phenomenon cited.

In the suprasegmental system (Table 1), you can see that input is higher pitched, shows more intonation variation in pitch, is louder in volume, contains more and longer pauses, and is much slower than speech among adult native speakers. It has been suggested that these pitch and volume features help to cue the learner that *this,* of all the speech noise, is language to be attended to. It serves as both an attention getter and an attention retainer (the latter is especially important for the learner or relearner who has a short attention span). Garnica (1977) showed that adults use high pitch to two-year-olds, somewhat lower pitch to five-year-olds, and lowest pitch to other adults. DePaulo and Bonvillian (1978) say that this special pitch marking may have a negative effect if learners ignore lower pitched conversations carried on between adults and so miss valuable linguistic data. Adults speaking with second language learners frequently use volume rather than pitch to mark speech as *for* the learner.

Broen (1972) showed that adult speech rate dropped to half normal rate when adults addressed children. Further, children best understood language delivered at a rate that matched their own relatively slow rate.

Second language studies also comment on the slow rate of speech addressed to second language learners, whether children or adults. Henzl (1975), for example, showed that teachers telling stories to beginners, advanced students, and to native speakers consistently varied speech rate to the level of proficiency of the hearers (see Table 2).

Table 1 Research on Features of Motherese and Foreigner Talk

Features	Motherese	Type*	Foreigner Talk	Type*
SUPRASEGMENTALS				
Exaggerated	Casagrande	A-C	Ferguson	A-A
intonation	Kelkar	A-C	Hatch	A-A
	Sachs & Johnson	A-C	Chaudron	A-A
	Moerk	A-C	Katz	C-C
	Clark & Clark	A-C	Peck	C-C
	Weeks	C-C		
Gesture	Kelkar	A-C	Ferguson	A-A
	Moerk	A-C	Henzl	A-A
	Clark & Clark	A-C	Hatch	A-A
High pitch or	Kelkar	A-C	Andersen	C-C
wide range	Garnica	A-C		
	Moerk	A-C		
	Clark & Clark	A-C		
	DePaulo & Bonvillian	A-C		
Loud speech	Kelkar	A-C	Ferguson	A-A
			Hatch	A-A
			Henzl	A-A
			Andersen	C-C
Onomato-	Austerlitz	A-C	Ferguson	A-A
poeia	Kelkar	A-C	Peck	C-C
	Phillips	A-C		
Pauses	Clark & Clark	A-C	Ferguson	A-A
	Newport	A-C	Hatch	A-A
			Henzl	A-A
			Chaudron	A-A
			Arthur et al.	A-A
Slow rate	Kelkar	A-C	Ferguson	A-A
	Broen	A-C	Hatch	A-A
	Moerk	A-C	Henzl	A-A
	Clark & Clark	A-C	Arthur et al.	A-A
	DePaulo & Bonvillian	A-C	Heidelberg Proj.	A-A
	Remick	A-C	Ramamurti	A-A
			Trager	A-A
			Steyaert	A-A
			Andersen	C-C
PHONOLOGICAL				
Clear	Casagrande	A-C	Ferguson	A-A
enunciation	Moerk	A-C	Henzl	A-A
	DePaulo & Bonvillian	A-C	Hatch	A-A
	Weeks	C-C	Freed	A-A
			Heidelberg Proj.	A-A
Phonological	(more simplification)		(less simplification)	
simplifica-	Casagrande	A-C	Hatch	A-A
tion	Austerlitz	A-C	(more simplification)	
	Clark & Clark	A-C	Katz	C-C
	DePaulo & Bonvillian	A-C		

Table 1   *continued*

Features	Motherese	Type*	Foreigner Talk	Type*
SEMANTIC				
Lower type—	Broen	A-C	Arthur et al.	A-A
token ratio	Drach	A-C	Trager	A-A
	Remick	A-C		
Concrete	Phillips	A-C	Hatch	A-A
lexicon	Clark & Clark	A-C	Henzl	A-A
	DePaulo & Bonvillian	A-C	Wong-Fillmore	C-C
Unique	Casagrande	A-C	Ferguson	A-A
lexicon	Austerlitz	A-C	Snow et al.	A-A
	Kelkar	A-C		
	Clark & Clark	A-C		
	DePaulo & Bonvillian	A-C		
	Sachs & Devin	C-C		
Definitions			Chaudron	A-A
			Hatch	A-A
			Wong-Fillmore	C-C
SYNTAX				
Fewer coordi-	Drach	A-C	Ferguson	A-A
nate, subor-	Shatz et al.	C-C	Hatch	A-A
dinate or	Snow	A-C		
embedded	Newport	A-C		
clauses	DePaulo & Bonvillian	A-C		
	Phillips	A-C		
	Vorster	A-C		
More impera-	Corsaro	A-C	Hatch	A-A
tives	Blount	A-C	Scarcella & Higa	A-C
	Sachs & Devin	C-C		
No + Verb			Ferguson	A-A
Neg.			Hatch	A-A
			Wong-Fillmore	C-C
			Katz	C-C
Omission of	Snow	A-C	Ferguson	A-A
articles	Kelkar	A-C	Hatch	A-A
			Ramamurti	A-A
			Clyne	A-A
			Snow et al.	A-A
			Katz	C-C
			Andersen	C-C
Ommission of			Ferguson	A-A
copula			Hatch	A-A
			Clyne	A-A
			Snow et al.	A-A
			Wong-Fillmore	C-C
			Katz	C-C
			Andersen	C-C
Omission of	Snow	A-C	Ferguson	A-A
possessive			Hatch	A-A
(or use of			Snow et al.	A-A
Noun +				
Noun)				

Table 1 *continued*

Features	Motherese	Type*	Foreigner Talk	Type*
Omitted or incorrect word endings	Kelkar	A-C	Ferguson	A-A
			Hatch	A-A
			Clyne	A-A
			Snow et al.	A-A
			Valdman	A-A
			Ramamurti	A-A
			Andersen	C-C
			Katz	C-C
Omitted pronouns or use of nouns	Snow	A-C	Ferguson	A-A
	Clark & Clark	A-C	Hatch	A-A
			Henzl	A-A
			Clyne	A-A
			Valdman	A-A
			Wong-Fillmore	C-C
More tag Qs			Ferguson	A-A
			Jordan & Fuller	A-A
			Hatch	A-A
Greater use of 1-word utterances	Clark & Clark	A-C	Katz	C-C
More questions	Clark & Clark	A-C	Hatch	A-A
	Corsaro	A-C	Peck	A-A
	Blount	A-C	Long	A-A
	Holzman	A-C	Freed	A-A
			Katz	C-C
			Scarcella & Higa	A-C
Fewer questions	Sachs & Devin	C-C	Peck	C-C
Shorter preverb length	Snow	A-C		
	Sachs & Devin	C-C		
Shorter MLU or words per T-unit	Snow	A-C	Henzl	A-A
	Phillips	A-C	Freed	A-A
	Nelson	A-C	Gaies	A-A
	Moerk	A-C	Chaudron	A-A
	Clark & Clark	A-C	Ramamurti	A-A
	DePaulo & Bonvillian	A-C	Chaudron	A-A
			Arthur et al.	A-A
			Long	A-A
			Wong-Fillmore	C-C
			Scarcella & Higa	A-C
			Snow & Hoef-nagel-Hohle	C-C
Fewer verbs and more content words	Snow	A-C	Henzl	A-A
	Phillips	A-C		
	Drach	A-C		
Few compound verbs	Snow	A-C	Henzl	A-A
			Ferguson	A-A

Table 1 *continued*

Features	Motherese	Type*	Foreigner Talk	Type*
COMMUNICATION DEVICES				
Repetition of	Kelkar	A-C	Ferguson	A-A
words and	Snow	A-C	Hatch	A-A
phrases			Freed	A-A
			Long	A-A
			Katz	C-C
			Scarcella & Higa	A-C
More correc-	Clark & Clark	A-C	Peck	C-C
tion of Truth			Katz	C-C
and phon.			Wong-Fillmore	C-C
than syntax				
Occasional Q's	DePaulo & Bonvillian	A-C		
Sentence	DePaulo & Bonvillian	A-C	Hatch	A-A
fill-ins			Freed	A-A
Sentence	Clark & Clark	A-C	Hatch	A-C
frames				
Rephrasing	DePaulo & Bonvillian	A-C	Hatch	A-A
			Long	A-A

*A-C = adult to child; C-C = child to child; A-A = adult to adult.

Table 2 Speech Rate in Words/Minute

			Audience		
Language	Teacher	Story	Native Speaker	Advanced Learner	Beginning Learner
Czech	1	1	109.1	61.0	46.7
		2	89.4	90.0	58.3
	2	1	115.0	51.8	55.5
		2	120.0	88.0	58.4
	3	1	110.0	81.4	56.8
		2	142.2	103.4	54.5
	4	1	113.1	70.0	63.6
		2	146.2	87.7	63.5
	5	1	123.0	84.0	33.1
		2	114.0	63.0	50.6
English	6	1	236.8	143.9	98.7
		2	288.5	163.0	117.2
	7	1	157.1	130.7	56.0
		2	147.5	103.1	52.2
	8	1	226.2	206.1	179.1
		2	166.7	167.8	144.5
German	9	1	187.2	166.4	83.8
		2	174.0	125.7	93.8
	10	1	98.0	105.3	81.2
		2	88.0	110.3	106.9
	11	1	123.3	105.8	96.1
		2	155.1	146.7	135.0

Henzl, 1975, p. 10.

Teacher 10 must be one of the few teachers in the world who has really internalized our teacher-training directions on using a natural rate of speech when teaching beginners. Few, if any, of the teachers I have observed during practice teaching maintain a natural rate of speech. Rather, they naturally adjust their rate of speech. And that slowing of rate means clearer articulation, fewer reduced vowels, less consonant cluster simplification, more fully released final stops, and stronger voicing of voiced consonants in final position. All of these should make the teacher's language "easier" for the learner to process. I suspect it also accounts for why students say they understand everything their ESL teacher says but have trouble understanding English in their other classes. In their other classes the speakers are not addressing the foreign student specifically and therefore are using a normal rate (presenting less clearly articulated messages).

Slower rate also means longer pauses between major constituents. This should help learners, not only because it gives them more processing time but also because it could help them identify major constituent boundaries. Garnica believes that the preponderance of rising-pitch terminals may also help the learner delineate sentence and other major constituent boundaries.

In syntax we also find clearer "articulation." Utterances are simpler syntactically. They are also more grammatically correct than performance data found in adult-adult conversations. There are fewer false starts and less repair so that, generally, one might say that the learner receives more examples of "good" sentences on which to build hypotheses about language structures. Freed, in her paper on "foreigner talk" (1978), also found that utterances to foreigners were highly grammatical and syntactically simple. Sentence length showed most dramatically how speakers took into account the language ability of the listener, as can be seen in Table 3 (in this table, Ss = sentences, not subjects).

The research, then, shows that there are marked similarities in language addressed to learners whether they are first or second language learners. The

Table 3   Syntactic Comparisons

Sentence Complexity	Motherese Mean %	Foreigner Talk		Adult Native Speakers Mean %
		Low Lrn. Mean %	High Lrn. Mean %	
No. Ss with 1 S node	.82	.71	.55	.41
Mean length of Ss with 1 S node	4.54	5.34	6.10	6.90
No. S nodes per average sentence	1.16	1.38	1.81	2.24
Mean length of sentence in words	4.24	6.74	9.66	12.13

Freed, 1978.

low MLU (Mean Length of Utterance) found in language to learners means that there will be few complex sentences, few subordinate clauses, few complimentizers, and so on. However, we ought to remember that spontaneous conversation has few of these to begin with. The increased number of tag questions in motherese and foreigner talk can easily be accounted for by the need to check comprehension more frequently when the addressee is a learner (e.g., "On Westwood Boulevard, right?"). Tags also present the learner with possible answers (e.g., "What didja see there, a horse?"). The limited use of pronouns is also easily explained. If we want to be sure we are understood, we will keep the referent in the foreground longer. Once we are sure the referent has been identified and can be kept in mind by the listener, it is easier to change to a pronoun form.

Even among adult native speakers, conversation appears to rely less heavily on complex syntactic development than does more highly planned speech or written text. Therefore, we must be careful in claiming that language to learners is syntactically simple, unless we have a comparison set of data for adult-adult conversation. As Long (1981a) has shown, many of the characteristics of language addressed to the learner also appear in the conversation of adult native speakers. The difference is a matter of degree. His study checked differences on sixteen input features. Table 4 shows that eleven features were significantly different from those obtained in native speaker baseline data.

These data were collected in six different tasks: (1) informal conversation, (2) vicarious narrative, (3) giving instructions for two games, (4) playing the first game, (5) playing the second game, and (6) discussing the supposed intent

Table 4 Differences Between NS-NS and NS-NNS Conversation Across Six Tasks

In NS-NNS conversation, there was/were:	p level
INPUT	
1. shorter average length of T-units	.005
2. lower number of S-nodes per T-unit	NS
3. lower type-token ratio	NS
4. higher average lexical frequency of nouns and verbs	NS
5. higher proportion of copulas in total verbs	NS
INTERACTION	
6. more present (versus nonpresent) temporal marking of verbs	.001
7. different distribution of questions, statements and imperatives in T-units	.001
8. different distribution of question-types in T-units (more WH-questions)	.001
9. more conversational frames	NS
10. more confirmation checks	.005
11. more comprehension checks	.005
12. more clarification requests	.005
13. more self-repetitions	.005
14. more other-repetitions	.005
15. more expansions	.005
16. more of 9 through 15 combined	.005

Long, 1981a.

of the research. Table 5 shows that the degree of modification of the sixteen features was related to the task (whether the task required a two-way exchange of information or not). Task makes a difference, for more modification of the interaction factors takes place when the conversation requires an exchange of information. In these tables, Long separates modification of language addressed to learners into input and interaction rather than considering them all as input factors. As we shall see later in this chapter, this allows him to test claims regarding the importance of language simplification versus simplification of the interaction task.

Social Interaction and First Language Acquisition

The adult speaking to the learner also adjusts speech to the "cognitive" level of the learner. Another way of saying this is that we all obey the "rules of conversation" in nominating topics and responding to the topic nominations of others. For example, if the child nominates "this" pointing to a fish in a fish tank, the child and adult seem to talk about "this" as a topic in a very few, very limited number of ways: "What? Fish. What's this? It's a fish. Where's the fish? Whose fish is that? What's the fish doing? He's (it's) swimming. Can he swim? No, it's not a fish." There are not many "etc.'s" possible.

The rules of conversation allow the adult only two kinds of relevant responses: (1) what information about "this" is shared by adult and child; and (2) what are the attributes of "this" that one can talk about? There is nothing immediately obvious about "this" to allow the adult to make a relevant remark about much of anything beyond what, where, whose, what color, how many, what doing, can X Verb, is X Verbing. And the first constraint prevents the adult

Table 5 Relationship Between Task-type and NS-NS and NS-NNS Conversation

The degree of difference between NS-NS and NS-NNS conversation in performance on:				
	Tasks 1, 4, & 5 (+ info. exchg.)		Tasks 2, 3, & 6 (− info. exchg.)	
INPUT				
1. average length of T-units	$p < .025$	NS	$p > .025$	NS
2. number of S-nodes per T-unit	$p < .01$	NS	$p < .025$	NS
INTERACTION				
3. distribution of questions, statements & imper. in T-units	$p < .001$		$p < .005$	
4. number of conversational frames	$p > .025$	NS	$p > .025$	NS
5. number of confirmation checks	$p < .005$		$p < .01$	NS
6. number of comprehension requests	$p < .005$		$p > .025$	NS
7. number of clarification requests	$p < .005$		$p > .025$	NS
8. number of self-repetitions	$p < .005$		$p < .005$	
9. number of other-repetitions	$p < .005$		$p > .025$	NS
10. number of expansions	$p < .005$		-------	NS
11. number of 4 thru 10 combined	$p < .005$		$p > .025$	NS

Long, 1981a.

from saying such things as "Didja know the price of tuna went up again?" or "What's an angel fish doing in a salt-water tank?"

One can conclude, then, that it is not really so much that the adult is consciously aware that the child cannot answer questions with complex syntactic forms and, therefore, consciously or unconsciously simplifies the input to the learner. Rather, the frequency of what, where, whose, is X Verbing, etc., is controlled by the child's conversation topics. Those topics, for young children, seem to be limited in most cases to the here and now. As the child matures, the range of possible topics gradually expands. In the initial stages the constraints that "relevancy" places on conversations insure simplicity in the input.

The data on motherese contains a variety of possible teaching devices, beyond those of presenting simple syntactic structures with high frequency. DePaulo and Bonvillian mention "occasional questions" consisting of the "say CONSTITUENT again":

Child: I want milk.
Mother: You want what?
Child: Milk.

and "constituent prompts":

Mother: What do you want?
Child: (no answer)
Mother: You want what?

and "fill in the blank" sentences:

Child: I want milk.
Mother: You want...?
Child: Milk.

(DePaulo and Bonvillian, 1978)

The authors feel these devices draw the child's attention to the missing constituent and, in effect, aid the child's understanding of syntactic structure.

In interactions adults recast, repeat, and expand child learner utterances in ways that may teach syntax and add content information as well. It has been suggested that use of "sentence frames" also assists syntactic development by making the subject-verb rule more apparent. Clark and Clark, for example, note the use of sentence frames such as:

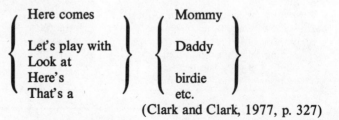

(Clark and Clark, 1977, p. 327)

These look very similar to the frames (also called chunk-learned, prefabricated, or formulaic speech) found in early second language learner data. That they should appear in speech addressed to child first and second language learners simply shows us the other side of communication script.

Snow (1972) states that the frequent use of semantic repetition (paraphrase) by adults such as: "Pick up the red one. Find the red one. Not the green one. I want the red one. Can you find the red one?" not only provides the child with many repetitions but also is similar to language games that children themselves play with newly learned words.

We must, of course, be cautious in claiming that simplified syntax of motherese and foreigner talk to children is meant to teach. DePaulo and Bonvillian (1978) state that, although there is no strong evidence that particular features of motherese are necessary for language acquisition, some features are more useful than others. They feel, for example, that the affective features (e.g., squeaky voice, phonological distortions, diminutives, unique lexicon in baby talk) do not play a role in acquisition, while many other features of simplified input might help.

Phillips (1973), in discussing the longer MLU in mothers' speech to infants of eight months as compared with their speech to eighteen-month-old infants, states that, when playing with an eight-month-old infant, mothers appear to be talking to and for themselves. However, even this early speech may be directed to the child to "teach" conversational turns:

Mother: Hello. Give me a smile then. (gently pokes infant in the ribs)
Infant: (Yawns)
Mother: Sleepy, are you? You woke up too early today.
Infant: (Opens fist)
Mother: (Touching infant's hand) What are you looking at? Can you see something?
Infant: (Grasps mother's finger)
Mother: Oh, that's what you wanted. In a friendly mood, then. Come on, give us a smile.

(Snow, 1977)

Once the child does begin to speak, there is a sharp reduction in the length and complexity of the mother's speech. DePaulo and Bonvillian and others have suggested that this simplification stops short of a match with the language of the child. Rather, they claim it "stays a step or so ahead" of the child's language and that this facilitates acquisition. This may, indeed, be the case, but at this point it is not clear whether that step or so ahead consists of utterance length, syntactic complexity, lexical choice, or what. It seems more likely that the match of language between mother and child is due to the process of negotiation of conversation. Before the child speaks at all, there is nothing to negotiate. (That's not strictly true, for there is much to be negotiated and much negotiation is going on, as seen in Snow's example above.) Once the child does begin to speak, conversations must be negotiated on another level; out of this negotiation come the characteristic markers of motherese.

In summary, adult speech to young children may facilitate language acquisition as well as communication in a number of ways. These are presented in Table 6.

Table 6   Adult Speech to Children

Adult Modifications:	Possible Roles in Acquisition		
	Identifying Conversational Turns	Mapping Ideas onto Language	Identifying Linguistic Units
Name of child	X		
Exclamations	X		
High pitch	X		
Whispering	X		
Exaggerated intonation	X		
Baby talk words		X	
Selection of vocabulary		X	
Omit word endings		X	
Avoid pronouns		X	
Model dialogues	X		X
Expatiations	X	X	
Prompt questions	X		
Corrections for truth	X	X	
Slow speech			X
Pauses			X
Short sentences		X	X
Frames		X	X
Repetitions		X	X

Clark & Clark, 1977.

From the literature we can conclude that language input in adult-child interaction must in some way assist language learning. While this input may not be a necessary component, language acquisition cannot proceed in a normal manner without it. This is supported by the report of Sachs and Johnson (1976) of a hearing child of deaf parents who was exposed primarily to television as the major input, though he did play with other children on occasion. At the age of three years, nine months the child had an extremely small vocabulary and his language development was severely delayed. Linguistic interaction between adult and child is important.

According to Harkness, in Guatemala, due to certain beliefs regarding child-rearing, a "quiet, sickly child might be ignored by a mother who interacted frequently with the child's more lively sibling. Individual differences among children might logically be accentuated by this treatment, and in fact it was not unusual to find three-year-old children who were less linguistically advanced than their one-and-a-half or two-year-old siblings" (1976, p. 111). Moerk stressed the importance of "encounters between parent and infant during care-giving activities which may attract the infant's special attention to the verbal stimuli, while much of adult conversation overheard by the infant may have little effect" (1977, p. 209).

Such statements are echoed in comments by Ervin-Tripp and others in second language learning research. If exposure were all that one needed, most Americans would know several languages. The idea that one can learn a second language spoken in the home simply by osmosis doesn't seem to work. Children of deaf parents do not learn from television. (Payton Todd, in a personal communication, has suggested that these children think TV actors are simply very poor signers or that they use some other sign language.) Despite the success of one of the good language learners in the Naiman et al. study (1978), few people learn French by watching French movies. In fact, Long (1981), as we shall see later, argues that one cannot acquire a language (in untutored conditions) without interaction.

Social Interaction and Child Second Language Acquisition

Negotiation in the initial stages of second language acquisition by children shares many aspects with that of child first language learning. Ochs Keenan (1974) claims that the first step the child must make in conversation is to get the attention of the person with whom she or he wishes to talk. This can be accomplished in nonverbal ways (banging a spoon, pulling at mother's hand, etc.) or through verbal gestures. If immediate response is not forthcoming, the child usually becomes insistent in the repetitions ("mama, mama, mama") until she or he does get a response, and may use additional nonverbal gestures to add to the attention-drawing verbalization. The child does not continue talking until contact with a listener is established. This first step is also clear in data of second language learning children:

Paul:	(To Kenny) You-you-you-you
Kenny:	Huh?
Paul:	I-see-you Kenny

(Huang, 1970; Paul, 5 yrs., Taiwanese)

Miki:	Ryan, Ryan, Ryan
Ryan:	Huh?

(Yoshida, 1976; Miki, 3 yrs., Japanese)

Paul:	Oh-oh!
Jim:	What?
Paul:	This (points to ant)
Jim:	It's an ant.

(Huang, 1970)

This does not mean that every time the second language learner wants to nominate a discourse topic he calls the first language learner's name, says "oh-oh" or "hey," or any of the usual attention-drawing markers (though Keller-

Cohen and Gracey, 1976, report a large number of "lookit's" in beginning conversations of children learning a new language). When a child is being studied, the investigator is almost always attending to the child (unlike a more natural situation). We would expect to find more attention-getting expressions in child-child interactions; and we would further expect that the second language learners would have a far wider range of nonverbal signals to check for listener-attention than have first language learners.

Once the learner has secured the attention of his conversation partner, the second task is to get the partner to attend to the topic of discourse. This can be done by pointing (Paul, pointing: cat) or by the use of other deictics. Many children (cf., Young, 1974) seem to favor "that" /dæt/. Paul's favorite was the demonstrative "this": Paul (pointing toward drum) "this, this, this!"

In a frame, then, the first task is to get attention, the second is to identify the topic referent:

(1)	*Paul:*	lookit	*(2)*	*Paul:*	oh-oh
	Jim:	What?		*Jim:*	What?
	Paul:	ball		*Paul:*	that (points at box)

One might claim that it is from these conversational exchanges that connected utterances of more than one word develop:

Paul:	this
Jim:	A pencil.
Paul:	(echo) pencil
	this+++pencil (falling intonation on each word)

It is possible that such two-word utterances (or two one-word utterances which follow each other) are propositions ("there exists a pencil"). It is more sensible, however, simply to gloss them as establishing the topic "notice the pencil." (In the same sense that Atkinson's "There goes a mouse!" hardly seems to be other than "notice mouseness" since *"There doesn't go a mouse" is quite impossible.) In turn (unless the task is one of looking at picture books and naming the objects seen), the adult does not interpret such utterances as "this+++ NOUN" as a piece of information. Rather, the adult accepts it as a topic of conversation. Adults do not seem to react as if children were telling them names of objects in such interactions.

If one can accept that a call for attention ("oh-oh!," etc.), a pointing out of a topic ("this," etc.), and the learner's and partner's identifying remarks serve to nominate a topic for conversation, then we have accounted for the presence of such utterances as "this+++NOUN" in the early data. That is, we can say that this particular structure evolves out of discourse interaction. It evolves, not because of some magical Language Acquisition Device which automatically operates on input, but because of the conscious desire of the child to say something, to talk about something.

Once the child has secured the listener's attention and has nominated a topic, what happens in the discourse? Scollon, in his dissertation on a child learning English as a first language, shows how the learner and the partner together build a conversation once the topic is established. In first language acquisition, of course, there is a good deal of difficulty in getting the topic understood:

Brenda: (a car passes in the street. R does not hear it at the time) /kʰa/
            (repeated four times)
R: What?
B: /gɔo/
            /go/
R: XXX
B: /bəiš/ (nine repetitions)
R: What? Oh, bicycle? Is that what you said?
B: /na?/
R: No?
B: /na?/
R: No—I got it wrong (laughs).

(Scollon, 1979)

Children learning second languages do not seem to have the same trouble in getting their topic nominations recognized (perhaps because I have only been looking at sequential second language data; there may be examples of this in Leopold or other simultaneous acquisition studies); their problems in control of the vocal apparatus are much less severe. They do, however, have problems in getting close to the adult model for specific words (cf., Itoh, 1978, where the child Takahiro makes repeated attempts at "square," yielding /skueəl, skuəl, škuwee, fukueer, šukuwel, skweyl, skweə, šuwel, kuweəl/).

When the adult does recognize the topic, he responds to it appropriately:

Brenda: Kimby
R: What about Kimby?
B: close
R: Closed? What did she close, hmmm?
Brenda: (looking in picture book which shows an old woman at a stove)
            cook
            say
R: What'd the cook say?
B: something

Out of these interactions (which Scollon, 1979, calls vertical constructions) develop syntactic structures (which Scollon calls horizontal structures). That is, the words that the child produces one at a time *are* semantically linked. When the adult asks for more information with questions, he or she asks for a *constituent to fill out the construction.* It appears quite clear that the adult takes the child's first utterance as a topic nomination and then asks the child to clarify it or comment on it.

Brenda:	hiding
R:	Hiding? What's hiding?
B:	balloon

The clarification or comment is semantically related by these questions and the relationship is later made more explicit through syntax. Scollon believes, therefore, that "this interaction with other speakers may well be the means by which Brenda has learned how to construct" syntactic relationships.

The child also produces vertical constructions without adult prompting:

Brenda	my turn	this way	bathtub
see that	do it	hold it (3 X)	scrub it (2 X)
		holding	paper napkin

but adult questions also help her get all the relationships out in the appropriate order:

Brenda:	tape corder
	use it (2 X)
R:	Use it for what?
B:	talk
	corder talk
	Brenda talk

Similar examples of cooperative dialogues between adults and children can be found in Shugar (1978), Atkinson (1979), Ochs Keenan (1974), Ochs Keenan and Klein (1975), Ochs Keenan and Schieffelin (1976), and Ochs Keenan, Schieffelin, and Platt (1978).

From many such examples, Scollon has built a convincing argument that these vertical constructions form the prototypes for longer horizontal structures at a later period of development. *"This suggests that . . . discourse structure is at the heart of sentence structure from the beginning of its development."*

Is there evidence for this same sort of progression in the data of second language learners? If we look back at one of the first examples given for Paul:

Paul:	oh-oh!
Jim:	What?
Paul:	this (points to ant)
Jim:	It's an ant.
Paul:	ant

(Huang, 1970)

it seems that we have similar evidence. If you glance through the following examples, it should look like there are direct parallels; and I believe that to be the case. However, there is a difference that must be taken into account. Second language learners have already learned to make syntactic constructions (Scollon's horizontal structures) in the first language. Why don't they immediately do so in the second language? Such learners have little difficulty physiologically in getting out long streams of speech; therefore, we can't say that the problem is completely in controlling the vocal apparatus. Two explanations seem possible: (1) learners need more time for their automatic Language Acquisition Device to work on the input in building up syntax; or (2) conversation is what they are learning and the syntax grows out of it. Perhaps it is some combination of the two, but let's test the second explanation to its limits to see just how strong a case could be made. Let's look at the first examples:

(1)	Paul:	this boat.	(2)	Paul:	this
	Jim:	mmhmm boat.		Jim:	Yes?
	Paul:	this		Paul:	this you?
		my boat		Jim:	It's Kenny's.

Why doesn't Paul start immediately with "my boat" or "this my boat"? It would not be beyond his ability to do so. But if we look at conversation function, we know that he must first make sure that the adult has identified the referent for the following discourse (much in the same way that an adult might say, "You see that boat?" "Mmhmm." "Well, it's mine."). In the other example, Paul again identifies the topic of discourse before he asks who the ball belongs to..

In the following example, Paul tries to establish a topic, but the adult, in turn, nominates another to which Paul must then respond.

Paul:	fish
	see?
Jim:	Where's the turtle?
Paul:	turtle
Jim:	Mmhmm. Is he in there?
Paul:	no turtle
	fish

The next example from Huang's data shows the child establishing a topic and defending his vocabulary choice for that topic:

Paul:	this
Jim:	What?
Paul:	window (looking at fish tank)
Jim:	Where's the window? (challenging lexical choice)
Paul:	window
	this
Jim:	Another window. Show me.
Paul:	another window (echo)
Jim:	Hmmm. Is this a *window* here?
Paul:	yah
	window fish
	not window car

Paul even responds to requests for imitations as though they were topic nominations on which he should elaborate:

Jim:	Paul, can you say "teacher"?
Paul:	teacher
Jim:	Right, teacher.
Paul:	teacher
	Elsie (name of his teacher)
Jim:	Very good.

The data from Huang, then, show a wealth of examples similar to Scollon's, and the conclusions I draw from the examples are the same. The child wishes to interact, to say something with language, and, in negotiating conversations, produces first vertical and then somewhat later syntactic constructions.

A number of researchers who work in the field of conversational analysis have said that the first rule of conversation must be to "say something relevant." The data that we have looked at so far shows that the child is doing just that. However, what happens when the child knows this rule for conversation from his first language but knows absolutely none of the second language? How does the learner "say something relevant" when wishing very much to negotiate a conversation with a speaker of a language he or she does not understand? What can a learner say that will be relevant?

Itoh's data (1978) show the very first interactions between her two-and-a-half-year-old subject, Takahiro, and his aunt. The child very much wanted to interact verbally with his aunt but he did not know any English. His strategy was to "say something" even though he did not understand what he said. The only possible way for him to interact verbally was to repeat her utterances after her. However, the intonation of the repetitions made the repetition "relevant." He echoed her statements with rising intonation and her questions with falling intonation:

(Takahiro and his aunt are parking toy cars and airplanes.)

Aunt:	Make it one at a time.
Takahiro:	one at a time? ↗
Aunt:	Park everything.
Takahiro:	/ɛvrišin/ ? ↗
Aunt:	Park them.
Takahiro:	park them? ↗
Aunt:	Does it fly?
Takahiro:	fly. ↘

As the data collection sessions continued, repetitions became less echolalic:

Harumi:	Do you want to race also?
Takahiro:	Also racing car.
Harumi:	That's all. That's all.
Takahiro:	Okay, that's all.

He then began nominating topics:

Takahiro: /graːz/
Harumi: Garage. OK. I'll make a garage.
Takahiro: OK
             /flɔ/
Harumi: Flower. Green flower.
Takahiro: green flower.
Harumi: Oh, what color is this?
Takahiro: green
             green flower.

He repeated, used, and recombined parts of the conversation:

Takahiro: this
             broken
Harumi: Broken.
Takahiro: broken
             This /əz/ broken.
             broken
Harumi: Upside down.
Takahiro: upside down
             this broken
             upside down
             broken

As in Scollon's data, vertical constructions took place even without adult interaction:

Harumi: House.
Takahiro: this house?
Harumi: House.
Takahiro: house
             to make the house.
             to make the house.
             to make the house
             this?
             house.
             garage.
             garage house
             house
             big house
             oh-no!
             broken.
Harumi: Too bad.
Takahiro: too bad.
Harumi: Try again.

Takahiro: I get try.
                I get try.
Harumi: Good.

While repetitions always played an important role in Takahiro's learning, immediate repetitions began to die out:

Harumi: It's a garage. Come in garage.
Takahiro: /kəmən/ garage.
                /nay/ your. (=not yours)
Harumi: This is yours.
Takahiro: /nay/ yours. (note morphology correction)
                Come back.
                You do garage /tə/ here.
Harumi: No, the garage is too small.
Takahiro: small garage?
Harumi: Mmmm. I can't come in. Right?
Takahiro: OK. You'll can.

The Itoh data appear to supply supporting evidence that syntactic constructions may grow out of conversation. It is quite possible that other studies of early acquisition, if input data (rather than only learner production data) were available, would show the same thing.

The negotiation of conversations is not limited to the three- or four-year-old. Peck (1978), in her study of Angel, an older child, identified two kinds of interactions—language play and language during play—and the focus that each might give to language learning, in contrast to adult-child interactions.

Language play gives the older child a great deal of practice with sounds of the new language. Sometimes the language play consists of simple sound repetition (e.g., native speaker: /nə/, Angel: /nə/). Sometimes it consists of prosodic shift (e.g., native speaker: I—will-*do*-it. Angel: I *will* do it.). Sometimes it is a delightful free wheeling variation on sounds as in the modification of the word "pieces" (used while working a puzzle) into the Pepsi-Cola song:

(Angel and Joe are working a jigsaw puzzle.)
A: (frustrated) Ooooh!
J: Ooooh!
A: Only one piece.
J: Only one /piš/ /piš/ /piš/ /piš/   //I can't stop//
A: //This a old// piece. Piece.
J: /piš/ /piš/ . You like /pišəš/ ?
A: No. I like pieces.
J: What? Whatta you mean—you like /pišəž/ //I like// /pišəž/
A: //Pizza/
       I like pieces, pizzas.

J: /pɛpsiš/ ?
A: (sing-song) Pepsi-Coli—yeah.
J: /pɛpsi koliš/   (laugh) /pɛpsi kolis/ /pɛpsi/   cola!
       /pɛpsi/ cola!

(Peck, 1978)

Play with language is not limited to the phonological level. The bedtime monologues described by Ruth Weir (1962) for a first language learner are very much like those found in language play of second language learners. Mazeika shows Carlito (a Spanish-speaking child acquiring English) engaging in many of the same kinds of buildups and breakdowns of sentence structure:

C: in the boat
       go in the boat
       Mommy, him go in the boat
       Mommy, go in the boat in a con esa
       Mommy, go in the boat
       Mommy, go in the boat con esa Daddy ride in the boat.

(Mazeika, 1971)

Language play then gives the child learner practice with phonology and perhaps also with syntax. It serves a conversational function of keeping talk going, which may be very important for the child learner. Once the child begins nominating topics and enlarging or commenting on them, he can use language play as a way of practicing or playing with these new forms for his own amusement or for the pleasure of those around him. Such behavior is accepted by other children and by adults (even though adults do not seem to be able to play the other part of language play dialogues very successfully).

Language during play, Peck suggests, gives the child learner another special focus. The language of games is predictable and repetitive (e.g., *my turn, my side, give it to me, next, throw it here, I win, get out of here,* etc.). Such chunks are quickly learned and their use gives the learner easy access to social interaction on the playground. More formal indoor games also have many high frequency formulas that the child can use to perform a part in these mini speech events. Lily Wong-Fillmore's data (1976) showed the very large number of "formulaic utterances" (not all of them are from language during play, but certainly a high percentage appear to be). These chunks give the child a way to interact, but they also are grist for the mill of acquisition. It isn't long before the child is stringing these chunks together and then operating on the units to break them down.

Social Interaction and Adult Second Language Acquisition

In contrast to these successful ways of negotiating conversations among children, negotiation for the adolescent and adult can be very difficult. In Chapter 8, we looked at a number of examples of adult second language learners negotiating meanings of lexical items in order to make certain that both had identified the correct topic (or at least the meaning of a particular word). These negotiations can be very protracted and often end in frustration if not total communication breakdown:

NS: Who is the best player in Colombia?
L: Colombia?
NS: Does uh . . . who is *the* Colombian player?
L: Me?
NS: No, in Colombia, who is *the* player?
L: In Colombia plays. Yah.
NS: No, on your team. On the Millonarios.
L: Ah yah, Millonarios.
NS: No, on the Millonarios team.
L: Millonarios play in Colombia. In Sud América. In Europa.
NS: Do, do they have someone like Pele in Colombia?
L: Pele? In Colombia? Pele?
NS: In Colombia? Who is, who is "Pele" in Colombia? Do you have someone?
L: In Bogotá?
NS: Yeah, who is the best player?
L: In Santo de Brazil?
NS: OK (gives up) and are you center forward?

(Butterworth, 1978)

The learner, Ricardo, a teenager learning English, responded to many questions with what appear to be irrelevant answers. However, it is often possible to reconstruct from his answers what he thought the topic and subsequent questions were about (e.g., whether the Bogotá team played in other countries besides Colombia and whether Pele actually played in Bogotá on the team). The small amount of communication accomplished is in sharp contrast to much of the adult-child talk reported on for first and second language learners, and the language play and language during play described in Peck's work.

This does not mean that adult learners never receive topics based in the "here and now." Long (1980) found more present tense marking in native speaker-learner conversations than in conversations between native speakers—evidence of concern with the "now." However, input to the adult second language learner differs in many ways from that of language to child learners. We assume much more shared information and the range of possible topics is not limited to simple, concretely represented or contextualized possibilities. Yet, the form of topic nominations and comments on topics are, in some ways, similar to the child learner's. Brunak, Fain, and Villoria's (1976) study of an adult Spanish speaker shows how difficult it is for the learner to carry out the turn:

NS: You're not working right now?

Rafaela:	No.
NS:	No?
Rafaela:	Ahhh
	for one week
	I ...
	the ...
	comp-any?
	the company ...
	is inventory
	inventory
	aha
	for one week.
NS:	Oh.
Rafaela:	Monday I work
	I work
	Monday.
NS:	You're going to start working Monday again.

Perhaps because the nominations and comments are so slow, the native speaker seems driven to paraphrase everything that has been said in one sentence.

Rafaela:	I like men American but I no no ...
	I no ...
	have nothing ...
NS:	Oh, I see. You don't have a boyfriend here.
Rafaela:	No boyfriend American.
Rafaela:	Before here 3, 2 months
	I live my mother.
NS:	For two months you lived with your mother.

The learner tries to solicit vocabulary from the native speaker and drives the native speaker to restate topics and comments in a summary, thus giving the learner a "correction," a syntactic model.

Foreigner Talk in Adult Interactions

One interesting fact is that many researchers have found no instances of "ungrammatical foreigner talk" in their data. A number of writers have doubted the existence of real "Me Tarzan, you Jane" foreigner talk. For fun, you might like to try Ferguson's (1975) "Foreigner Talk Elicitation Test"*:

---

*For further examples, including replication studies in German, French, and English, see Meisel (1977) and McCurdy (1980); Andersen (1977) also worked out a similar task where children were asked to talk with puppets, one of whom was designated as a foreigner.

Administrator reads: I am asking you to tell me how you think an English-speaking person might act in trying to communicate with some non-English speakers. The person whose speech I want you to describe is acting as the spokesman for a group of three and he is addressing a group of non-English speakers who are obviously non-European. They may have heard some English before but they are not really able to understand it or speak it. You have already discovered that they cannot read or write. I will read you a sentence in normal English, and I want you to write down the way you think the English speaker might say it. I'll repeat each sentence as many times as you like before going on to the next.

Sentences
1. I haven't seen the man you're talking about.
2. He's my brother not my father.
3. Did you understand what she said?
4. Come and see me tomorrow. Don't forget!
5. Yesterday I saw him and gave him some money.
6. He's working with me. He'll work with you too.
7. Who is that man? Is he your brother?
8. He always carries two guns.
9. Where's the money I gave you yesterday?
10. She's going tomorrow.

Administrator asks:
A. Would you use this kind of language yourself in this situation?
B. Would you make any special use of gestures in connection with this kind of language?
C. Are there any other features of this communication situation you would like to comment on?

If you wrote down "many moons" and "talkie-talkie," you've seen too many movies. Having given this task to classes a number of times, and also similar ones using real data (in order to compare perceptions of what one might do with what was done), a number of features of "foreigner talk" which promote comprehension have emerged. The responses to the Ferguson task almost always turn out to be closer to Tarzan talk, at least in lexical choice, than do those elicited from real language examples. Yet, they share many other characteristics.

Topics get moved to the beginnings of utterances where they are more salient. For example, "I haven't seen the man you're talking about" becomes "The man, you want a man? I no see him." "He always carries two guns" becomes "Guns (boom-boom) (gestures) one-two, man carry guns." Using data from Butterworth's study, I found native English speakers did much the same thing when asked how they would respond to the learner's language. For example, after Christmas, Butterworth asked Ricardo: "Did you have a nice holiday?" To which Ricardo replied "huh?" Twenty-four native speakers changed holiday to Christmas, and topicalized it. The actual repair in the

Butterworth data was: (slower) "Nice Christmas . . . was your Christmas nice?" In conversational data, WH-questions were changed to or-questions or to yes/no questions. These kinds of repairs by the native speaker make it easier for the learner to take a turn in the conversation, since the required answer is, in effect, supplied. This places all the burden of the conversation on the native speaker who must then take up the turn again. When we can't get rid of the turn, we can end up feeling exhausted after five minutes of such conversation with second language learners.

In order to make conversations with learners possible at all, native speakers make many adjustments. One technique for making messages clear that all native speakers used in our foreigner talk data was repetition of their original utterance with minimal change:

(Midori has not understood the directions to the restaurant.)
NS: Well, you can ask anyone how to get here.
M: What? What?
NS: Most, most people know how to get here. Many people know how to get here, okay?
M: How to what?
NS: Many people know how to get here.
M: How together?
NS: Yeah, how to get to the restaurant.
M: An get to the restaurant.
NS: Yeah, okay?

(Hatch, Shapira, and Gough, 1978)

When simple repetition did not clarify the conversation, restatements were made, often with several synonyms being used in one exchange:

(Pauline is asking a typist to type her thesis.)
NS: Well, is it typed?
P: Uh, pardon me. Excuse me?
NS: (very slowly) Is-it-hand-writ-ten?
P: I, I don't understand.
NS: Is-your-the-sis-now-handwritten?
P: Ummm, I don't understand.
NS. Mmmm. Is y— Is your thesis now *type*-written or did you write it by hand?
P: Ah, yes, by hand?
NS: By hand.
P: I I me I write my copy by hand but uh uh I like you type for me. You understand?
NS: When. When do-you-need-the-the-sis? When do you-want-to-have-it-typed?
P: Yes, when.
NS: When.
P: When ah maybe ah two ah weeks.

One native speaker first slowed down, eliminating contractions, then changed to separate word articulation, and finally separated syllables. The data is also full of comprehension checks, most usually expressed by "do you understand?" and "OK?":

M: I uh I I live Santa Monica.
NS: Okay, Santa Monica. Take Wilshire Boulevard, OK?
M: Take uh . . .
NS: Wilshire.
M: Take what?
NS: Wilshire Boulevard.
M: I see. Wilshire Boulevard.
NS: Do you understand?
M: Yes.
NS: Okay. Wilshire Boulevard east.
M: East?
NS: To Westwood.
M: Oh.
NS: OK?
M: Okay.

The learners frequently requested vocabulary items via a "fill-in-the-blank" technique. This allowed them to say as much as they could with the hope that the native speaker would complete the sentence for them, filling in expressions they could not produce:

Pauline: How much uh all . . . (laughs)?
NS: All together?
P: Yes, all together.

Native speakers who were particularly good at this "analysis by synthesis" game sometimes out-predicted themselves, filling in meanings that the foreign student had not intended.

Amazingly, considering the difficulty most of the native speakers in our study had in making their messages clear, very few "gave up." While impatience was exhibited by some native speakers, this almost always disappeared once the speaker realized the student did not understand. Then an opposite sort of response was given. Sympathetic sighs greeted "I no understand," and terms of affection were used:

Pauline: Oh excuse me. I don't understand.
NS: Ohhh (sigh of sympathy) you don't understand. MMMM.
Midori: How much manuscript handwriting paper?
NS: I . . . I don't understand you now for a minute. (laugh) What, dear?
Midori: Thank you very much.
NS: You're very welcome, dear. Goodnight.

They also complimented the foreign students on their English:

(After negotiating the typing of the thesis)
NS: What country are you from?
Midori: Japan.
NS: Oh, that's nice. An uh I thought there was—
M: I can't um uh speak English uh.
NS: Oh, you're doing fine. If I went to Japan, I couldn't speak Japanese as well as you speak English.
M: Uh thank you.
NS: I (laugh) never—
M: You are kind.
NS: No, I meant it. English is so difficult, you know.
M: Yeah.
NS: How long have you been in this country?
M: Mmm, just uh three months.
NS: Oh well, you're doing fine. You're doing very, very well.
M: Thank you.

The above native speaker, perhaps the most sympathetic, was the only one who not only used all the devices of slowed speech, restatement, vocabulary repair, confirmation-checking, and occasional word-by-word stress, but also adopted some features of the foreign student's speech in adjacent pairs:

(Having settled that the final copy costs $1.00 per page, Midori wants to know how much a rough draft costs.)
M: And another?
NS: I beg your pardon?
M: Not final?
NS: Oh, the not final is 85¢.
M: Eighty-five.

All of the above data exemplify ways that adjustment can make communication possible. But does simplification have a "teaching" value, or is it useful only as a communication strategy? Even in segments of the data where the foreign student solicits and is given vocabulary items (even in cases where the words are spelled out for them on request), it seems unlikely that those vocabulary items are always learned.

Since the above data is illustrative, perhaps another anecdote will not be out of place. On returning to my office, I met our janitor who is one of the few people with whom I have a chance to practice my very limited Arabic. I wanted to thank him for cleaning my file cabinet since he had both washed and waxed it. But I couldn't think of the word for "file cabinet." So, I elaborately elicited the vocabulary item, saying (in Arabic) "Thanks for cleaning my desk and, and this?" (pointing to the file cabinet). He immediately supplied the word and I went on to thank him for cleaning the file cabinet. The conversation continued for a few moments and I happily left the office. As I went down the stairs, I tried to recall the new vocabulary item. Alas, it was nowhere to be found. I had consciously elicited the word and planned to "learn" it. Yet, communication had taken over and once I got the word I needed, I used it, and left it (lightly pencilled in) wherever my short-term memory routes such things.

Yet some kinds of negotiation of meaning may be useful. It's clear that foreigner talk does contain more high frequency vocabulary, vocabulary that is more clearly referential. Beyond that, Chaudron (1979) showed that teachers use particular markers (e.g., "It's a kind of X." "this means X," etc.) which make definitions salient. If not explicitly marked as definitions, we often use "try marking"—that is, rising intonation (e.g., a nickle? a 5¢ piece?) to check for comprehension. The definitions themselves often give form class information (e.g., funds or money), semantic feature information (e.g., a *hummingbird,* you know, like a *little tiny* bird that goes *hmmmm*) or collocation information (e.g., the *library* keeps *books* on *shelves* called *stacks*). It is difficult, then, to make claims about just exactly what in the input helps us learn and what helps us to communicate. Perhaps there can be no dividing line.

Adjustment in language among learners and native speakers is negotiated, and that negotiation is also frequently marked by a special affective bond. Motherese and foreigner talk may both support language learning via this affective bond. But foreigner talk may, I think, work in unexpected ways.

First, the native speaker may be the one who does all the "learning" in order to create the affective bond. Ferguson suggested that: "In both baby talk and foreigner talk the responses of the person addressed affect the speaker and the verbal interaction may bring some modification of register from both sides. . . . The usual outcome of the use of foreigner talk is that one side or the other acquires an adequate command of the other's language" (1971, p. 144). In exchanges between Zoila, a Spanish-speaker learning English, and her friend, Rina, it is Rina rather than the learner who adapts. She incorporates the learner's Interlanguage forms into her talk:

Zoila:	Do you think is ready?
Rina:	I think is ready. (Zoila's Interlanguage form)
Zoila:	Why she's very upset for me?
Rina:	She is upset for you?
Zoila:	Yeah, is.
Zoila:	These no . . . no /ha/ . . . much nicotine.
Rina:	No much nicotine?
Zoila:	No. . .these. . .no. . .uh. . .11 mmmm. . .nicotine 8.
Rina:	Mmmm.
Zoila:	I think for not too much.
Rina:	You think not too much better?
Zoila:	Yeah, I wait for my cake pero I . . . I don't know . . . ah . . . what time is coming.

Rina: You think is coming or you think maybe no coming.
Zoila: I think maybe no . . . I don't know.

When the native speaker did use grammatically correct forms, Zoila did not respond to the model but rather to the meaning.

Zoila: No, no is yours.
Rina: *It's* mine?
Zoila: Yes.

If the native speaker did not immediately use Zoila's favorite verb forms, she did so a few exchanges later. In the following example, she was then reinforced by Zoila for using the Interlanguage form.

Zoila: He's unhappy. He no liking.
Rina: He no like what?
Zoila: Ummmm, when I change. He no liking.
Rina: Well, I don't know.

.
.
.

Rina: I no liking this story.
Zoila: I no liking either.

While Rina's speech mirrored that of the learner in most respects, it was not a complete match. For example, her possessive pronouns were always grammatically correct while Zoila's were not. However, there is no evidence that this, then, served as a cutting edge for learning on Zoila's part. That is, the foreigner talk used by Rina was simplified to the point of matching, plus "one step ahead," if that step can be identified as possessive pronouns. There is no evidence that Zoila was moving toward correct use of possessive pronouns. It seems clear that the function of foreigner talk in the data could not be used to support the notion that foreigner talk has an explicit or implicit teaching function for the learner. Rather, the exchanges between Zoila and Rina are examples of foreigner talk promoting easy communication and helping to establish an affective bond.

While foreigner talk helped establish and sustain an affective bond for Rina and Zoila, the use of foreigner talk can have a negative effect in other circumstances. Many foreign students are insulted when the simplification is obviously a mismatch, far more than is necessary. Perhaps the most insulting is the affective intonation of motherese that sometimes appears in foreigner talk as well. Simplified syntax and highly referential vocabulary use may be appreciated for the clarity they can give to discourse. Baby talk intonation, however, does not make meaning clearer, nor does it promote the acquisition of normal intonation. It is rightfully resented. (But for many native speakers it's very difficult to control this shift in intonation, even when the shift and its insulting quality are clear.)

In first language literature, older children talking with babies simplify their speech. However, older children talking with child second language learners (of the same age) do not seem to simplify to the same extent. Katz (1977), for example, found the native speaker child he studied did not use ungrammatical foreigner talk. She did not slow down her rate of speech to accommodate the child learner playmate. And other aspects of foreigner talk also were not clearly expressed. Wong-Fillmore includes samples of foreigner talk of native speaker children in interactions with child learners; however, it is not consistent. Rather, it occurs under communication stress, as in the following:

NS Child:	You robber! (=you have to be the robber)
Learner:	No!
NS Child:	Si!
Learner:	Le's go teacher. (=I'm gonna tell the teacher)
	Teacher, teacher—
Teacher:	What?
Learner:	(pleading tone) Gimme da cowboy. Es Kevin da robber.
	(=let me be the cowboy and K the robber)
NS Child:	You robber.
Teacher:	You wanna be the robbers?
Learner:	No! No! Es me da boys. (=cowboys)
NS Child:	No! You robbers.
Learner:	C'mon, Kevin!
NS Child:	No, you robbers.
Learner:	OK, I no wanna play.
Teacher:	C'mon, you two guys can both be what you want.
Learner:	(trying to convince K) Dese a robber—es good, Kevin.
NS Child:	OK, I'll be the robbers.
Learner:	Oh! (holds up finger) Lookit that me. It me!
NS Child:	One cowboy—this me.
Learner:	Teacher, lookit . . . pow! pow!
NS Child:	Hey Alej! Me shot both.

(1976, pp. 697–698)

The variation in foreigner talk/motherese, when we compare children with adults, may have to do with the amount of negotiation needed to carry out communication. Children's interaction may be successful without much negotiation, while adult conversations with learners may require much more negotiation before meaning is clear. (This is just a guess.) There is, of course, a great deal of variation in how successfully each person (regardless of age) can negotiate the exchange and get, or give, useful input for learning.

Summary of Benefits of Simplified Talk for Learners

While foreigner talk does vary from native speaker to native speaker, there can be little doubt that we do adjust our speech in response to the language proficiency of our listeners. And that adjustment helps promote communication, helps establish an affective bond, and can serve as either an explicit or implicit teaching mode. Table 7 summarizes the benefits which might accrue to the second language learner from simplified input, the adjustments described in this chapter. Of course, not all interactions show all these aspects of foreigner talk.

Table 7   Summary of Foreigner Talk

Slow Rate = clearer articulation (less "sandhi variation")
- Final stops are released, voiced final stops are voiced.
- Some glottal stops used before words beginning with Vs.
  (Benefit: learner should be able to identify word boundaries more easily.)
- Fewer reduced vowels and fewer contractions.
  (Benefit: Learner receives the full word form.)
- Longer pauses.
  (Benefit: Learner gets more processing time and the major constituent boundaries are more clearly marked.)

Vocabulary
- High frequency vocabulary, less slang, fewer idioms.
  (Benefit: Learner is more likely to know and/or recognize topic.)
- Fewer pronoun forms of all types.
  (Benefit: Reference should be clearer.)
- Definitions will be marked:
    Explicitly by formulas (This means X, it's a kinda X).
    Implicitly by intonation (a nickel? a 5-cent piece?).
  (Benefit: Marking should make definitions salient.)
- Derivational morphology frames (miracle—anything that's miraculous? sum up—summarize?).
  (Benefit: Gives learner information on morphology class membership.)
- Form class information (funds or money, industrious and busy).
- Semantic feature information (a cathedral usually means a church that's a very high ceilings).
- Context information (If you go for a *job* in a *factory* they talk about a *wage* scale.).
- Gestures and pictures.
  (Benefit: Learner gets information on lexical form class, features, and vocabulary sets.)
- Endearment terms.
  (Benefit: May give an affective boost to learning.)

Syntax
- Short MLU, simple propositional syntax.
  (Benefit: Should be easier to process and analyze.)
- Left dislocation of topics (Friday, Saturday, you have a nice *weekend*?).
  (Benefit: Should help learner identify topic.)
- Repetition and restatement.
  (Benefit: More processing time and relationship of syntactic forms may be clearer.)
- Less pre-verb modification.
  (Benefit: New information should be at the end of the utterance where it is more salient.)
- Native speaker summarizes learner's nonsyntactic utterances.
  (Benefit: Provides a model of syntax.)
- Native speaker "fills in the blank" for learner's incomplete utterance.
  (Benefit: Provides a model of syntax.)

Table 7   *continued*

Discourse
- Native speaker gives reply within his question (WH-questions restated as yes/no or or-choice questions.).
  (Benefit: Learner is able to stay in the conversation by using the model supplied.)
- Native speaker uses tag questions.
  (Benefit: Identifies ends of utterances and supplies learner with model for response.)
- Native speaker offers correction.
  (Benefit: Identifies trouble source the learner should work on.)

Speech Setting Interaction
- Child-child language play.
  (Benefits: Practice on the possible sounds, their range of articulation, and combinations with other sounds. Practice with syntax via buildups, breakdowns, and transformations.)
- Language during play.
  (Benefit: Many chunk utterances to stockpile for later analysis.)
- Adult-child interactions.
  (Benefit: Vocabulary negotiation and question-answering helps build sentence syntax via interactions.)

Some native speakers use only those simplifications listed under discourse. Others use slow rate or vocabulary simplification. Nor is the shift always toward a simpler form when trouble occurs in the interaction. A WH-question may go to a yes/no question and then back again to a WH-question.

Based on these data and the motherese literature, Krashen (1980) proposed an Input Hypothesis for second language acquisition. If this hypothesis includes both input and interaction, then—as with the study of pragmatics in first language acquisition—the focus would be on the learner's ability to use the socio-interpersonal context to create and interpret language. The input would be negotiated by the learner through social interactions in ways which I have tried to exemplify in this chapter. In much of the first language literature, social interaction and language development are so tightly interwoven as to seem inseparable. In its strongest form, an Input Hypothesis would not see social interaction and language development simply as interwoven but would see interaction as causally related to language acquisition.

Long (1980, 1981b) argues that we ought to separate input factors from interaction factors on the grounds that modification of one is possible without modification of the other. That is, interaction factors (see those listed in Table 4) can be modified without modifying the input. (Modified input without modified interaction is less likely, though it could conceivably occur in work settings— e.g., ungrammatical foreigner talk of foreman to foreign workers in factories. Long believes, however, that the resulting pidginized second language may be due as much to lack of sufficient input as to its foreigner-talk characteristics.) Long proposes, then, that it is modified interaction, not modified input, that facilitates second language acquisition. And the modified interaction features occur most frequently in conversations where a true two-way information exchange is taking place. This is important, because he also believes that, for most learners, conversational interaction is the only experience they have with the target language (and so must provide sufficient data for successful language acquisition).

While the data presented in this chapter appear to support an Input/Interaction Hypothesis, we must match this evidence against that to the contrary. Let's take anecdotal evidence first. One can at least acquire basic receptive skills in another language without interaction. I acquired French comprehension skills (enough to pass the ETS French test) by reading a daily newspaper while living in a country where that was the only available paper. Larsen-Freeman (1980) cited an adult who claimed to have successfully acquired Dutch via television, again without interaction. Long argues that in such cases the languages are so similar that basic competencies in one can be substituted for the other.

Snow and Hoefnagel-Hohle (1982) also contest the importance of input/ interaction to language acquisition. They studied the language input in classrooms where American children were learning Dutch via immersion. They found that language addressed specifically to the child learners (whether by their teachers or classmates) was simpler. That is, speech to the learner had a smaller mean length of utterance. However, for the six learners for whom pre- and post-test scores were available, neither the amount of language heard by the child nor the amount directed specifically to the child showed any relationship with success in language learning (measured by gain scores over a period of approximately five months).

Ochs (1980) has suggested that motherese, language simplification to first language learners, may be a "Western" phenomenon. She claims that children in Samoan cultures are not spoken to in a simplified register. If it is the case that neither mothers nor older children serving as caretakers simplify their language in interacting with young children, then we cannot say that simplified input is a prerequisite to language acquisition. The children do acquire Samoan.

A final counter-example is the case study of Blank et al. (1979). John, the three-year-old subject, acquired language without acquiring social interaction skills. This case study shows that social interaction skills are not prerequisite to language development, in fact, that they need not even be tightly interwoven (though, of course, that is usually the case). While his language represents an adequate description of the physical world (he can describe objects and events accurately), it is inappropriate in a communicative sense. He does not follow conversational themes in a coherent manner and seems basically uninterested in the content of his partner's speech. He appears incapable of understanding nonverbal communication. For example, the pointing gesture (which we noted earlier as important in child topic nominations) is completely lacking from his repertoire and he seems bewildered when others use such gestures. Rather than look at the object pointed to, he would follow the line of movement from the adult's finger to the shoulder. He has never interacted in games of peek-a-boo and has not acquired social greeting terms (hi, bye bye).

In this case, we might wonder how John learned language at all. The authors believe that it came about through symbolic play. Once the child learned the word "car," for example, the parents would tend to say such things as "Oh, let's take a ride" or "We'd better get gas for the car." Gradually, John produced similar phrases and sentences when presented with the car. None of the sentences were exact copies of parent talk though they were, of course, influenced by the input. When the car reappeared, it elicited sentences such as "Park the car. Get a ticket. There's a toll booth. Can get to another toll booth." If the toy that was eliciting the language was withdrawn, John would stop speaking. If another toy was introduced, the language associated with that play object would appear. Again, silence would ensue when the toy was withdrawn. Once language was well established in such play routines, John gradually transferred it to nonplay situations.

While John's case is certainly atypical, it does show that language development is possible without social interaction. Obviously, more empirical studies are needed to help us clarify the role of interaction in language development. Social interaction (conversational interaction and interaction in the second language classroom) leads, I believe, to useful input—in Krashen's terms, comprehensible input. However, that interaction alone cannot account for acquisition. While social interaction may give the learner the "best" data to work with, the brain in turn must work out a fitting and relevant model of that input. If the input contains all the features presented in Table 7, the task should not be as impossible as we may have thought. The brain must have rules for guiding the development of language. If these rules for guiding development are innate, they must also already be overlaid and transformed in the learning process, first, for initial language development and, now again, during second language acquisition. Perhaps we have reached a stage where we can say that both "camps" of the '60s were right. The learner is neither a language-producing machine working on unrestricted input nor the grand imitator of unanalyzed input. To once again quote Stern and Stern:

We believe that the proper position is a synthesis. . . . In his form of speech a child learning to speak is neither a phonograph reproducing external sounds nor a sovereign creator of language. In terms of contents of his speech, he is neither a pure associative machine nor a sovereign constructor of concepts. Rather his speech is based on the continuing interaction of external impressions with internal systems which usually function unconsciously; it is thus the result of a constant "convergence." (1970, p. 87)

In addition, from the discussion of discourse (Chapters 7, 8, 9) and the language comprehension models (Chapter 5), we must also see that neither an imitation and analogy or a LAD model of language acquisition is sufficient. They are crude models at best, for all mental life is involved in the interactions that produce language acquisition. It's clear that second language learners, as well as children learning their first languages, do comprehend language they themselves cannot produce. With world knowledge, however limited, and the use of inference, learners can understand a great deal. If language acquisition were limited to basic comprehension, then a model based on speech setting, world knowledge, pragmatics, and general cognitive capacity might suffice. For some second language learners (at early stages of acquisition) this may be the case. However, in true language acquisition, an overall complete and autonomous grammar must be created. Its creation must rely, at least in part, on input, interaction, and inference. The autonomous grammar must be formed through linguistic hypothesis testing. However, other processes which are nonlinguistic may be critical to the learner's discovery of linguistic elements that make up that system. Such processes may make the formation of linguistic hypotheses possible. The relationship between nonlinguistic and linguistic hypothesis testing is, therefore, a crucial area of research for language acquisition, both first and second.

10 Individual Factors—Age

In previous chapters we noted the ways language addressed to children and adults who are learning languages differs. Age is a factor to consider in many areas of learning. In fact, it is the most commonly cited determiner of success or failure in second language learning. In psycholinguistics we should take this truth (which is a folk belief, supported by experience over centuries) and look for the research to either support or disconfirm it. Tables 1, 2, and 3 summarize papers that speak to this issue.

Table 1 Age Factor in Acquisition, Natural Environment—Observational Studies

Children	+/− success	L1 Dominant	L1 or L2 Forgotten
Leopold	+	+ (alternating)	alternately
Kenyeres	+	+ (alternating)	alternately
Ronjat	+	−	no
Burling	+	+ (alternating)	L2
Huang	+	?	L2; relearned
Yoshida	?	L1	L2
Itoh	?	L1	L2
Celce-Murcia	+	+ (alternating)	alternately
Berman	+	+ (alternating)	L1; relearned
Young	−	L1	—
Older learners			
Shapira	+ communication − morphology	L1	—
Schumann	−	L1	—
Hanania	−	L1	—
Sorenson	+	no information	no information
Salisbury	+	no information	no information
Kessler & Idar	−	L1	—

Table 2 Age Factor in Acquisition, Experimental Studies—Second Language Environment

Researcher	Ss	Results	Measures
Fathman	200; age 6–15; equal time	oldest for syntax & morphology; youngest for pronunciation	SLOPE
Eckstrand	2, 189; age 8–16; Swedish as L2	direct r. with age, except free oral	pron, dict, list comp, read, free oral, free written
Snow	42; age 3–5, 6–7, 8–10, 12–15, adults	rate of acq. favors older, but diff. wash out with LOR.* Teens, adults, then children	pron, list. comp, morph, PPVT, sent repet, translation
Heidelberg Project	48; arival age, 15–55	neg. r. with age of arrival. LOR less important	Syntactic Index
Genesse (approx. 10 studies). Also Bruck & Troue	high school +/- FLES*	early FLES no sig. advantage over later start	skills vary across reports
Grinder, Otomo, & Toyota	2, 3, & 4th grade	pos. r. with age	listening/speaking
Asher & Garcia	71 Cubans; arrival age 1–6, 7–12, 13–19.	neg. r. with age of arrival but LOR not controlled	pronunciation
Oyama	60 Italians; age 14–37; grouped 6–10, 11–15, 16–20	early age of arrival most related to successful repetition	sent. repetition (heard under noise mask)
Patkowski	67 foregn; 15 nat. spkr.	age of acq. best predictor	FSI oral interview, Ling. Intuitions

*FLES = foreign language instruction in the elementary schools; LOR = length of residence.

Table 3 Age Factor in Acquisition, Experimental Studies—Foreign Language Learning

Researcher	Ss	Results	Measures
Thorndike et al.	?n; age 9–57	oldest = best	unknown
Justman & Nass	200 +/− FLES*	+FLES ns for French +FLES better for Spanish (also higher IQ for group)	
Dunkel & Pillet	3, 4th grade; college	college best; ns between 3rd & 4th grades	read, listen, read aloud, vocab, gram. writing
Eckstrand	1,200; 1, 2, 3, & 4th grades	older better after 1 semester AV course	all skills
Stern	Age 7–11	11-yr. group best	listen/pron.
Brega & Newell	High school +/− FLES	+FLES better but also higher IQ	
Blank & Keislar	4 preschool & 6 grade 5	time to criterion on Lang. Master cards; Grade 5 fastest	
Asher & Price	Age 8, 10, 14, 18–20	adults & 14 yr. group best	response to oral commands
Weber-Olsen & Ruder	10: age 4–5 10: age 23–28	adults better at lexical learning task	Japanese locatives production tests

*FLES = foreign language instruction in the elementary schools.

Diary Studies

The diary studies of second language learning almost universally portray the child as the successful learner and the adult as the nonlearner. The evidence against this is sparse: Alma, Young's subject (1974), appears to be a genuine nonlearner. After a year of kindergarten in an American school she could speak only a few words of English and gave little indication of comprehension. And, in non-data-based claims, Sorenson (1967) and Salisbury (1962) write of successful adult learners in cultures that highly value bilingualism after adolescence. However, if we look at the child studies, we find a number of interesting facets which also separate them from adult learners. In most simultaneous acquisition studies (e.g., Leopold, 1939; Kenyeres and Kenyeres, 1938; Burling, 1978; Celce-Murcia, 1978) we find that acquisition is never balanced; the child predominantly uses either one language or the other. That is, Leopold's Hildegard used almost all English in America and almost all German in Germany. She protested and cried when asked to use English in Germany. Kenyeres and Kenyeres also wrote that Eva, while in Geneva, protested (once she had learned French) that she had forgot Hungarian (and the reverse when she returned to Hungary). Ronjat is a strong counter-example, for he shows that the child Louie was perfectly balanced in production of the two languages, never stronger in one, and claims there was little or no influence of one language on the other. Most of the short-term studies of child second language acquisition (where the child is in the States for one year and then returns home) have shown that once the child returns, he or she appears to lose the language even more rapidly than he or she learned it. The problem with "forgetting" claims is that we have no real data to show how much and what has been forgotten (that is, whether it is only production that is lost or whether comprehension is also involved). However, re-remembering has been documented for Caroline by Celce-Murcia (1978) who has watched the re-emergence of English each fall as Caroline returns from her summer in France. The only case of apparent re*learning* is the current study of Berman (1979). The child, Shelly, accompanied her parents to the States and became a fluent English speaker. Now, returned to Israel, she is relearning Hebrew. In the Celce-Murcia study (and in others as well) re-entry into the language community appears to trigger a fairly rapid return to the first language. These children appear simply to re-access the "forgotten" language, or perhaps it is more accurate to say that they reactivate the production system while comprehension may have continued all along. In the Berman case, the subject appears to be regaining the language very slowly, perhaps really *re*learning it.

In contrast, we do not find that adults forget their first language when they acquire a second. (There are a number of studies that look at the new directions in which adults elaborate their first language. Most immigrants, returning to their homeland, find that they are readily identifiable as Americans on a number of traits including language change.) I know of no case where an adult simply replaces the first language with a second (a claim that could be made for some of the child learners, those who never again use the first language—for example, Burling's, 1978, child with Garo). The Pennsylvania project on language attrition may give us more specific information on language loss across age groups.

The diary studies that present the child as the good learner do not specify exactly what the child learner is able to do with the language. A child can do things that are necessary for a child to do; but the range of topics, the kinds of discourse required, may be very different from that of an adult. It may be that children are highly successful because of the small range of types of communication they require, while adults may appear highly unsuccessful because of the large range necessary for interaction at the adult level. I suggest it is because adults must read, write, speak, and understand the language in a very wide range of topics, and must participate in interactions that require understanding personal interactions and communication rules, that they fail to acquire the same phonological and morphological accuracy as children. Such a claim would be similar to that made by audiolingual methodologists: keep the vocabulary/content very limited and work on nativelike pronunciation and morphology. While this is a possible explanation of the problems of adult learners, most researchers would reject it as an adequate explanation of lack of success in phonology and morphology for adult language learners.

The strongest evidence from the diary studies comes from Cazden et al. (1975). Their Ss were two adults, two young adolescents, and two children, all Spanish-speakers learning English in the States. On their measures, the best learner was the ten-year-old and the least proficient was Alberto, one of the adult subjects. In several papers on Alberto, Schumann claimed that it is social and psychological distance that accounts for Alberto's poor second language performance. While I believe that social and psychological distance factors are *age related*, I don't believe the evidence is conclusive that age alone accounts for the differences. Kessler and Idar (1979), too, discuss the differences in learning of a Vietnamese mother and child in terms of both age and age-related issues.

Experimental Studies

Experimental studies also give evidence regarding optimal age for second language learning. These are divided in Table 1, for convenience, into studies that look at learning in the second language environment and studies that investigate foreign language learning.

Experimental studies must have some sort of "test" by which one can judge success or failure in language learning. In observational studies, the measure has almost always been morphology and/or Aux development. In considering the experimental studies, it is important to keep in mind just which skills are being tested; these are presented in Table 1.

The Fathman study (1975b) was concerned with many factors, age being but one. The Ss ranged in age from six to fifteen years, but all had had equal in-school exposure to English. So the question is: Does age of arrival (or, age at onset of learning) predict language learning success? The measure used to test success was the SLOPE (Second Language Oral Proficiency Exam). The results showed that the learners who began school exposure to English at a later age got higher scores on syntax and morphology. Those who began at a younger age scored higher on pronunciation.

The Eckstrand study (1975b) is similar, for it looked at immigrants learning Swedish in Sweden and was also done in the school setting. A battery of tests covering pronunciation, dictation, listening comprehension, reading, free oral data, and free written data were given. The findings show a direct correlation with age. That is, the older the learners the better they did—except for production of free oral data. A major finding was that length of residence (LOR) was not significantly correlated (that is, showed no direct relationship to performance) except for free oral data. This seems to mean that the longer you live in a country, the better you will be in communicating your ideas (probably a practice/opportunity effect). Again, this points out that one can gain communicative ability without necessarily simultaneously acquiring grammatical or phonological accuracy.

The Eckstrand study also considered other factors along with age and length of residence. Teachers were asked to rate the students' Swedish proficiency. Those ratings were more strongly related to the learner's social adjustment scores than to language proficiency. Secondly, the LOR did not directly correlate with the learners' social adjustment scores. This is an interesting finding in light of Schumann's acculturation claim. You might look at these data in two ways. Either the teachers' ratings of students' language proficiency are accurate (that is, they are more accurate than the proficiency test battery) and, since they correlate with adjustment to the culture scores, this is evidence for the acculturation claim. Or, you could say that the language battery accurately measures language and language learning is separate from social adjustment—evidence against the acculturation claim. It's also possible to say that the social adjustment scores are not measures of acculturation or that teachers give inaccurate estimates of acculturation and simply disregard these data as not speaking to the acculturation issue.

The Snow and Hoefnagel-Hohle study (1978) looks at Americans in five different age groups learning Dutch in the Netherlands. The measures include pronunciation, listening comprehension, morphology, the Dutch version of the Peabody Picture Vocabulary Test, sentence repetition, and translation tasks. Their findings are that the rate of acquisition favors older learners in the beginning stages of learning but that these differences wash out with length of residence. In this report, teenagers do best, then adults, then young children in all areas of the test battery.

The Heidelberg study (1978a) works with a Syntactic Index (see discussion of the Index in Chapter 5) as its measure of language learning. There is a negative correlation ($r=.56$) on the Syntactic Index with age of arrival. That is, the earlier Ss arrived in Germany, the better their Syntactic Index score and thus the younger the start the better. The effect of length of residence is not seen as an important variable since it has a lower correlation (r=.20) with the Syntactic Index score than age of arrival. However, ":contact with Germans at work place" also proved to positively correlate (r=.53) with Syntactic Index scores. Thus, the age at which one begins second language learning and the amount of interaction with native speakers are seen as important factors in language learning.

The other study showing a direct inverse correlation with age of arrival is the Oyama study (1976). The task in this study is listening comprehension under noise conditions (a type of task frequently used in psycholinguistic research dealing with the analysis by synthesis model of comprehension). Again length of residence fails to show up as *the* strongest predictor of success. Age of arrival is again the factor which correlated most strongly with comprehension and repetition of sentences.

Age of arrival again is seen as having a strong negative correlation with *pronunciation* ability in the Asher and Garcia study (1969)—results corroborating Oyama's findings. Examining the lists in Table 1, it is puzzling to see that pronunciation is better the earlier one begins to learn the language; yet find that, in other studies that look at initial learning, sometimes older Ss do as well or better than younger Ss in all skills including pronunciation, while in others young Ss do as well or better than older Ss, *especially* in pronunciation. The reversal effect reported for children in second language immersion classes where language is *not* the community language should also be considered. That is, apparently young children in the St. Lambert's studies were judged to have attained nativelike pronunciation in the early grades, only to become less nativelike in French at around grade four. Obviously, something other than age and/or age of arrival is at work.

One of the most impressive studies of the effect of age on second language learning is that done by Patkowski (1980). Using highly educated Ss, he compared their ratings (and T-unit counts) on an FSI oral interview. In addition he developed a Linguistic Intuitions Test which required Ss to select one odd sentence from a group of three (e.g., John expected Mary to go home/John persuaded Mary to go home/John promised Mary to go home). The 25-item test is sophisticated in form and meaning (as well as sophisticated in what each item is designed to test), in keeping, perhaps, with the educational status of his Ss. He found that those Ss who began acquiring English before age fifteen were, in fact, still discernible from native speakers, but that those who began English after age fifteen showed markedly lower scores. All the Ss had resided in the United States for at least five years, all were highly educated, and all presumably were well motivated by professional interests to acquire the language. Yet, the only factor associated with syntactic proficiency was the age at which acquisition began. Practice and instructional variables showed little or no association with the test results.

There have been many reports done on the effectiveness of foreign language instruction in the elementary schools (FLES) as promoting success in foreign language learning at the high school level. That is, does instruction in French at the elementary school level mean that Ss will do better in high school French than those who begin French at the high school level? Most of the studies show that FLES instruction does not improve chances of success at the high school level. This is not very popular research among those of us who want children to have second language classes in the elementary schools. However, we can argue that other very important benefits can accrue from such early language exposure.

The studies listed in the third section of Table 1 are research reports of success in foreign language learning outside the country of the target language. The Thorndike et al. study (1928) has no target language country since it involves Esperanto. Perhaps this study should not have been included since it is no longer available. However, it is mentioned in one of Burstall's studies (1975) and is reported as showing that for the age range 9–57, the oldest Ss did best. (This leads me to think that my next language to be learned should be Esperanto.) A number of the studies listed in this section of the table are for short-term teaching programs and so the findings that "the older the better" may simply reflect initial efficiency in problem solving rather than ultimate language learning success. The Dunkel and Pillet study (1957), the Blank and Keislar study (1966), the Asher and Price study (1967), the Eckstrand (1964) (English as a foreign language in Sweden this time), and the Olson and Samuels (1973) studies may all be a reflection of such short-term exposure to language learning. That is, it may be that it is not that older is better, but rather that older is better in the beginning stages. This view is supported by the Florander and Jensen (1969) results as compared with the Mylov (1972) results. The Ss are learning English as a foreign language in Denmark. At the end of eighty hours of instruction, the oldest group (6th graders) did best on their test battery. Mylov, looking at the same Ss after 320 hours of instruction, found that while 6th graders were still best, the level of significance of that difference had dropped. It appears that the younger Ss were beginning to catch up and might ultimately surpass the older group.

Again, there are a number of studies which look at the effect of FLES on later proficiency. The results of these studies conflict. Justman and Nass's (1956) results are the strangest of all. They found it made no difference whether one began French in elementary school (and continued it in high school) or whether one began such study in high school. Yet, for Spanish they found that if the Ss had Spanish in elementary school, they did better than new beginners at the high school level. Surely there is nothing about the languages themselves or the learning task that could account for conflicting findings. Brega and Newell (1965) found that elementary school language instruction helped when test results were compared with those of new learners at the high school level. One might want to consider once again the "savings" literature reported in Chapter 4 in trying to find some explanation for these findings.

The most sophisticated study of all those that look at age is the Burstall NFER report which followed British children learning French as a foreign language. There are several papers on this research project which cover various parts of the total study. To simplify the massive amount of work into one relevant line, Ss who began French later did better than those who began at a younger age. For example, Ss beginning French at age eight and continuing to age thirteen did less well than Ss beginning at age ten and continuing to age fifteen. The difference held for all skill areas. FLES does not appear to promote French learning better than somewhat later instruction. This study, since it has unpopular results, has come under a great deal of criticism (similar to the criticism heaped on Head Start's national evaluation). However, given the unusual level of sophistication of the research design, it is difficult to criticize it from an evaluative research standpoint. It is carefully done; there is more information on the children, the parents, the teachers, the principals, the schools, and the districts than anyone would ever want to know. Socioeconomic status, attitudes, aspirations, and so forth are all included. In addition, the findings are replicated in Carroll's (1975) comparisons of French instruction in eight countries. When other time factors were controlled, no advantage was found for beginning French instruction early and in the U.S. and Sweden, students starting in later grades did better.

The general picture that emerges is this: The research does not strongly support an optimal age hypothesis that says "the younger the better." Nor does it support a contrary hypothesis, "the older the better." We may state another hypothesis, "the older *child* the better," but even that is not clear from the data.

Krashen, Long, and Scarcella (1977) believe that the conflict among the studies can be explained in a number of ways. Primarily, they believe that the research should first be separated into studies that look at *initial* learning and studies that look at ultimate, long-term language *attainment*. In a careful review of the literature they give evidence for three generalizations regarding age, rate, and eventual attainment in the second language: (1) adults proceed more rapidly through the initial stages of syntactic and morphology development than children; (2) older children acquire faster than younger children; and (3) acquirers who begin second languages in early childhood through natural exposure achieve higher proficiency than those beginning as adults. Their basic position is that adults do better in initial learning but that younger is better in the long run.

In looking at many of the same studies I feel that it is still too soon to make strong claims. First, we need to accumulate findings from more carefully carried out research, research that clearly specifies which skills are being tested and how, that clearly identifies all the possible subject traits that might be important, and that clearly specifies the kinds of exposure or instruction the Ss have had. When research findings as sophisticated as the NFER reports all concur, then we might want to begin giving explanations. Until then, our explanations are really only complaints that the authors didn't find the results expected because they didn't control x, y, or z.

Meanwhile, folk belief "truths" are not to be put aside lightly. I would, in spite of this chapter, prefer to start my own children in a second language program at the early elementary stage rather than later. I don't make that decision on the basis of physiological age. Rather, I think the *more* exposure to language learning the better. And the more practice the better. The more interaction in the language the better. I don't think that the aging process itself causes one to become a less proficient learner once one gets beyond adolescence. Rather, I think all the age-related variables change the possibilities for a good language learning prognosis. If there is to be an optimal age hypothesis at all, I think it must be based, not on age or aging, but on age-related variables.

Let me hedge a bit on this statement. Pronunciation and inflectional morphology are areas where we may continue to find differences with age. I am puzzled as to how to explain it. Intuitively, I buy physiological explanations, rather than age-related factors, for this phenomenon. If this is neurologically based, then where in neurology does the problem reside? To reiterate from Chapter 2, if adults are less proficient in pronunciation than children, is it because the adult learner is unable to intake—hear—the incoming material accurately (e.g., are the cochlear hairs worn down)? Is she or he able to hear accurately but unable to analyze the system underlying what is heard? This seems unlikely, given what we know about language function and the brain. Are hearing and analyzing all functioning, but something is no longer available for motor command programs? This seems most likely if we agree that the phonological and morphophonemic plans are almost completely automatized, as Whitaker suggests. Or does it mean that everything works except that when the motor commands go to the articulators, they are somehow "resistant" to the commands? If nothing changes in any of these areas with aging, then is it safe to turn to other possible explanations? Before giving a qualified yes answer, let's turn to the field of neurolinguistics to see what information it can give us, both on this question and in support of the psycholinguistic plan levels discussed in previous chapters.

11 Neurolinguistics and Bilingualism

Whatever we may say about plan levels, we know that language messages do more than just enter learners' ears. Where messages go and what happens to them are two of our most intriguing unanswered questions. We do, of course, know a great deal about the brain, but although we have learned to name all its parts, we still do not truly understand what happens to language input or how language output is formed.

Brain Structures and Functions

The brain is not just one monolithic organ, but a series of organs, and it is possible to describe the anatomy of each. But language teachers and psycholinguists are not so much interested in the descriptions as they are in understanding the functions of the parts—specifically, can we locate various language functions in the brain? If we can, does it tell us anything about our psycholinguistic plan levels? Unfortunately, it is precisely when we assign functions to locations that we run into the most disagreement. Some neurolinguists believe we can pinpoint functions fairly well (see Geschwind, 1979); others insist that such a localist view is inadvertently misguided at best, that the observations on which a localist view is built are simply a reflection of other phenomena at work.

With this initial caution, we'll begin with the most generally accepted statements of function, after which you may consider whether you agree with assignment of function to parts, disagree totally, or wish to take some intermediate position.

Consider first the two major parts of the brain—the right and left hemispheres. They are major parts for they take up most of the brain area (see Figure 11.1). Most of the rest of our anatomy comes in pairs—we have two arms, two legs, two ears, two eyes—and the two members of each pair have fairly similar functions. It is surprising, then, to discover, that the right and left hemispheres of the brain do not seem to be nearly as perfectly matched in function. The left hemisphere has special strengths that the right does not have,

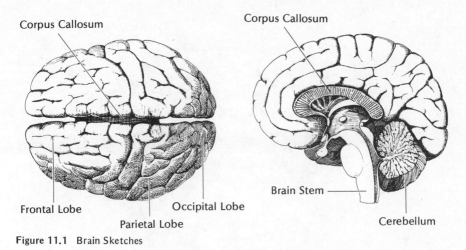

Figure 11.1 Brain Sketches

Source: *Language and Speech,* George A. Miller (San Francisco: W. H. Freeman and Company, 1981), p. 28. © 1981 by W. H. Freeman and Company.

and the right has special talents that the left does not have. The right hemisphere appears to have a special talent for music and for recognition of complex visual patterns. And the left hemisphere appears to have special analytic ability including special language capacities.

Figure 11.2 shows the outer layer of tissue—the tissue called the cortex— of the left hemisphere. As in the side view in Figure 11.2, the front of the brain is to the left and the back is to the right. Arching from ear to ear across the top of the hemisphere is the motor strip, a strip of cortex which controls voluntary muscle movement. A fairly large area of the motor strip is taken up with the control of the muscles of the tongue, lips, jaw, and those for swallowing—all of which are extremely important in the production of language. Directly behind this strip is a parallel strip of cortex which receives the sensory input of nerves from the skin, bones, muscles, and joints. As we talk, the sensory strip receives feedback from the lips, tongue, and jaw. If you have ever had a shot of Novocain at the dentist's, you know how important that feedback is to speech. Like the motor strip, a relatively large area of the sensory strip is involved with the face.

Every elementary text on the brain includes a homunculus, a drawing that makes clear the disproportionate development of the motor and sensory strips for the face and the articulators. This delineation of the motor strip (only the part on the left hemisphere) and the sensory strip (only a view of the right hemisphere) can be seen in Figure 11.3. Imagine this as an ear-to-ear cross-section viewed from the front. As you can see, the face and articulators use up much of the "space" in these areas.

Input received *visually* goes, via optical nerves, to the inner surface of the occipital lobes, to the primary *visual* cortex. And the *heard* language input goes mainly to the primary *auditory* cortex. The auditory nerves carry this information to the underside of the frontal lobes. These areas are shown in the

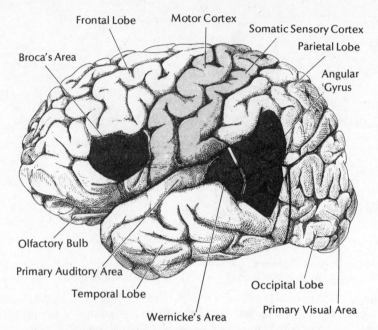

Figure 11.2   Cortex of the Left Hemisphere

Source: "Specializations of the Human Brain" by Norman Geschwind, *Scientific American, 241*:3 (September, 1979) p. 186. © 1979 Scientific American Inc.

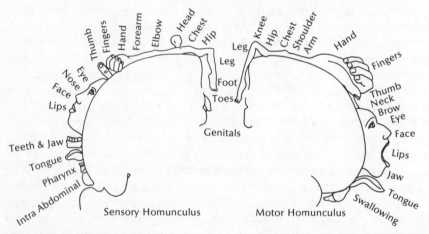

Figure 11.3   Homunculi

Source: "Specializations of the Human Brain" by Norman Geschwind, *Scientific American, 241*:3 (September, 1979) p. 182. © 1979 Scientific American Inc.

"map" of human cortex in Figure 11.4. So we know roughly where input goes: auditory input is carried via nerves to the auditory area; visual input is carried via nerves to the visual area; and sensory nerves carry input to the sensory strip. But what happens then?

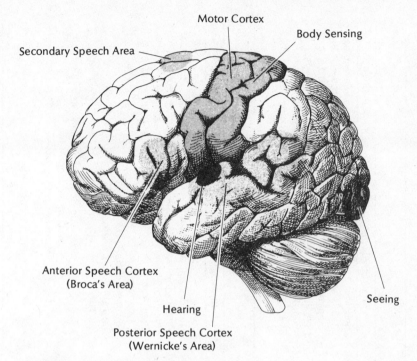

Figure 11.4 Cortex Showing Major Processing Areas

Source: *Language and Speech,* George A. Miller (San Francisco: W. H. Freeman and Company, 1981), p. 30. © 1981 by W. H. Freeman and Company.

Next to the "face" area of the motor strip (the part of the motor strip that controls the lips, tongue, jaw, etc.) is an area of cortex called Broca's area (see Figure 11.2. When a person has a stroke, the arteries shut off and the surrounding tissue dies. Death of tissue in this area results in language problems. Usually the stroke also affects part of the face area of the motor strip so there may be some weakness or partial paralysis of the face. But there is a disruption of speech production as well from damage in Broca's area. That disruption is *not* just a reflection of weakness of face muscle control. The patient can still move these muscles while eating, and patients with Broca's aphasia can often still sing very familiar songs, thus operating all the muscles well enough to produce speech in song. Second, the speech resulting from damage to Broca's area has special characteristics, only some of which have to do with problems of articulation (for a speech sample, see Table 1). Speech may be slow and labored, but more dramatic is the lack of morphology and syntactic organization. Damage to Broca's area results in speech that is often called "telegraphic," since much of the syntactic marking is gone. The patient's writing often reflects this telegraphic style as well. Damage to the corresponding area of the right hemisphere does not result in a similar language disorder. Broca's area is, then, located only in the left hemisphere. While language *production* may be severely impaired when Broca's area is damaged, language *comprehension* may remain

Table 1   Samples of Aphasic Data

Broca's—Nonfluent Aphasia (poor production, better comprehension)
Lesion site: base of 3'rd frontal convolution, "motor"

Spontaneous Picture Description	Language Comp.	Repetition
Monotone Intonation Reduced No. of words Telegraphic, Agrammatic Syntax Uses more nouns than verbs Well... mess... uh /sgæðɚ/ cookie jar fall down... and uh the girl and the cookie—uh, oh, fall... wife spill water... and uh /dɪsɪz/ ... and uh tsups and saucer and uh plate... I uh... no... done!	Good ↑1, 2, 3 stage commands Complex ideational material ↑(yes/no Q's) Token Test ↑87% correct	Poor artic: mama→maba, baba, etc. tip top→tic toc hammock→kəmɪt Poor Sent. Rep: I got home from work I am, I come home work

Wernicke's—Fluent Aphasia (poor comprehension, better production)
Lesion site: Posterior 2/3 of Superior Temporal Gyrus, "sensory"

Spontaneous Picture Description	Language Comp.	Repetition
Normal Intonation Increased No. words Paragrammatic Syntax (Extra Morphemes) Literal Paraphrasias (Sgl. sound substitution): pretty→britty Verbal Paraphrasias (Sgl. word substitution: just a very small put-together (= picture) Well that's a little kid, the little boy on the... getting his cookie, cookie jars (jar) off the stool falling off his little girl wanting some from her (him) and his mother's washing dishes and the dishwater is running water (over) she doesn't notice... and dishes on (are) being done but she's got a bit of a mess there now... and looking outdoors and uh she's busy and she's not really watching as clozley as close as she should have... and pretty britty dangerous the way the boy is stooling (falling) on the stool... so I guess that's about all there is, just a very small put-together.	Poor: ↑1, 2, 3 stage commands Complex Ideational Material ↑(yes/no Q's) Token Test 77% correct Show me a circle /sə mi/, there is no /səmi/ Syntactic Comprehension Test: Easy: Gender, Neg/Affirm Hard: rev. active/passive pres/future direct/indirect obj. subord. clauses	mama→mama, emphasize↑ /ɛmfrsaɪd/ I got home from work→I got urns from urn. The spy fled to Greece.→ the fly /fleyd/ /fleyd/ to /kid/

Neurolinguistics and Bilingualism 203

Table 1 continued

Conduction Aphasia
Lesion site: Arcuate Fasciculus—white fiber bundle connecting Wernicke's and Broca's areas, deep to supra-marginal gyrus

Spontaneous Picture Description	Language Comp.	Repetition
Normal intonation Circumlocutory, empty speech Literal Paraphasias (Sgl. sound substitution) Phon. Sequence Problems: tool, kool, for stool k, k, kuh, cookies Here's a cookie jar. The boy's falling down his *tool, kool*, I mean his uh, whatever he may be being. And uh, his uh little girl is having some k, k, kuh, cookies. And this uh... somebody or other... is now the is... uh *cleaning* water all over the floor.... OK?	↑Good Token Test ↑96% correct	Good articulation Good single word repetition, except for numbers. Sent. excessively impaired: *Pussy willow*→possy willer, water, etc. *He asked where he was when we were there.*→How, no... h-how, no, he he asked when we were there. No. (repeat) He ... asked what where we were, when we when we ... *No if's and's or but's*→If's no if's uh ... hii, hif, no ridiculous! No if's but's... but's.... no it's but no ... it's buts, what's the matter with that 1 (repeats)

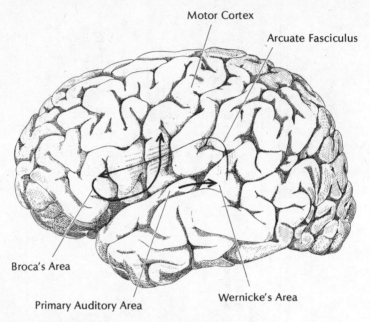

Figure 11.5   Possible Route in Repetition Task

Source: "Specializations of the Human Brain" by Norman Geschwind, *Scientific American*, 241:3 (September, 1979) p. 190. © 1979 Scientific American Inc.

relatively good. Broca's area appears to be extremely important for production of syntactic and morphology plans.

The second area of importance for language in the left hemisphere is Wernicke's area, next to the primary auditory area (see Figure 11.5). As in Broca's area, a lesion in this area produces language disorder but the disorder is of a very different type (for a sample, see Table 1). While Broca's aphasia is sometimes called telegraphic or agrammatic, patients with Wernicke's aphasia are still fluent, their speech still grammatically organized, but the sense of the utterance is difficult to process. Nonsense words may be used and/or word choice may be inappropriate. Even when word choice is correct, meanings seem to be expressed in a vague or roundabout way. Even more marked is the deficit in language *comprehension*. Comprehension of messages seems to be much impaired for such patients. From such symptoms, then, it appears that messages received in the auditory area pass through Wernicke's area for processing of some sort (comprehension), while Broca's area is more crucial to syntactic organization and language production. The fact that comprehension can remain good when Broca's area is damaged says something about syntactic versus semantic processing (comprehension) models discussed in Chapter 5. However, perhaps comprehension does deteriorate (that is, has not been accurately assessed in cases of Broca's aphasia) and one can get by with semantic processing. Another possibility is that comprehension and production sites both have syntactic elements in them. Then, the loss of syntactic markers in Broca's area would not mean that Wernicke's area did not still have some syntax accessible for comprehension (but not production).

Geschwind claims we can trace a simple "route" that might be followed during a simple repetition task (see Figure 11.6). You might think of the learner first receiving the input which is carried from the ears by nerves to the auditory cortex. It goes then to Wernicke's area in some form and is somehow transformed in processing. It next passes through a bundle of nerve fibers called the arcuate fasciculus to Broca's area. There production planning takes place and is sent to the adjoining face area of the motor strip which, in turn, transmits—and perhaps transmutes—the motor plans to the articulators which repeat the message.

If there is damage to the bundle of nerves that connects Wernicke's and Broca's areas (the arcuate fasciculus), the message cannot be transmitted. The result is called conduction aphasia. As you can imagine (and can see in Table 1), persons with damage to this connecting bundle of fibers have severe problems in repeating verbal stimuli. Though the Wernicke's area may be functioning normally and the patient may understand the input, there is little chance of the message being transmitted successfully to Broca's area. If it were, Broca's area (which is also functioning well) would be able to send the message to the motor strip, allowing for correct repetition.

Messages received visually rather than auditorily must be carried through the area called the angular gyrus (see Figure 11.6) to Wernicke's area. The

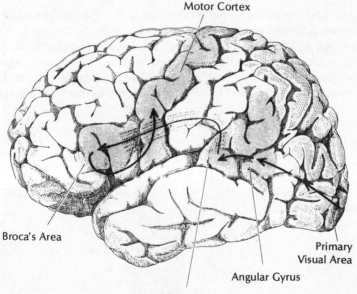

Figure 11.6   Possible Routes in Reading Tasks

Source: "Specializations of the Human Brain" by Norman Geschwind, *Scientific American*, 241:3 (September, 1979) p. 190. © 1979 Scientific American Inc.

angular gyrus may change the visual message in some way so that it evokes the auditory form of the message in Wernicke's area, though this is speculation. But somehow, the message must also be deciphered in much the same manner as auditory input at Wernicke's area.

It is clear that areas other than the cortex are also involved in language development and language performance. For example, we know that another part of the brain, the cerebellum (see Figure 11.1), is important in smoothing out all motor activities. It allows us to make a golf swing or a tennis stroke as a single flowing movement rather than a series of jerky sequences (as in old-time movies) or as one over-run of a movement sending us spinning into space. Cerebellar speech is usually characterized as excessively sloppy, mushy-mouthed, like the speech of comics pretending to be alcoholic. The cerebellum works like a quick-erase computer, taking care of the total plan efficiently, synchronizing the movements of groups of muscles. If you are interested in other vertebrates, consider the importance of the cerebellum to birds in flight. Their ability to fly through trees without touching the branches is due in part to the marvelous working of the cerebellum. You might also think about how complex many of our motor patterns are. For example, if you write with your left hand instead of your right, the motor plan is automatically adapted and sent to those muscles. If you try to write with a pen stuck between your toes, or even between your teeth, the plan is still available to you. It can't be the case, then, that plans are specifically made for only certain muscles but, rather, are much more abstract sets of rules.

Figure 11.7 shows the limbic area, which appears to regulate many of our basic functions. The drawing is of the inner side of the hemisphere, like a cut down through a "center hair part" which has been opened outward. Animal experiments show that limbic stimulation results in the show of alarm, aggressive behavior, panting, growling, head jerking, dilated pupils, and so on. Human limbic cries—the cries of fear or of sex, for example—have been equated to

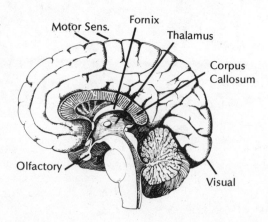

Figure 11.7   The Limbic Area

limbic cries of other mammals. However, even these cries are, in humans, language specific. Pain cries differ over languages; even sneezing seems to be culturally determined. Only severe pain cries appear to be universal rather than language specific. There are very strong connections between the outer cortex and the deeper limbic areas; these connections may be even more important for language than the connections across the outer cortex.

An important part of the limbic area for language is the hippocampus. The hippocampus seems to play a role in memory, perhaps selecting material from the input for long-term storage. An interesting case study is that reported by Milner et al. (1968). The patient, who had parts of the hippocampus removed, could attend to ongoing input but was unable to hold the material in memory for long periods of time. For example, he was unable to learn his street address and can only remember facts by constantly rehearsing them. Once distracted, the memory trace is gone. Obviously the hippocampus is very important in language learning, but what and why certain things are stored and others not is unclear. For example, while on a short visit to Finland, my constant rehearsal of how to say "I want a NOUN" in Finnish did not help me to retain the frame overnight, yet the nouns that went into the frame were still easily accessed the next day.

Learning supported by emotion seems to be long retained. For example, everyone remembers where they were and what they were doing when President Kennedy was assassinated (as I remember sitting in our grape arbor when FDR's death was announced). Some people report strong associations of scent and memory or of color and memory. This also appears to be limbic association at work. Learning, including language learning, supported by these associations seems to be strongly printed in memory.

Again, many neurolinguists believe that it is the connections from the cortex (from Broca's and Wernicke's areas) to the thalamus in the limbic area that are important for language rather than the cross-cortical connections. That is, they don't believe that the connections between the visual processing area, the angular gyrus, Broca's area, Wernicke's area, and the motor strip are as crucial as the many connections of these areas with areas much deeper in the brain.

Matching Functions and Structures

How strong a claim can one make concerning matching functions to brain structures? Where can one find evidence to support these claims? The four major positions lie along a continuum. At one extreme, the strong localist position contends that there are three major speech areas: Broca's motor association area (which plans and then delivers the plans to the motor strip directly behind it), Wernicke's area (the auditory association area, apparently involved with language comprehension), and the angular gyrus (connecting the visual and auditory areas). A second position is that the limbic area is important and that the connections to this area are more important than tracks that connect various areas of the cortex. A third is the holistic approach. This position suggests that both left and right hemispheres are capable of language processing

208 PSYCHOLINGUISTICS: A Second Language Perspective

(both comprehension and production), but that the two handle language data in slightly different ways. The left hemisphere is concerned with analytic tasks of all sorts, of which language is just one. The right hemisphere is more holistic or gestalt-like in dealing with language input. Yet, the whole brain is seen as "plastic"; different areas can take over functions once handled by other areas. The fourth model, at the other end of the continuum, holds that both hemispheres are capable of language but that the right hemisphere is inhibited in some way from capturing the language channel.

Advocates of all four positions look for evidence from similar sources. The most obvious source, as can be seen from our discussion so far, is evidence from brain damage. When the brain is injured through accident or stroke, the patient almost always shows some sort of language impairment. If the symptoms of impairment can be matched to a brain lesion, then it should be obvious what function the area once performed; that is, the language function that is impaired. Using this kind of evidence, Broca successfully showed that the third frontal convolution of the left hemisphere caused severe language impairment, as described in Table 1. (He also tried to show—with little success—that women are less intelligent than men because their brains weigh less.) A similar recording of language symptoms, later matched to lesion sites from postmortem examinations, established Wernicke's area as important in language comprehension. (Actually, Wernicke—twenty-six when he published his paper—noted the different symptoms of patients who had damage near the auditory input area. His drawings showed the area in the *right* hemisphere, and it was up to others to put it correctly in the left hemisphere!)

In the past symptoms were not always recorded carefully. When they were, often no postmortem was done. So we're not always sure that the surmised damage was real or that the damage site was accurately recorded. The extent and depth of lesions are not always given. And most neurosurgeons emphasize the amount of variation found among individuals. In fact, this matching may have puzzling results. For example, the literature mentions cases where ablation (that is, removal) of tissue may cause a particular language deficit. One might therefore surmise that the particular area involved is responsible for the particular language function. Later, the same patient may require a second operation. More tissue is removed, and the function that had disappeared following the first operation now reappears. So matching claims must be taken with some degree of scepticism; not total disbelief perhaps, but with some scepticism.

Fortunately, new procedures now allow for better information on the exact site and depth of lesion prior to surgery. High speed light waves are used to scan the body and send back information on speed of light waves through tissue. Light waves pass through certain types of tissue faster than others, and the difference in speed at each change of tissue type is then transferred to a picture of lesions, tumors, and healthy tissue, a picture far more accurate than anything obtained before.

Staining is another method used for understanding the connections among the areas of the brain. Apparently, all the areas are connected to everything else, but the stain technique shows that some parts are more strongly connected than others. This has allowed us to learn more about the interconnections among the various language areas.

Probes have also been used successfully to increase our knowledge of brain anatomy and language function. The brain itself does not experience pain. It is possible then to painlessly stimulate various parts of the brain and thus discover whether such disruption at any pressure point affects language. This technique made it possible for Penfield and Roberts (1959) and other neurosurgeons to literally map out areas of the motor and sensory strips, as well as to gather more information on Broca's and other areas important for language.

Matching lesion sites to language disorder symptoms, and the probe technique, established the doctrine of functional asymmetry of the right and left hemispheres. Supporting evidence for functional asymmetry also came from the Wada test, a test given to epileptics to establish language hemisphere dominance prior to surgery. The test includes a fairly dangerous procedure— injecting sodium amytal into the carotid vein to block out one hemisphere entirely. The patient is then asked to count, identify objects, and follow simple directions such as raising or lowering the arm or pointing to objects. With the left hemisphere blocked, most patients are unable to do these tasks. This led to the belief that there is no language in the right hemisphere, that it is "silent" or "dormant." Since we believe that language is a left-hemisphere function, you might wonder why epileptic patients are subjected to this test at all. There is a fairly high incidence of left-handedness in epileptic patients, and it is thought that more bilateral representation of language exists for persons who are left-handed than for those who are right-handed. So if there is doubt, it is important to establish language hemisphere dominance prior to surgery.

One operation which has been performed on patients suffering from severe epileptic seizures is to sever the corpus callosum. The corpus callosum is a series of fibers connecting the two hemispheres (see Figure 11.1). This is the major pathway between the two hemispheres. Through it information from one brain can pass over to the other.

It is interesting that information from the right ear does not go to the right hemisphere, and that left ear input is not to the left hemisphere. In fact, the opposite happens. Information from the left ear and the left visual field goes to the right hemisphere. Right ear input and right visual field information go to the left hemisphere. This is called a contralateral pathway. The same contralateral effect works for the motor and sensory strips. To share information between the two hemispheres, the information has to cross from one side to the other across the corpus callosum. When the pathway is cut (in order to prevent massive and continuing seizures in epileptic patients), that information cannot cross to the opposite hemisphere and the brains become separate in some more severe sense than before. (There *are* weaker bilateral connections, however, as well.)

If, in patients who have had such split-brain operations, input from the left ear goes to the "silent" right hemisphere, what happens? The early literature reported that nothing happens; that the right hemisphere is "deaf" to language. Input to the right ear is still processed by the left hemisphere, as usual. We seldom (except in experiments) receive input from just one visual field or just one ear, so language impairment in split-brain patients is thought to be slight.

If such patients are asked to pick up something they cannot see in their left hand (the right hemisphere sensory strip receives the information), they can identify the object by pointing to a picture or by spelling it with the left hand. *Asked* (to the left hemisphere as well as the right) to name the object, the patient would err in naming it. The left hemisphere would not know, would not have received the input, and therefore could not correctly identify the object. However, there is much variation in the data from these experiments, and the reasons for it are interesting. An anecdote is told of a patient who felt the object in the left hand without seeing it. The right hemisphere knew the object was a matchbox, looked for a similar object in the room, and focused on it. The left hemisphere picked up the cue, and reported the object correctly. This is called cross-cuing. Gazzaniga et al. (1969) instructed a patient to report verbally whether a light flashed to his left visual field was red or green. (Remember that information to the left visual field goes to the right hemisphere.) In the beginning the left hemisphere responded at chance level, since it didn't receive the information. Then the patient's performance picked up dramatically. What had happened was that the right hemisphere (which knew the answer) began to make facial grimaces every time the left hemisphere made an error. Feedback on the grimace went to the left hemisphere, allowing it to correct itself.

Through a number of experiments Gazzaniga showed that these split-brain patients, when information is given only to the right hemisphere, are unable to recognize the relationships between subject-verb-object, future and past tense, or singular and plural. Levy et al. (1971), in their experiments, gave contradictory evidence. They changed the task requirements, thereby showing that the right hemisphere can react to commands to manipulate toy objects with the left hand. They showed that the right hemisphere can carry out responses to commands that make these syntactic distinctions. They suggest that the right hemisphere may understand, but that the left hemisphere normally blocks its attempt to gain control of the motor pathways. To account for Levy's data, Gazzaniga and others claimed that the weak interconnections (the corpus callosum isn't the only connection between the hemispheres, nor is it always completely severed in such operations) allow the left hemisphere to inform the left hand, and that therefore Levy's data are still really the result of the left hemisphere, not the right.

So far I have talked about evidence gathered from patients with brain disorders, and it may be unrealistic to surmise from that data how the normal brain functions. Data from normal subjects have been obtained from dichotic listening and visual field tasks. In the dichotic listening task, the person receives simultaneously two messages through a headset, one to the left ear and one to the right. The onset time must be perfectly matched. The S is then asked to report the words presented on the headsets. Most right-handed Ss report more of the words that are directed to the right ear, which the left hemisphere receives first. This is called the right ear advantage (REA) for language. The REA in normal (corpus callosum intact) Ss is not great, but differences are large enough to be statistically significant. Krashen (1976) claims this advantage reflects left hemisphere dominance for language. Furthermore, he reports that children show no right ear advantage until age five. Others have shown that the "advantage" for language to the right ear (and thus the left hemisphere) does not appear consistently until age nine and that it continues to increase until age eleven. The REA is strong for processing consonants, but there is a gradual continuum to a left ear advantage (right hemisphere) for vowels. Stops are stronger than fricatives for REA and fricatives are stronger than nasals. Nasals may be stronger for left ear advantage and vowels are even more left ear (right hemisphere). Apparently intonation is more successful with the right hemisphere. So it may be that not every feature of language is processed best or only by the left hemisphere.

A similar visual test has also been used to look at left versus right hemisphere language claims. Each eye has a right and a left visual field. The right visual field of each eye goes first to the left hemisphere; the left visual field of each eye goes first to the right hemisphere. This information is then transferred across the corpus callosum to the other side. Early experiments on eye field required that one fixate on a spot and then a word was flashed either to the left or the right visual field. The problem was that involuntary saccadic eye movements are so rapid that the technique wasn't exactly foolproof. Zaidel then invented a special contact lens which blocks out either the right or the left visual field. Zaidel's lens allowed for experiments similar to dichotic listening, and the procedure is clearer in some ways. The eye field tests conducted by Moscovitch (1977) led him to conclude, as had Zaidel, that the right hemisphere does process visual material. However, Moscovitch also suggested that it is accomplished by template matching. Levy et al. found that the right hemisphere will match words like *nose* and *rose* and say that they rhyme, but will not match *knows* and *rose* as rhyming words. Again, this suggests template matching of shapes. From a variety of sources (not just the eye field tests), Van Lancker (1975) and others claim that the right hemisphere does seem to be able to process language to some extent. Certainly the right hemisphere has access to formulaic language; e.g., chunk-learned utterances (even such large items as the Pledge of Allegiance), content words, and especially swear words. This has led people to wonder whether initial second language learning might not be unanalyzed chunk learning done by the right hemisphere plus a variety of content words of high frequency. The right hemisphere should be able to take care of such input without ever having to treat it analytically in the left hemisphere. This might account for bilingual aphasia patients who, after left hemisphere damage, lose their first language but do remember tenth-grade, high school French, using these high frequency utterances, parts of dialogues, and vocabulary items to carry out their communicative needs. Probably all of us remember whole dialogues from language classes we've taken. My son can recite whole dialogues in Russian but has no idea what they mean except in a very global sense. He also could never respond to an exchange taken from the middle of a dialogue. Rather, he would have to begin at the beginning and say it up to that point before he could continue. This is like the right hemisphere data from an aphasia patient who could only answer "What's the number after 11" by counting up to that number and then giving the next. Or answer "What's spangled?" by singing the entire "Star Spangled Banner" and then saying, "That's it."

The right hemisphere does appear to have "automatic" language. Broca believed that it could also process language. Moscovitch also believes that the right hemisphere can process language (although differently from the left), *and* that it is inhibited from doing so. The culprit is the corpus callosum. Moscovitch thinks that one function of the corpus callosum is to inhibit the attempts of the right hemisphere to meddle in language processing. Once a patient has the corpus callosum cut, the right hemisphere should then be able to take over and function relatively unhampered in linguistic pursuits. This would help explain why people with left hemisphere damage aren't always able to use right hemisphere language abilities to compensate. The corpus callosum is still blocking the right hemisphere. It also might explain why focal lesions sometimes result in deficits which are no longer found when the entire cortex of the left hemisphere is removed.

A final source of information about language and the brain is the most impressive of all. The brain, like the rest of the body, is fed by blood. Regional blood flow varies according to the amount of activity or metabolic rate needed to sustain activity. Xenon 133, a radioisotope in the blood stream, can be followed, and the recording of the flow rate can be converted into pictures of nerve-cell activity. The photographs of blood flow while the person is resting, listening, speaking, reading, moving the hands, and so on can be shown (see the dramatic color photos in *Scientific American,* October 1978). When the subject watches a moving object, the visual association cortex in the rear of the brain is shown as active. When listening to spoken words, the auditory cortex and Wernicke's area are active. Asked to count, the mouth area of the motor strip lights up, as does the auditory area which is listening to the words. During silent reading, four areas are shown to be active: the visual area, the frontal eye field, the motor area, and Broca's area. Reading aloud adds the mouth motor area and the auditory areas. If you look at the photographs, however, you will see that the right hemisphere is also active, perhaps working in other ways on the visual and auditory input. It is clear that the right hemisphere is not "silent" or "dormant" in any way.

The evidence from all these sources is, I think (because it is cumulative), quite convincing. Some areas of the left hemisphere are more involved in language processing than others. The right hemisphere is also involved but appears to process quite differently from the left. Perhaps the left hemisphere is an analytic device and the right hemisphere a gestalt device. Both of these are used in most problem solving, whether language-related or not. Damage to either hemisphere must lead to deficits in problem solving of some sort, though they may not be immediately obvious to researchers.

While the photographs of blood flow through the cortex are impressive, we still have much to learn about the subcortical areas of the brain and their importance to language learning and language behavior. What we have learned about the brain and how it handles input does give us, once again, some evidence for psycholinguistic claims about language. Syntax and morphology seem to be handled quite differently from lexicon; content words are handled differently from function words. Consonants seem to be handled differently from vowels. Nasalization and intonation also seem to be processed somewhat differently from segmentals. It is true that we have not "localized" each of these parts of language. It is also clear that in trying to locate functions, we have made no mention, for example, of discourse. (Though, again, there are case reports in the literature—e.g., Blank et al., 1979—of patients who seem to have acquired syntax, morphology, phonology, and so on, but have not acquired the "grammar" of communication.) Where in the brain might these "rules" be processed/ produced? Disease to other areas important to normal language (e.g., Parkinson's disease) have not been mentioned here, though they too are important in understanding language function in the brain. All in all, we can be sure of at least one thing: There is no single "black box" for language in the brain. The machinery of the brain is much more complex than that. Perhaps that is what makes it so fascinating.

Again, consider how much more complicated the problem of locating language function in the brain must be if the person knows more than one language. One of the interesting hypotheses made in bilingual literature is that, in the brain, second languages are represented differently from first languages. To test this, Maitre (1974) did a dichotic listening test on Americans studying Spanish at the university level. She found a right ear advantage for words in Spanish and for words in English. However, she found that the advantage was statistically stronger for English than Spanish. However, no significant difference was found when short sentences rather than single words were used as stimuli.

Obler et al. (1975) also performed a dichotic listening test on fluent bilinguals. They found, as had Maitre, that all Ss showed a right ear advantage (meaning left hemisphere location of language processing). However, they showed a stronger right ear advantage for the first language, whether English or Hebrew, than for the second. They speculated, then, that the first language becomes lateralized to the left hemisphere, "but something about the process of learning a second language involves the right hemisphere of the adult learner more than we might have expected."

Galloway (1981) then searched the literature on bilingual aphasia, checking for lesion evidence which might show that second languages, at least in the beginning stages of acquisition, are more right hemisphere than left. She hypothesized that if she could find evidence of right hemisphere lesions, those patients would be as impaired in the second language as the first, if not more so. Unfortunately, from the approximately 200 cases reported, none documented the combination of right lesions and information on both first and second languages. So, she formed a second guess, that the second language would be less impaired than the first (or would be recovered before the first language) after left hemisphere lesions. Five case studies were found with appropriate information for this hypothesis.

Galloway's first study was of a Polish male who, having worked in Berlin, was in the army in the Soviet Union. He was in a Polish squadron but he did learn some Russian. For ten months following injury—a bullet wound in his left hemisphere—he appeared to understand nothing; then he began to speak a few words in Russian. Hospital attendants began to teach him Russian. Although he complained bitterly that he had forgotten his Polish, his comprehension of Polish remained intact. German, apparently, was completely gone. This study might be evidence for right hemisphere representation of early second language learning, since Russian reappeared and developed while the production of the first language was severely impaired.

The second case was a German woman who at age nineteen briefly studied Italian as a second language. She visited Italy occasionally and, just before her injury (due to a fall from a horse), spoke Italian approximately two to three hours a day with an Italian-speaking friend. She had also studied French as a high school student but had few opportunities to speak French thereafter. Following her injury, she began to count in Italian for several hours during the third and fourth day. Then she uttered French spontaneously. She could repeat the alphabet in German, her first language. She named objects in Italian and could translate text from German to Italian. After a few days, she preferred French. As French reappeared, Italian regressed. Questions posed in German were answered in French. French remained her major language until two weeks after the injury when German began to re-emerge. As German reappeared, French regressed. Again, the second languages came back first when damage was to the left hemisphere, suggesting support for the hypothesis that the right hemisphere is involved in second language learning.

Case 3 was a German male who had learned French as an adolescent. The *S* had third-stage syphillis and possible basal meningitis affecting the right side of the body (thus left lesions likely). During the early aphasic stage, the patient could only speak French. Then he recovered his first language, German. Again, this supports the notion that the right hemisphere was active for second language learning. The fourth case Galloway discussed was a Swiss-German who was injured in a motorcycle accident. Although educated only to the elementary school level, he was an avid reader of German history and German literary classics (High German). He knew some Italian and some French which he used while in the military service. The patient recovered his Swiss German and High German. He was unable to produce or comprehend all but the most common and simple utterances in French and Italian. This is counter evidence for the hypothesis.

The final case was a thirty-three-year-old Russian officer. French was his second language, and Serbian was a second language which he did not speak fluently though it had been his business language for three years. Following syphillis with seizures, the first language recovered was Serbian and later Russian with a Serbian accent. This case is difficult to interpret as either support for or against the hypothesis.

Failing to find strong evidence in the case studies, Galloway turned to data from Obler and others on the importance of the right hemisphere for second language learning. Obler followed sixty-three patients who suffered brain damage in childhood. Thirty-six had lesions in the right hemisphere. Four of these, despite normal I.Q.'s, displayed severe difficulties in second language learning, even at the college level. Galloway points out that many normal individuals have problems with second language learning as well, so such statements must be interpreted with caution. Galloway cites a final source of possible support for right hemisphere involvement in second language learning; the descriptions of brains (postmortem) of six polyglots. Four showed strong development in the right temporal lobes, one showed no special development, and the last contained no mention of special development. Galloway concludes that, while the notion of right hemisphere involvement in second language learning is an attractive one (at least for initial learning), and while there are many hints in the literature which are intriguing, the evidence that she found in support of the notion is not strong. Much of it could be interpreted in many other ways. As both she and Paradis have noted, we need much fuller case records on bilingual aphasia before we can make strong claims.

Paradis (1977) has presented the most complete review of case histories of bilinguals who have suffered brain damage. Many bilinguals, in fact the majority, recover the languages in parallel. However, there is tremendous variety in the case records reviewed. Some bilinguals recover first one and then the other language; some recover one language and, as the second begins to come back, lose the first one again; some retain/recover parts of each of the languages—perhaps reading and writing skills in one language, comprehension in the same language, but production only for the other language. To account for the wide variety of data presented, hypotheses other than those proposed by Galloway should be considered.

One hypothesis is that the last learned language should be recovered first (Ribot's Rule). In the survey of the literature, Paradis found equal numbers of cases where the first or last learned languages were recovered. In some cases it was the language of the hospital that was recovered first (possibly though, no one spoke anything else to the patient, so this is not very good evidence).

Another hypothesis is that the language most used will be recovered first. We already know from the discussion of Galloway's search that this is not always the case. Psychological reasons have also been cited in attempting to account for recovery patterns. For example, a psychological explanation was given for a patient's recovery of the language spoken by the housemaid in his family but not the language of his wife.

Unfortunately, the review does not include complete information on the site of injury, but this is not Paradis's omission. The records in most of these case histories are very incomplete. Paradis has included a table of information questions which he hopes will be used in the future by researchers working with bilingual aphasia. One problem is that language proficiency prior to brain injury is difficult to assess; responses of relatives may be less than accurate, but it is important to at least attempt to get as much information as possible both on language proficiency and language use, and on the nature of the lesion(s).

Another type of hypothesis has also been made to explain bilingual aphasia data, a concentric circle explanation. That is, in the early stage of language development, large areas of the language cortex may be involved with language. As the representation of language becomes more abstract, less redundant, and more automatized, less and less wiring should be necessary for the plans. Therefore, the area used for various plans becomes smaller and smaller (concentric circles). Then, when one wants to learn a new language, again a large area of the language cortex may be involved. It should not be surprising then, if one uses the probe technique, to find differences in location for the two languages. Ojemann and Whitaker (1978), for example, have reported that word naming frequently seems to overlap for the two languages with other places being specific to one or the other language. Unfortunately, no one has yet given us photographs of Xenon in blood flow to show a person speaking first one language and then a second. It would be exciting to see if many differences were found. Meanwhile, a concentric circle explanation seems appealing. This shows the brain to be fairly plastic, with functions becoming more and more concentrated in area as they become more and more automatic. However, such an explanation would really say that second languages are being handled as first languages once were, by larger areas of the brain. This may or may not be the case. Such an explanation would not account for Albert and Obler's (1975) case study of a Hebrew and English bilingual patient whose left hemisphere damage caused Wernicke's aphasia symptoms in one language and Broca's aphasia symptoms in the other. (Paradis suggests that the case may be one of differential recovery and that, if data were available, we would find a difference of degree rather than of nature of aphasia.)

I conclude this chapter with a few leftovers which I think are interesting, even though they do not fit in nicely with any of the above data.

Whitaker (1976) has mentioned a very interesting syndrome associated with lesions in the Rolandic area. This is the so-called "foreign accent" syndrome. A native speaker of English sounds like a foreigner because of an "accent" which occurred after brain damage. Whitaker's patient placed glottal stops between word boundaries to make the syllable pattern which has often been called the universal open syllable (but which is typical of many foreign accents in English). She devoiced final stops, the vowels were fronted and raised (so she has no clear *i/I* distinction, which sounds like a Spanish speaker's English). This patient could hear that her output didn't match her rules for English pronunciation, but she could not control her output to correct her speech. Many foreign students also seem to recognize the inaccuracy of their phonological output but are not able to change the commands. Now, it seems illogical to say that the two are the same and that both are neurophysiologically determined (in one case by lesion and the other by nonplasticity of cortex, caused by age of acquiring the second language). However, the parallels are interesting.

Via case studies, Whitaker has also been able to show that lower level grammar rules are entirely automatic. He has mentioned the study of a subject with a viral brain disorder who would automatically correct morphology in sentence repetition as well as correct the phonology of an utterance given to her to repeat. (For example, given "it's a ling" to repeat, she said "it's a ring." Given "the boy hit herself" she corrected it to "the boy hit himself.") She understood nothing of what she said and yet made all these "automatic" changes in phonology and syntax. The undiseased portions of her brain still continued to process lower level syntax and phonology for her. Whitaker suggests that it is this automatic system from the first language which continually gets in the way of second language morphology and syntax rules; interference, for him, is from this automatic system. This does not explain why many second language learners do not have interference problems, or why parts of the "automatic system" should interfere more than others.

Another interesting thought that didn't fit in anywhere above is the often noted similarity of early second language data and American Sign Language data. It has been suggested that users of Sign are more right hemisphere in their language use. This makes sense, since the system is visual-spatial in nature. Written English data of native speakers of Sign is, of course, second language data in a real sense. And it is similar in many ways to that of other second language learners. Is Sign, and most early second language data, really processed by the right hemisphere? Again, we have no answer, but Sign like all languages has system to be analyzed. While the right hemisphere may be more suited to dealing with visual-spatial organization, the left hemisphere must still be actively analyzing the data as language. Nevertheless, the idea of parallels between Sign and second language data is interesting to consider.

In spite of my early warning, in this chapter the connection between language function and anatomy appears strong. This may be misleading. The early data on which many of these claims are based may be shaky and the claims no more than conjectures. For example, in most brain damage cases, it's not just one area that is damaged but usually a constellation of other areas as well. Injury in one area may set off damage in others which is not easily seen. To the extent that many of the proposals of localists depend on brain damage evidence, they must be taken with at least a grain of scepticism. Data from blood flow pictures of healthy persons is an exciting breakthrough for research relating language function and brain site. However, they only give us information on the outer cortical layers, not on the subcortical tissue. Again, many neurolinguists believe that the data on cortex activity only reflects subcortical activity and that we must turn to these areas if we are ever to understand the nature of language acquisition and language processing.

12 Cognition, Cognitive Strategies, and Language Acquisition

Now that we have reviewed the research on language functions and the brain, we can turn to another area psycholinguists look to to explain language learning abilities and the order of acquisition of particular parts of language systems. That area is cognition.

The term "cognition" is a vague one (as are many others in most fields). In its nontechnical sense it appears to mean any mental process. Surely, one would not argue against language learning as a mental process. In a more technical sense, however, cognition is seen as covering the problem-solving abilities of humans. A major claim in child language research is that language is only one of many analytic activities which all depend on cognitive development. Language acquisition is seen as having certain cognitive prerequisites or co-requisites. That is, the child will not develop linguistic forms before acquiring the cognitive bases for those forms. For example, the child is expected to learn the where-question/location answer prior to the when-question/time answer because the concept of place is acquired prior to the concept of time, and this order is cognitively determined. For many researchers, language development is but one manifestation of more general cognitive or perceptual capacities. For example, Bates says:

We are suggesting that there is Great Borrowing going on, in which language is viewed as a parasitic system that builds its structures by raiding the software packages of prior or parallel cognitive capacities. (1979, p. 9)

Greenfield (1978), in support of a strong, causal link between cognition and language acquisition, has shown how action and language are hierarchically related. Her claim is that there is parallel development of action and language features and that cognition is a common underlying mechanism for both.

While Greenfield, Bates, and others have amassed a great deal of evidence in support of the link between language and cognition, the causal relationship between the two has been questioned on a number of points.

First, let's consider the reverse claim on the connection between language and cognition—that language is causally related to cognitive development. Such a relationship can be easily discredited by the research on non-signing deaf children which shows cognitive development can proceed in the absence of language. Carey (1979), too, has shown that children have words for concepts before concepts and vice versa. Curtiss (1977), in her research on Genie, also shows that this child, while linguistically and socially deprived during a long period of isolation, did develop nonlinguistic cognitive abilities in the absence of language development.

Claims, however, are now made primarily in the other direction. That is, cognition is seen as underlying language skills: The order in which particular structures are acquired by child language learners reflects their cognitive growth. Many researchers have written on the cognitive prerequisites for language acquisition. Surprisingly, many of these prerequisites focus on language learning strategies rather than on the relationship between cognitive and linguistic strategies. These strategies, since they are stated in linguistic terms, could be considered as separate from cognitive strategies. For example, Slobin's (1973) strategies include such principles as "pay attention to the ends of words" or "pay attention to word order," and so on. These directions do not necessarily appear to be cognitive strategies. They could as easily be called language strategies.

While cognitive and language development may be interrelated, let's consider evidence that argues against any strong position that cognitive growth is causal to language development. The first area is covered in case studies of first language acquisition summarized by Yamada (1981). She reports that individuals with Turner's syndrome have been reported to have normal or superior language ability alongside cognitive problems in visual-spatial tasks, temporal sequencing tasks, numerical operations tasks, and logical operations. (Turner's syndrome is a sex chromosomal anomaly.) Hydrocephalics with linguistic ability far exceeding their nonlinguistic cognitive abilities have also been reported. However, in these cases, language may not develop uniformly. While syntactic abilities may be quite developed, semantic abilities are reported to be less fully developed. Turner's and hydrocephalic speech may be fluent but bears little meaning, and has therefore been termed "cocktail party speech." This suggests that semantics may be more directly related than syntax to cognitive abilities.

In line with these findings, Curtiss, Fromkin, and Yamada (1979) have shown that, for Genie and other language-impaired individuals, semantic knowledge may correlate with concept knowledge while syntax does not. There seems to be a possibility, then, that different plan levels of language may be differentially linked to cognition.

Yamada (1981) reports on the high syntax/low cognition profile of a severely retarded adolescent, "M." This girl (18 years old), on Piagetian tasks, placed at a level prior to concrete operational (7–11 years) and at the end of or just beyond the sensorimotor period (0–2 years). Thus, she appears to be functioning cognitively somewhere in the 2–7 year range. In both formal and informal observations she showed problems with numbers and with numerical and time concepts. While she can recite numbers, she has not mastered the concept of counting or numerosity. She is unable to consistently give her correct birth date or age, nor can she name the days of the week or demonstrate other common knowledge abilities. In spite of her low cognitive abilities, M uses sentences that are complex syntactically. That is, she uses subordination (relativization, complementation) and coordination:

M: She does paintings, this really good friend of the kids who I went to school with last year, and really loved.

M: Last year at (name of school) when I first went there three tickets were gave out by a police last year.

Some of M's utterances are quite well formed both syntactically and semantically, and are appropriate to the context, while others are not. M's numerical references in spontaneous speech reflect that her numerical concepts, like her temporal ones, are extremely limited:

M: I was like fifteen or nineteen when I started moving out o' home. So now I'm like fifteen now, and I can go.

S: How many nights did you stay there? (at a hotel)

M: Oh, about four out of one.

Yamada's case study, then, shows that M's linguistic abilities place her well beyond that of the normal preschooler, while her cognitive capacities still fall within that age range. Case study evidence suggests that a strong version of cognitive development as causal to language development is not tenable.

A second area of evidence on the separateness of language and cognition is that of second language data. Sequential second language learners, those who acquire a second language after the first, are, one assumes, cognitively developed. This greater cognitive development has been used to explain differences in the order of acquisition for certain morphemes in second and first language data. Such an explanation for differences has been questioned in two ways. First, some studies show a high degree of correlation with first language orders. A more basic question, however, is why there should be *any* similarity between first and second language data if cognitive development were the driving force behind order of acquisition of language features. That is, with greater cognitive development, the orders in which second language learners acquire parts of the language would logically be radically different. Time should not be learned after place. Why/because relationships should not be acquired later than where/location relationships. In spite of cognitive development, however, the order of acquisition of these and many other features agrees substantially with that of first language acquisition. Since this is the case, the influence of cognitive development on language acquisition must be somewhat suspect.

While it is true that cognitive development and language development may grow side by side in early childhood, an interrelational model that sees cognition as the basis (or causal factor) for language development does not seem to be without pitfalls. Evidence in support of this model may be strong in child language research. However, research in second language acquisition and in case studies of high language/low cognition individuals have posed problems which must be solved before language can be seen as simply one of several cognitive capacities dependent on cognitive development.

Cognitive Style

However, the link between cognition and language development is seen in other ways as well. There is a growing body of literature that looks at cognitive style as important to success in second language learning. Wittrock (1978) has defined "cognitive style" as the relatively stable way that people "perceive, conceptualize, and organize information." This style is seen as stable over time, though dependence on one cognitive style can be shifted over time (e.g., in response to education requirements). Field dependence/field independence is, perhaps, the dual factor most mentioned in discussions of cognitive style in second language research.

According to Witkin et al. (1977), *field dependence* is a global cognitive style where the individual fails to differentiate parts of a "field" from the general background (i.e., can't see the trees for the forest). *Field independence* is the cognitive style used by people who identify, organize, and impose structure on the parts of the field (i.e., see the trees and organize them within a forest). Second language teachers and researchers both comment on the global way in which some of their learners appear to produce language (e.g., Gough's 1975 case study of Homer) in contrast to the analytical approach of others (e.g., Huang's 1978 case study of Paul).

The psychological test for field independence/dependence is the Embedded Figures Test, or the Rod and Frame Test. In the visual mode, some people are extremely good at locating "hidden figures." Perhaps you remember the puzzles in *Jack and Jill* and other children's magazines which required you to find ten smiling faces in a landscape (hidden in tree foliage, ocean waves, curtains, etc.). If you could see them all immediately, you would probably score high on the ETS (Educational Testing Service) version, the Hidden Figures Test. In this test you are shown a figure and then asked to find it again in an array of figures. For example, try to find this figure in the array.

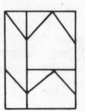

Field independence/dependence can also be tested with objects tactilely presented. Having once felt an object, the S must then find it again within the total assembled object. It has also been tested aurally, where the S is asked to isolate three tones in a ten-tone melody. The ability to separate out pieces from a whole may be useful in language learning in some way. Perhaps one is more easily able to attend to such things as morphemes or other function markers. Interestingly, women, persons over fifty, and members of some ethnic groups appear to be more field dependent than men, people under fifty, and members of majority groups. This is puzzling, since field independence has been shown to be one of the best predictors of second language learning success. Since field independence reportedly increases with age in a gradual upward slope until age fifty and then levels off and declines, the optimal age hypothesis would be in real trouble if field independence were related in any causal way. Older women from ethnic minority groups should also be the least adept second language learners (a prediction that I have never seen substantiated). Of course, tests of language learning have always been general proficiency tests, so perhaps high field independence really means good test-taking ability.

Hartnett(1980), in an excellent review of the literature, also lists other dual sets within cognitive style. One of these, the *verbal/imaginal* cognitive style, has been researched by Paivio (1971). Individuals are thought to process verbally in a sequential, linguistic manner, or they may process using a visual/spatial imaginal style. This dual coding again is related to hemispheric preference in problem solving—verbal being left hemisphere and imaginal being right hemisphere. The generative instructional method proposed by Wittrock and others seems to combine these two processing styles. Students are asked to verbally process and then transform what has been processed into imaginal, pictorial, visual-spatial memory as well.

A third dual style is the *analytical/relational* dichotomy. Analytic learners are those who tend to group objects by function or by abstract qualities that objects share. Relational learners depend much more on the global qualities in processing. Zelinker and Jeffrey (1976) found that reflective learners have an analytical cognitive style, while impulsive children use a more global cognitive style when matching figures by their salient characteristics. In this style dichotomy, according to Hartnett, the analytic cognitive style is associated with abstracting information from a stimulus to reality, while the relational mode sees meaning only in the global characteristic of the stimulus associated to some total context. The relational mode is also described as self-centered in its orientation to reality.

Pask and Scott (1972) have identified another dual set: *serialist/holist* cognitive competencies. In the serialist mode, the individual consistently assimilates long sequences of information, being intolerant of irrelevant material. The holist competency is one where the individual learns and recalls information as a whole, imaging entire principles and being able to deal with extraneous information.

Luria (1966) believed that memory and reasoning are guided either in a linear or a simultaneous fashion. These two cognitive processing modes have been called *sequential successive/simultaneous synthesis.* Das (1973) and others who describe this dichotomy claim that neither cognitive style is superior (that is, marked by higher intelligence).

Hartnett summarizes all these characteristics as follows:

Analytical Cognitive Styles	*Holistic Cognitive Styles*
1. field-independent (Witkin)	1. field-dependent
2. verbal (Paivio)	2. imaginal
3. analytic (Zelinker & Jeffrey)	3. relational
4. serialist (Pask & Scott)	4. holist
5. sequential-successive (Das)	5. simultaneous-synthesis

She then relates these to what neurolinguists and psychologists suggest are left hemisphere and right hemisphere functions:

Left Hemisphere Functions	*Right Hemisphere Functions*
1. propositional thought (Bogen)	1. appositional thought
2. time-related judgments (Carmon & Nachson)	2. spatial relations (Levy-Agresti & Sperry)
3. linear processing (Efron)	3. gestalt-synthetic processing (Kimura)
4. abstracts essentials (Bogen)	4. part-to-whole judgments (Nebes)

It has also been suggested that eye movement is a reliable predictor of hemispheric preference in problem solving. That is, almost everyone has to pause a moment to think when asked "What is your grandmother's maiden name?" or "Count backward from 100 by 7's." As we pause, our eyes move characteristically either to the left or right. This is an indirect test of hemispheric preference in problem solving. Hartnett has summarized these characteristics as follows:

Right Eye Movement	*Left Eye Movement*
1. higher scores on the math subscales of the SAT (Bakan)	1. self-report clearer imagery (Bakan)
2. higher scores on concept identification tests (Weitan & Etaugh)	2. classical/humanistic majors (Bakan)
3. majors in science/quantitative areas (Bakan)	3. easier to hypnotize (Bakan)
	4. creative, artistic, social (Bakan, Weitan & Etaugh)

From this summary and a comparison of the sets of terms, Hartnett claims that two cognitive styles can be identified, analytic and holistic. Since, according to Hartnett the two are separate (rather than the two ends of a continuum), it is quite possible for one to use different cognitive approaches at different times and still show a preference for one style over the other.

In second language research, as mentioned earlier, field independence (which Hartnett relates to analytic style) has been found to correlate significantly with language learning success. Brown (1977) suggested that field independence/field dependence differences might be related to Krashen's learning versus acquisition distinction, with field independence being more important in classroom instruction than in natural acquisition. Researchers working on cognitive style emphasize that neither style is superior to the other, but it is clear that instruction emphasizes analytic over holistic approaches.

Hartnett (1975) tested students learning Spanish in a university setting. Using the eye movement measure, she divided the learners into two cognitive style groups—analytic and holistic. She then found that most students selected Spanish classes that used methods that agreed with their cognitive style preferences. That is, analytic students selected classes that emphasized grammar rules and grammar explanations, and holistic learners selected more direct language classes with little or no emphasis on grammar rules. In addition, students who did not enroll in classes that matched their style did less well than those who picked matched classes. Nevertheless, the group with analytic cognitive style did better overall than the holistic group.

In a follow-up to this study, Hartnett (1980) looked at adult ESL students, this time using a ratio of their analytic to holistic scores to identify learner cognitive style. Students were then taught and tested on the form and function of the English passive voice on the basis of one of two treatments. One treatment emphasized a visual, holistic approach and the other a more rule-oriented analytic step-by-step presentation. Students, regardless of their cognitive style ratio, did better if instructed by the analytic treatment. Hartnett suggests that a variety of explanations could be given for this finding, but among them we must consider that perhaps cognitive style is not as critical as methodology, at least in short-term treatment studies.

Intelligence

Finally, cognition has been considered in terms of what we might call intelligence. Certainly, in the discussion presented at the beginning of this chapter, cognition relates to intelligence. The problem is how to define intelligence and its relationship to language learning, particularly second language learning. Wechsler (1944) defined intelligence as the ability "to act purposefully, to think rationally, and to deal effectively with the environment." This coincides with Piaget's emphasis on adaptive behavior as basic to intelligence. Others define intelligence as the ability to think abstractly. One would assume, then (if one believes in Piagetian stages in which the ability to think abstractly is acquired very late), that the young child has no intelligence. Early theorists believed that intelligence is an all-encompassing factor influencing one's abilities in all areas. The more intelligent you are, the better you are at everything. Spearman (1927) suggested that intelligence consists of two factors, a general factor (the g factor), which he believed underlies all performance, and a specific factor (the *s* factor) which influences specific abilities (thus accounting for the fact that one's math scores might be much higher than verbal scores). Thurstone and Thurstone (1941) expanded the number of factors included within intelligence. Using factor analysis techniques, they found seven factors which they labeled memory, reasoning, number, perceptual speed, space, verbal comprehension, and word fluency. Taking factor analysis several steps further, Guilford (1959) proposed a 3-dimensional model of intelligence. This model gives us 120 separate components for intelligence (see Figure 12.1). The three dimensions, *operations, contents,* and *products,* are shown in Table 1.

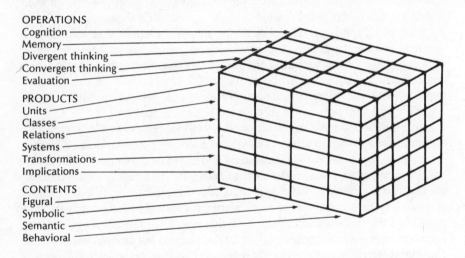

OPERATIONS
Cognition
Memory
Divergent thinking
Convergent thinking
Evaluation

PRODUCTS
Units
Classes
Relations
Systems
Transformations
Implications

CONTENTS
Figural
Symbolic
Semantic
Behavioral

Figure 12.1   Guilford's 3-dimensional Model of Intelligence

Using Guilford's model, tests have been devised for many different facets of intelligence. The Street test is a common one used to determine cognition of figural units. In this test one is asked to recognize pictures of familiar objects even though parts of the silhouettes of the objects are missing. (This test, along with eye-movement tests, has been used to identify persons with holistic cognitive styles.) To test the ability to make transformations of meaning in semantic relations, the child may be asked to state several ways in which two objects (oranges and apples, chairs and tables) are similar. To test divergent production of semantic transformations, students are asked to list as many appropriate titles for a story as possible. People who give lots of appropriate titles are credited with ideational fluency. But to get credit for originality or creativity, they have to come up with clever, unusual answers. There are, then, possibilities for testing all 120 cells in Guilford's model.

The question is how these components of intelligence relate to language learning. Oller (1979) has talked about the common, unitary underlying factor,

Table 1 Guilford's Three Dimensions of Intelligence

OPERATIONS are the *ways* we think:
1. Cognition (discovery or recognition)
2. Memory
3. Divergent thinking (seeking new answers by exploring different avenues of thought)
4. Convergent thinking (leading to one right, or best, answer)
5. Evaluation (deciding about adequacy of knowledge)

The CONTENTS of our intellectual functioning—*what* we think about—may be:
1. Figural (concrete information perceived through our senses)
2. Symbolic (words and numbers)
3. Semantic (verbal meanings or ideas)
4. Behavioral (social intelligence)

PRODUCTS are the *results* of our thinking. They result from the application of *operation* to *content*:
1. Units (a single word, number, or idea)
2. Classes (set of related units)
3. Relations (relationships among units or classes)
4. Systems (logically organized ideas)
5. Transformations (changes and modifications in arrangements, organization, or meaning)
6. Implications (see certain consequences from the information given)

Spearman's *g* factor, which influences all of language learning. Language ability has always correlated highly with I.Q. measures, and it has often been assumed that language tests, in fact, measure the same thing intelligence tests measure. However, it seems unlikely that one general factor can underlie all of language learning and all of intelligence. If that were the case, only the very gifted would be excellent language learners. Happily, this is not so (as has been amply demonstrated by the language learning abilities of mentally retarded children and children with other learning disabilities, and the failure of many highly intelligent adults to acquire second languages easily). Such a causal statement takes us back to the arguments presented earlier in this chapter. No one, however, has taken all the facets of intelligence identified by Guilford and tried to determine which factors, or sets of factors, are most clearly related to language learning success.

Memory

It is clear from the literature, however, that memory (Guilford's second operation) may be as important to second language learning as cognitive style. Despite all the research done on memory, it too is difficult to define. For many of us, memory is apparently a permanent record of our experiences. In this static view of memory, we believe that nothing is lost; everything is permanently stored somewhere in our brains. In recalling an event, we believe we relive it, and that all the surrounding meaningless details are still there, attached to the event. Others argue that we recreate a total recall from memory traces and that the traces seem "real" in the same way that vivid dreams appear to be totally recalled. Under hypnosis, some psychologists believe that one can be truly age-regressed and that this is a true return to that permanent memory record of one's experiences. Again, other psychologists claim that hypnosis only frees re-pressed memory traces, allowing one to recreate a memory of what would otherwise have been remembered anyway.

Penfield and Roberts, in reports on electrical stimulation of cortical areas of the brain, found patients often startled by sudden recall of such clarity that they felt that some stored experience was actually recurring. For example, one patient, J.T., who had come to Canada from his home in South Africa, cried out when his right temporal lobe was electrically stimulated: "Yes, Doctor! Yes, Doctor! Now I hear people laughing—my friends—in South Africa." Later, J.T. commented on his double awareness and expressed astonishment, for it had seemed to him that he was with his cousins at home and he and two women were laughing together. He did not, however, remember what they were laughing at. Penfield says that "doubtless he would have discovered that also, if the strip of experience had begun earlier, or if the surgeon had continued the stimulation a little longer." (1959, p. 50)

Paradis (1977) also comments on case studies where patients recovered "unavailable" languages during special states such as epileptic fits, delirium, and hypnosis. Such studies give some support for memory as a permanent record which may or may not be accessible. Is it the case, then, that children who once knew but have since forgotten a language actually have it permanently stored in memory? Case studies that mention quick retrieval of a seemingly once known but forgotten language abound in the anecdotal opinion of our field.

Reviewing the literature on age regression under hypnosis, Campbell and Schumann (1981) found four studies which relate to language remembering. The two most interesting are those of Reiff and Scheerer (1959) and Fromm (1970). Reiff and Scheerer described a twenty-six-year-old woman who had been a high school Latin champion. She no longer was able to do the tasks (verb conjugation, noun declensions, and translations) which had won her a medal at age sixteen. Under hypnosis and age regression, however, she once more accurately performed these tasks. Fromm, during a demonstration of hypnosis and age regression for a psychology class at the University of Chicago, found her twenty-six-year-old Japanese-American subject unexpectedly speaking a "stream of Japanese—he talked on and on for about fifteen to twenty minutes." Unfortunately, the session was not tape-recorded. The subject was just as surprised as the hypnotist, since he was unaware of any competence in Japanese. The experiment was repeated and no Japanese was exhibited when he was age-regressed to age seven, nor at age five. However, when regressed to age three, he again initiated a monologue about a puppy in Japanese. Fromm found that shortly after his birth the family had moved to a relocation camp. After the war, they moved to Utah where they had no Japanese contacts, nor was Japanese used as a home language. Does such data substantiate fixed memory, a permanent and full representation of experiences, or is this another example where a repressed memory has been released? The argument is not whether information is stored; certainly it is, in some way. But it may be reconstructed in recall, rebuilt and refleshed, and revisualized. That is, memory may be a constructive process rather than retrieval of something which was stored as a static whole.

Neisser strongly advocates the active "constructive" view of memory.

The cognitive approach to memory and thought emphasizes that recall and problem-solving are constructive acts based on information remaining from earlier acts. That information, in turn, is organized according to the structure of those earlier acts, though its utilization depends on present circumstances and present constructive skills. (1967, p. 292)

In order to use earlier experience selectively in reconstructing a memory, Neisser suggests there must be some agent that does the selection, searches memory, and processes and reconstructs it anew. Is it, Neisser asks, "the little man in the head," the homunculus? While it is difficult for us to consider some other self doing this for us, and while such speculation reduces us to talking about self within self within self, some agent has to do this work. Otherwise, "we" would have to consciously sort through memory, pull out or censor, construct and reconstruct. These constructive processes are never conscious, though their final product is. Neisser suggested that we could view this agent in terms of a computer model with executive routines and lower-level routines available for such work. Of course, the problem then is to discover who wrote the program for the executive to begin with. In this view of memory, we can see how closely related memory processes and language processes may be. And we can also understand why memory processes are important to language learning. The same sorts of processes seem to be called for in both.

Echoic memory is also seen as important to language learning. Tucker, Arthur, and others have suggested that a strong echoic memory may be a good predictor of second language learning success. Neisser has suggested that auditory memory may be rhythmically organized. This explains our ability to know what part of a series certain recalled numbers come from, even though we can't recall all the numbers in the series. In tasks that ask for recall of digits or words, it has often been noted that the last numbers or last words may be recalled while earlier ones are not. The inability to do backward recall, Neisser suggests, may be due to the distortion of rhythmic pattern when recall must be in reverse order. When long strings are to be remembered, and neither the beginning nor the end are specified in advance, the subject must wait for the end of the series, all the while attempting to organize and reorganize the relations between the numbers (or words) and rhythmic structures. If rhythmic structure does underlie immediate echoic memory, then disruption of rhythm should seriously affect recall. Since it does, one might wonder how rhythmic organization of a new language changes verbal memory. Students from syllable-timed languages (for example, Japanese or Spanish) should exhibit great difficulty in echoic memory of English.

When we hear a short span of language, we are able to recall it for some length of time so long as we are not distracted by other incoming messages. The question is: How many different levels of storage—"short-term store," "medium-term store," "long-term store," etc.—are there before information is truly "stored in memory" for use when recalled?

That memory is a cognitive process related to language learning is clear in this summary of Neisser's position:

1) Stored information consists of traces of previous constructive mental (or overt) actions. 2) The primary process is a multiple activity, somewhat analogous to parallel processing in computers, which constructs crudely formed "thoughts," or "ideas," on the basis of stored information. . . . Its products are only fleetingly conscious, unless they undergo elaboration by secondary processes. 3) The secondary processes of directed thought and deliberate recall . . . are serial in character, and construct ideas and images which are determined partly by stored information, partly by the preliminary organization of the primary processes, and partly by wishes and expectations. 4) The executive control of thinking in the secondary process is carried out by a system analogous to the executive routine of a computer program. It is not necessary to postulate a homunculus to account for the directed character of thought. 5) The secondary processes themselves are mostly acquired through experience, in the same way that all other memories—which also represent earlier *processes*—are acquired. 6) Failures to recall information which is actually in storage are like failures to notice something in the visual field, or failures to hear something that has been said. The executive processes of recall may be directed elsewhere, either deliberately or because of a misguided strategy of search; they may also lack the necessary constructure abilities altogether. (1967, pp. 303–304)

Clearly, such a definition of memory as part of cognitive structure is very similar in part to proposals made for procedural grammar. That is, it is this process of reconstruction of memory which must precede the start-up of the programs for lexically driven syntactic structures.

In his conclusion, Neisser suggests that truly satisfactory theories of higher mental processes can only come into being when we also have theories of motivation, personality, and social interaction. To that list we should also add theories of language. While cognition, memory, and language may all be separate in some sense, all are similar in the sense that all are *processes*. With Neisser's view of cognition as process, many of the earlier objections to an interrelated model of language and cognition become much less convincing. Although there may be no Great Borrowing taking place, it seems sensible to think that some raiding of systems is going on, as Bates proposed. The question is whether cognition and language processes have one common unified core, whether one develops from the other, or whether each develops separately but works in similar ways. Much may ultimately be learned about cognition, memory, and language development by comparing the kinds of models which might account for each.

13 *Plan Levels Revisited*

From a psycholinguistic perspective, language processing and language production can be thought of as involving several plan levels. I have presented each plan, one level at a time, beginning with the "lowest" levels and concluding with the "highest" levels. Although this suggests that plans are stacked like boxes one atop the other, you should not infer that each level influences *only* the ones below it. To do so would mean that speech setting controls speech event that controls syntax that controls lexicon that controls morphology that controls phonology that controls phonetics, like the house that Jack built. Yet, just as each event in the house that Jack built has some independence, so each plan has some independence. And we can, if we wish, reorganize the "house" in slightly different ways.

In Chapter 1 we saw how lower levels *can* affect higher levels. This is especially true for the intonation plan. We can change a sentence that seems to be affirmative into a negative by overlaying an ironic intonation curve on it. We can change the speech act value of the sentence by changing intonation. A statement may become a command; a question may become a complaint. Intonation plans frequently appear to override other, supposedly higher level, plans. It is, therefore, often separated from phonology and placed higher than syntax.

Syntax is a high level plan; however, lexical choice, a lower-level plan, may cause us to repair the syntax of the utterance. That is, we begin with a syntactic plan but, because of a lexical choice, we may have to repair it. We can think of this either as a "slip" (in which case, theoretically, we should repair the lexical items, *not* the syntax) or as a real reshuffling of levels with the lexical "box" momentarily slipping up over the syntactic "box." Or we may decide that syntax is really lexically driven and so move the lexical level above syntax.

A set of boxes stacked one atop another may not be the best analogy. A Slinky toy might be more appropriate. We can pick up the Slinky and hold it vertically, a spiraling set of interconnected circles. We can turn it upside down.

Or we can hold it in both hands, raising and lowering the sides at will. We can pluck out one circle of the Slinky and make that our focal point, letting everything else go for the moment. We can find lots of examples of one circle or plan capturing focus. Children, for example, may become momentarily (and delightfully) trapped in the *phonological* plan level during language play (Peck, 1978):

L2 child	Native speaker child
	Oooh, I got!—no—dong!
Doyng!	Doyng, I said darn!
No! I said doyng,	doyng
doyng, boom.	Doyng, doyng, doyng.
Doyng.	/ɪd/ Dong. Ding-Dong!
	That was—remember Dong?

When we are tired or in a playful mood we may do stream-of-consciousness talk that looks like play, trapped momentarily at the *lexical* level:

Call it anything you like—a method, a framework, a theory, a model, strategies, hypotheses, hyperboles—oh, god, I can't even think! Really, I don't care what you call it.

Children (first language learners in crib monologues or child second language learners in a variety of environments) engage in play at the *syntactic* level (Peck, 1978):

L2 child	Native speaker child
	I can't do it. I just...
	Do what? Do this. Do this-do what.
Do that.	Do what. Do that, do what D-D-D-D
	D-D-Ummm /də/ (4 X)
My daddy's in Mexico.	

And children also can use just the *discourse* level, filling in nonsense for lexicon. For example, arguments take certain forms. They can be rapid one-word exchanges (yes-no-yes-no) which build in volume to a peak, or the long build-up with increased volume may come from just one speaker in response to a challenge. Enrique, Young's (1974) second language learner, responding to an "I can beat your brother up" challenge, uses the discourse plan effectively, filling in all the rest with nonsense, building volume to the final crescendo required by discourse form:

You can beat him, huh. I can beat him to my party 'n you can beat him 'n you can beat my brother. He beat you up. You (noise building in volume) it. *I CAN BEAT YOU UP.*

A Slinky may be a more accurate analogy since it lets us see how learners use (or become trapped by) one level and how low levels on occasion can override other higher levels. Yet a Slinky still does not represent the plans in a very sensible way. Perhaps a traffic model is a better analogy. Think of all the plans as emptying output into a traffic system. As we talk, alternative and vying output may be produced at each plan level. A series of stop lights must be shunting off much of this alternative production before it even gets off the side streets into the mainstream of traffic. Then some sort of traffic director must be rerouting some of the more appropriate material onto on-ramps ready to go into the main message which has captured the communication channel. Other possible alternatives then get moved up to the on-ramps in case something goes wrong in the channel and the message needs to be repaired or reworked in some way.

Repairs along the way sometimes do result in better planned messages, but sometimes what comes out shows us that something somehow got by the stop lights and the traffic director. Take the following example from teacher talk (Chaudron, 1979):

> ...a weigh scale. You weigh a fish. You can weigh the scales off the fish.

What could the final sentence mean? Such an example is not a bizarre case. If you were to record class lectures, you would surely find many such examples where something has come up out of place, touched off by word or phonological associations. Some people seem much more prone to this sort of escape of vying messages, but it is not abnormal behavior by any means.

Such behavior becomes abnormal when the person is not able to get out of one plan level. That is, many of us do—either playfully, willfully, or when very relaxed—let lexical items touch off multiple associations. We may let sounds touch off other associations in word play. Or we may go around singing, "ii, ee, u, a, a, ting tang walla walla bing bang" for days on end. But we can do other things as well. These are only parts of a wide repertoire which we use for various functions. We are seldom limited or trapped by any one level or set of levels for long.

When speech pathologists talk about such speech as symptomatic of certain disorders, what they mean is that the speaker does not seem to use the same repertoire of plans that we use and that he or she seems to use certain plans much more than we do. All of us stutter at times, but not to the same degree as the stutterer, all of us make many repairs in our speech but not as many as others, all of us do sound and word play but not as much as others. When we see data representative of schizophrenic speech:

> My mother's name was Bill. (pause, low pitch as in an aside, but with marked rising question intonation)... and coo? (strong, loud) St. Valentine's Day is the official startin' of the breedin' season of birds. All buzzards can coo. I like to see it pronounced buzzards rightly. They work hard. So do parakeets.
>
> (Chaika, 1974)

The associations *(bill and coo, Valentine's Day, breeding, bill of birds that co, buzzards, parakeets)* seem remarkably rich. We might hope to achieve the same richness in writing poetry, but it is not likely that we would allow such associations to escape during normal conversation. It may happen on rare occasions, but we expect to have a range of language quite different from this as well.

In this volume I have tried to show that the plans have some reality, and that that reality is established by data from normal monolinguals, language disordered patients, and first and second language acquisition and use—in other words, from all language behavior. Somehow learners must be able to create the processing mechanisms for each plan as they acquire the language. The units within the plans and the rules (or processes) within the units may be quite different from those proposed in linguistic descriptions. Learners must also maintain control (unconscious control, to be sure) over all the plans, the interactions among them, and the rules within them while communicating. From a descriptive standpoint, the task seems formidable, and yet humans are amazingly adept at communication that follows these requirements.

In the same spirit, then, let us think of what must happen if we have within each plan level not just one but two languages. It may sound silly to say we must now have stop signs that work for both languages, albeit using slightly different rules or sets of conditions, or that we must have bilingual traffic directors. But something of this sort would be necessary if our traffic analogy is to work.

Consider the fluent bilingual who shifts rapidly back and forth, selecting effectively from each language. The traffic director would have no problem if the learner only wanted to insert a few "you know's" or "no?'s" in the correct places:

Atashi suki da yo, *you know.*
It's about the same, *no?*
Er du faerdig, you slow-poke? Saa korer vi.

(Hatch, 1976)

But consider the problems of the traffic director when both languages are fully utilized:

C: Cuéntame del juego.
R: Mmmm, primero they were leading diez pa' nada.
C: ¿Diez a nada? ¡Issh! ¿Y luego?
R: Then there was our team to bat and we made . . . 'cimos dos carreras. And then ellos fueron a batear. Hicieron una y then nosotros 'cimos cinco. Despues 'ciron six, 'ciron cinco.
C: Siete.
R: And then they made dos and then it was our time to bat and we made . . .
C: ¿Cuántas?
R: Ah . . . five or six. And then they beat us by five runs.

(Lance, 1969)

No wonder so few psycholinguists want to seriously consider second language data in building models of language production.

But before this skillful interplay of languages can take place, the learner must have acquired some fluency in the languages. The psycholinguistic notion of plans may not at first say much about how that process takes place. Yet it does present a framework for making certain predictions about language acquisition. It also makes us aware that investigation of language acquisition can occur within each plan but, in the end, must include *all* levels. Until one can control all plans, one really cannot be considered totally bilingual. Until our research considers more than just a few aspects of each plan, we really cannot claim to know much about bilingualism.

From the research reports presented in the preceding chapters, it should be clear that there are two major strands flowing through all levels for the researcher interested in second language behavior: first, a tradition of looking at language contrasts as being either between first and second language or among language typologies. The second strand is Interlanguage research. Interlanguage research has been mainly descriptive. That is, no strong claims have been made beyond some general universals of language learning. Within this strand, we find descriptions of naturalness theory and of the syllable as the universal unit in phonology, predictions on coreness or markedness in lexicon, predictions that basic syntactic propositions will be easiest to process, and claims for a natural order for acquisition of inflectional morphology.

To move beyond this requires another strand—one that is linked to sociolinguistics—(a) the study of the form of language addressed to the learner; and (b) the study of speech events in language use. Study of the input to the learner and the interaction that determines that input is now seen as a major way to understand how acquisition of languages is possible. Research on language use, particularly on the speech event, will undoubtedly become another major area.

Model building has also been restricted in important ways by our view of what is to be included within psycholinguistics and applied linguistics. In a sense, this depends on one's view of what linguistics is. Lewis and Cherry (1977) describe three major models. The first, the reductionist position, assumes that language and cognitive and social knowledge exist independent of one another (see Figure 13.1). From this point of view, social and cognitive factors are irrelevant to the study of language acquisition, comprehension, and production. One can ask many interesting questions about units of language

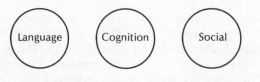

Figure 13.1   Reductionist Model

analysis, the sequence in which particular parts of language are acquired, the difficulty of syntactic structures, and so on. The model, however, limits the phenomena to be explained and the kinds of explanations that can be given. Since social and cognitive factors can be ignored, causality can be ascribed only to the individual's existing linguistic system. That is, language learners (first and second) acquire a new structure because the language system learned so far allows for the acquisition of the new form. A problem for those who prefer this model, according to Lewis and Cherry, is that there can be little communication among researchers in linguistics, psychology, language teaching, sociology, and language pathology (while suspicion of researchers in other fields may be promoted).

A second model is an interactionist model. This model assumes that language and social interaction and cognitive knowledge are interrelated in a unidimensional way (see Figure 13.2). Language is seen as derived from, or

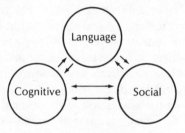

Figure 13.2   Interaction Model

strongly influenced by, cognitive and social interaction factors. Social and cognitive knowledge are each strongly influenced by language factors. Language, social interaction, and cognitive knowledge are still discrete, but each influences the others. Research within this model looks at the cognitive and perceptual requirements that are prerequisites or precursors of acquisition of parts of the language system. It also considers the socialization process as a prerequisite or precursor to language growth. Cognition and/or socialization are, to some greater extent, seen as causal factors in language learning. This model, like the reductionist model, limits what is to be researched. It ignores the parts of language, cognitive, and social systems that do not interact. This approach to research, Lewis and Cherry claim, encourages communication among linguists, sociologists, and psychologists, while keeping each field separate.

The third model is the unified model (Figure 13.3). Individuals have a highly integrated system of social, cognitive, and language knowledge that is basic, but, with age, may become differentiated and specialized. For this model, Lewis and Cherry draw the analogy of a tree: the trunk represents the unified system of knowledge, and the branches represent the separate, more specialized areas.

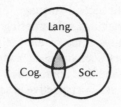

Figure 13.3   Unified Model

Some of the branches are independent, while others are interdependent. Researchers who follow this model are concerned primarily with discovering the common basis that makes all communication possible. Hymes (1972) has called this common basis "communicative competence." The investigation (and defining) of communicative competence has been a central issue in applied linguistics for several years. This model does not limit the field of research. Since it is holistic in approach, researchers are free to focus where they will. While their focus may be on some discrete point, researchers will always see language learning as a unified development with causal threads moving in and out of the three major areas of knowledge.

Adherence to any one of these three models (or to another) is likely to be based on training, on how convinced one is by evidence from one side or the other, on the area of interest, and on the degree of ambiguity tolerable in conducting research. Some student researchers feel uncomfortably fettered working within the reductionist model. They believe that too many factors which influence language learning, comprehension, and production must be ignored. Others, working in the integrated model, feel lost in some hazy, ever-changing fog, frustrated by a never-ending number of factors (all with different weights) which must be considered all at once.

The model we choose colors the areas of psycholinguistics or applied linguistics we look to for explanations of language learning, comprehension, and production. For the psycholinguist interested in second language acquisition, adopting a reductionist outlook would be simpler than trying to work out relationships between cognition and two languages; or trying to discover what the core of cognition, two language systems, and social systems might consist of or which parts are independent and/or interdependent. This text has, perhaps, tread an unsteady line between the reductionist and unified models. That is, the research reported here has been mainly within the reductionist school, while unified explanations have been sought or appealed for.

For the psycholinguist, the most interesting research must be that which tests models such as these or which tests linguistic theories and descriptions within plan levels. Second language research has not had this psycholinguistic perspective as its major focus. This is partially due to a generally held view of the reductionist school that performance data can't say much of interest to the theoretical linguist. It is also partially due to the frequently held view of language teachers that everything about second language learning is so unified that it is useless to try to look at discrete rules, rule ordering, and grammar models. With such a focus, however, perhaps some of the prejudice on both sides can be broken so that applied linguists, sociolinguists, and psycholinguists will see that their research is interrelated and that the research questions of each are valid. My hope is that a psycholinguistic perspective in second language research will make this possible.

REFERENCES

Abramson, A. S., & Lisker, L. Discriminability along the voicing continuum: cross-language tests. In *Proceedings,* VI International Congress of Phonological Science, 1967. Prague: Academia, 1970.

Adams, J. *Donald Copey of Harvard.* Boston: Houghton Mifflin, 1960.

Adams, M. The acquisition of morphology rules by kindergarten children in the process of learning a second language. 250K paper, March, 1972.

Albert, M., & Obler, L. Mixed polyglot aphasia. Paper presented at 13th Annual Meeting of Academy of Aphasia, Victoria, British Columbia, 1975.

Algeo, J. The voguish uses of non-. *American Speech,* 1971, *46,* 87–105.

Allwright, R. Turns, topics and tasks. In D. Larsen-Freeman (ed.), *Discourse analysis in second language research.* Rowley, Mass.: Newbury House, 1980, 165–187.

Al-Naggar, Z. An analytical study of errors found in English written expression of students of the English Section, Faculty of Education, Ain Shams University, M.A. thesis, 1977.

Amastae, J. The acquisition of English vowels. *Papers in Linguistics,* 1978, *11,* 3–4, 423–458.

Amastae, J. On markedness and sociolinguistic variation. In E. L. Blansitt & R. V. Teschner (eds.), *A festschrift for Jacob Ornstein.* Rowley, Mass.: Newbury House, 1981.

Ammon, P. The perception of grammatical relations in sentences. *Journal of Verbal Learning and Verbal Behavior,* 1968, *7,* 869–875.

Andersen, E. Learning to speak with style: a study of sociolinguistic skills of children. Ph.D. dissertation, Stanford University, Stanford, Calif., 1977.

Andersen, R. The impoverished state of cross-sectional morphology acquisition/accuracy methodology. *Working Papers on Bilingualism,* 1977, *14,* 49–82.

Andersen, R. An implicational model for second language research. *Language Learning,* 1978, *28,* 2, 221–282.

Anderson, S. Why phonology isn't "natural." *UCLA Working Papers in Phonetics,* 1980, *51,* 36–93.

Antinucci, F., & Miller, R. How children talk about what happened. *Journal of Child Language,* 1976, *3,* 169–189.

Aranoff, M. *Word formation in generative grammar.* Cambridge, Mass.: MIT Press, 1976.

Arthur, B. Short term changes in EFL compositions. In C. Yorio, K. Perkins, & J. Schachter (eds.), *On TESOL 79, the learner in focus.* Washington, D.C.: TESOL, 1979, 301–342.

Arthur, B., Weiner, R., Culver, M., Lee, Y. E., & Thomas, D. The register of impersonal discourse to foreigners. In D. Larsen-Freeman (ed.), *Discourse analysis in second language research.* Rowley, Mass.: Newbury House, 1980, 111–124.

Asher, J., & Garcia, R. The optimal age to learn a foreign language. *Modern Language Journal,* 1969, *53,* 5, 334–341.

Asher, J., & Price, B. The learning strategy of total physical response: some age differences. *Child Development*, 1967, *38*, 1220–1227.

Atkinson, M. Prerequisites for reference. In E. Ochs & B. Schieffelin (eds.), *Developmental pragmatics*. New York: Academic Press, 1979.

Atkinson, R. Mnemonotechnics and second language learning. *American Psychologist*, 1975, *30*, 821–825.

Austerlitz, R. Gilyak nursery words. *Word*, 1956, *12*, 260–279.

Austin, J.L. *How to do things with words*. Cambridge, Mass.: Harvard University Press, 1962.

Bach, E., & Harms, R.T. How do languages get "crazy rules"? In R. Stockwell & R. Macauley (eds.), *Linguistic change and generative theory*. Bloomington: Indiana University Press, 1972.

Bailey, K. Teaching in a second language: the communicative competence ·of the non-native teaching assistant. Ph.D. dissertation, UCLA, 1982.

Bailey, N., Madden, C., & Krashen, S. Is there a "natural sequence" in adult second language learning? *Language Learning*, 1974, *24*, 2, 235–243.

Bakan, P. The eyes have it. *Psychology Today*, 1971, *4*, 64–69.

Bakan, P., & Strayer, F. F. On the reliability of conjugate lateral eye movements. *Perceptual and Motor Skills*, 1973, *36*, 429–430.

Baker, L. The lexicon: some psycholinguistic evidence. *UCLA Working Papers in Phonetics, 26*, 1974.

Barik, H. A look at simultaneous translation. *Working Papers on Bilingualism*, 1974, *4*, 20–42.

Bates, E. *The emergence of symbols*. New York: Academic Press, 1979.

Beebe, L. Sociolinguistic variation and style shifting in second language acquisition. *Language Learning*, 1980, *30*, 2, 433–448.

Bellugi, U. The emergence of inflection and negation systems in children's speech. Paper presented at the New England Psychological Association, 1964.

Bellugi, U.The development of interrogative structures in children's speech. In K. Riegel (ed.), *The development of language functions*. University of Michigan Language Development Project, Report 8, 1965.

Bellugi, U., & Brown, R. (eds.) The acquisition of language. Monograph of the Society of Research in Child Development, 1964, *29*, 1.

Bennett, T. An extended view of verb voice in written and spoken narratives. In E. Ochs Keenan & T. Bennett, Discourse analysis across time and space. *Southern California Occasional Papers in Linguistics*, University of Southern California, 1977, *5*.

Berko, J. The child's learning of English morphology. *Word*, 1958, *14*, 150–177.

Berman, R. The re-emergence of a bilingual: a case study of a Hebrew-English speaking child. *Working Papers on Bilingualism*, 1979, *19*, 157–180.

Bertkau, J.Comprehension and production of English relative clauses in adult second language and child first language acquisition. *Language Learning*, 1974, *24*, 2, 279–286.

Bickerton, D. Quantitative versus dynamic paradigms: the case of Montreal "Que." In C. Bailey & R. Shuy (eds.), *New ways of analyzing variations in English*. Washington, D.C.: Georgetown University Press, 1973, 23–43.

Blank, M., Gessner, M., & Esposito, A. Language without communication: a case study. *Child Language*, 1979, *6*, 2, 329–352.

Blank, M., & Keislar, E. A self-controlled audio-lingual program for children. *French Review*, 1966, *40*, 266–277.

Bloom, L., Lifter, K., & Hafitz, J. Semantics of verbs and the development of verb inflection in child language. *Language*, 1980, *56*, 2, 386–412.

Blount, B. Parental speech and language acquisition. *Anthropological Linguistics*, 1972, *14*, 119–130.

Blount, B., & Padgug, E. Prosodic, paralinguistic and interactional features of parent-child speech. *Journal of Child Language*, 1977, *4*, 67–86.

Bogen, J.E. The other side of the brain II: an appositional mind. *Bulletin of the Los Angeles Neurological Society,* 1969, *34,* 135–162.

Bolinger, D. *Generality, gradience, and the all-or-none.* The Hague: Mouton, 1961.

Bolinger, D. *Meaning and form.* London: Longman's, 1977.

Bolinger, D. Pronouns in discourse. In T. Givon (ed.), *Syntax and semantics, Vol. 12, Discourse and syntax.* New York: Academic Press, 1979, 289–309.

Bowditch, L. Why the what's are when. *Berkeley Linguistic Society,* 1976, *2,* 59–77.

Bowen, J., & Haggerty, T.A contrastive analysis of a lexical split: Spanish *hacer* to English *do/make,* etc. In R. Nash (ed.), *Readings in Spanish-English linguistics.* Puerto Rico: Inter-American Press, 1971.

Bowerman, M. Learning the structure of causative verbs: a study in the relationship of cognitive, semantic and syntactic development. In E. Clark (ed.), *Papers and Reports on Child Language Development, 8.*Linguistics Department, Stanford University, Stanford, Calif., 1974, 142–178.

Brega, E., & Newell, J. Comparison of performance by FLES program students and regular French III students on Modern Language Association tests. *French Review,* 1965, *39,* 433–438.

Bresnan, J. A realistic transformational grammar. In M. Halle, J. Bresnan, & G. Miller (eds.), *Linguistic theory and psychological reality.* Cambridge, Mass.: MIT Press, 1978.

Briere, E. An investigation of phonological interference. *Language,* 1966, *42,* 4, 768–796.

Broca, P. Remarques sur le siege de la faculte des langage articule, suivres d'une observation d'ephemie. *Bulletin de la Societe d'Anatomie,* 1861, *6,* 330–364. Reprinted in H. Hecaen & J. Dubois, *La naissance de la neuropsychologie du langage.* Paris: Flammarion, 1969.

Broen, P. The verbal environment of the language learning child. American Speech & Hearing Monographs, 1972, 17.

Brown, H.D. Children's comprehension of relativized English sentences. *Child Development,* 1971, *42,* 1923–1936.

Brown, H.D. Cognitive and affective characteristics of good language learners. *Proceedings, Second Language Acquisition Research Forum,* 1977, 349–354.

Brown, R. *The first language.* Cambridge, Mass.: MIT Press, 1973.

Brown, R. Introduction to C. Snow & C. Ferguson (eds.), *Talking to children.* New York: Cambridge University Press, 1977.

Brown, R., Cazden, C., & deVilliers, J. Directions for scoring 14 English morphemes obligatory in some contexts. Mimeo paper, Harvard University, n.d. Reprinted in *Working Papers on Bilingualism,* 1974, *3,* 39–43.

Brown, R., & McNeill, D. The tip of the tongue phenomenon. *Journal of Verbal Learning and Verbal Behavior,* 1966, *5,* 325–327.

Bruck, M., Lambert, W.E., & Tucker, G.R.Alternative forms of immersion for second language teaching. *Working Papers on Bilingualism,* June, 1976, *10,* 54 pages.

Bruck, M., & Schultz, J. An ethnographic analysis of the language use patterns of bilingually schooled children. *Working Papers on Bilingualism,* May, 1977, *13,* 33 pages.

Bruder, M., & Paulston, C. *TESL: techniques and procedures.* Cambridge, Mass.. Winthrop Publishers, 1976.

Brunak, J., Fain, E., & Villoria, N. Conversations with Rafaela. Second language acquisition project, UCLA, 1976.

Burling, R. Language development of a Garo and English-speaking child. In E. Hatch (ed.), *Second language acquisition.* Rowley, Mass.: Newbury House, 1978, 54–75.

Burstall, C. An optimal age for foreign language learning? *English Teachers' Journal* (Israel), 1975, *14,* 23–26.

Burstall, C., Jamieson, M., Cohen, S., & Hargreaves, M. *Primary French in the balance.* Slough: National Foundation for Educational Research, 1974.

Burt, M., Dulay, H., & Hernandez, E. *Bilingual syntax measure.* New York: Harcourt Brace, 1973.

Butterworth, G., & Hatch, E. A Spanish-speaking adolescent's acquisition of English syntax. In E. Hatch (ed.), *Second language acquisition.* Rowley, Mass.: Newbury House, 1978, 231–245.

Bye, T. Aspects of the acquisition of communicative competence: the role of listener oriented presupposition in producing directions. Ph.D. dissertation, UCLA, 1976.

Campbell, R., & Schumann, J. Hypnosis as a tool in second language research. In R. Andersen (ed.), *New dimensions in second language research.* Rowley, Mass.: Newbury House, 1981, 80–91.

Cancino, H., Rosansky, E., & Schumann, J. The acquisition of English negatives and interrogatives by native Spanish speakers. In E. Hatch (ed.), *Second language acquisition.* Rowley, Mass.: Newbury House, 1978, 207–230.

Caramazza, A., & Grober, E. Polysemy and the structure of the subjective lexicon. In R. Rameh (ed.), *Georgetown University round table on languages and linguistics.* Washington, D.C.: Georgetown University Press, 1976, 181–206.

Carey, S. The child as word learner. In M. Halle, J. Bresnan, & G. A. Miller, *Linguistic theory and psychological reality.* Cambridge, Mass.: MIT Press, 1979.

Carmon, A., & Nachson, I. Effect of unilateral brain damage on perception of temporal order. *Cortex,* 1971, *7,* 410–418.

Carrell, P. Background knowledge in second language comprehension. Paper presented at AILA, Lund, Sweden, 1981.

Carroll, J.B. *The teaching of French as a foreign language in eight countries.* New York: J. Wiley & Sons, 1975.

Carton, A.S. Inferencing: a process in using and learning language. In P. Pimsleur & T. Quinn (eds.), *The psychology of second language learning.* London: Cambridge University Press, 1971.

Casagrande, J. Comanche baby talk. *International Journal of American Linguistics,* 1948, *14,* 11–14.

Cazden, C. Environmental assistance to the child's acquisition of grammar. Ph.D. dissertation, Harvard University, 1965.

Cazden, C., Cancino, H., Rosansky, E., & Schumann, J. *Second language acquisition sequences in children, adolescents, and adults.* Final report, U.S. Dept. of HEW, August 1975.

Celce-Murcia, M. The simultaneous acquisition of English and French in a two-year-old. In E. Hatch (ed.), *Second language acquisition.* Rowley, Mass.: Newbury House, 1978, 38–53.

Celce-Murcia, M. Contextual analysis of English: application to TESL. In D. Larsen-Freeman (ed.), *Discourse analysis in second language research.* Rowley, Mass.: Newbury House, 1980, 41–55.

Celce-Murcia, M., & Rosensweig, F. Teaching vocabulary in the ESL classroom. In M. Celce-Murcia & L. McIntosh (eds.), *Teaching English as a second or foreign language.* Rowley, Mass.: Newbury House, 1979, 241–259.

Chaika, E. A linguist looks at "schizophrenic" language. *Brain and language,* 1974, *1,* 257–276.

Chaudron, C. Complexity of ESL teachers speech and vocabulary explanation/elaboration. Paper presented at TESOL, Boston, Mass., 1979.

Chaudron, C. Foreigner talk in the classroom. In H. Seliger & M. Long (eds.), *Classroom language acquisition and use: new perspectives.* Rowley, Mass.: Newbury House, in press.

Chiang, D.L. Predictors of relative clause production: the roles of overall proficiency, language interference, and complexity of linguistic feature. Paper presented at Second Language Acquisition Research Forum, Los Angeles, Calif., 1978.

Chomsky, C. *The acquisition of syntax in children from five to ten.* Cambridge, Mass.: MIT Press, 1969.

Cicourel, A. Language and the structure of beliefs in medical communication. Paper presented at AILA, Lund, Sweden, 1981.

Clark, E. What's in a word? On the child's acquisition of semantics in his first language. In T. Moore (ed.), *Cognitive development and the acquisition of language.* New York: Academic Press, 1973, 65–110.

Clark, H., & Clark, E. Semantic distinctions and memory for complex sentences. Quarterly Journal of Experimental Psychology. 1968, *20*, 2, 129–137.

Clark, H., & Clark, E. *Psychology and language: an introduction to psycholinguistics.* New York: Harcourt Brace Jovanovich, 1977.

Clyne, M. Multilingualism and pidginization in Australian industry. *Ethnic Studies,* 1977, *1,* 40–55.

Cohen, A., & Aphek, E. Easifying second language learning. Hebrew University, 1979. Available through ERIC ED 163–753.

Cohen, A., & Aphek, E. Retention of second language vocabulary over time: investigating the role of mnemonic associations. *System,* 1980, *8,* 221–235.

Cook, V.J. The comparison of language development in native children and foreign adults. *IRAL,* 1973, *11,* 1, 13–28.

Cook, V.J. Language function in second language learning and teaching. Paper presented at AILA, Lund, Sweden, 1981*a.*

Cook, V.J. Some uses of second language learning research. Paper presented at the New York Academy of Science on Native Language and Foreign Language Acquisition, New York, 1981*b.*

Cornejo, R.J. The acquisition of lexicon in the Spanish of bilingual children. In R.P. Turner (ed.), *Bilingualism in the Southwest.* Tucson, Ariz.: University of Arizona Press, 1973.

Corsaro, W.The clarification request as a feature of adult interactive styles with young children. *Language in Society,* 1977, *6,* 2, 183–207.

Cowan, N., & Leavitt, L.A.Talking backwards: speech play in late childhood. Paper presented at Second International Conference for the Study of Child Language. Vancouver, August 1981.

Cowan, N., Leavitt, L.A., Massaro, D., & Kent, R. A fluent backward talker. *Journal Speech and Hearing Research,* in press.

Cromer, R.F. Children are nice to understand: surface structure clues for the recovery of a deep structure. *British Journal of Psychology,* 1970, *61,* 397–408.

Crystal, D. *Prosodic systems and intonation in English.* London: Oxford University Press, 1969.

Curtiss, S. *Genie: a psycholinguistic study of a modern day wild child.* New York: Academic Press, 1977.

Curtiss, S., Fromkin, V., & Yamada, J. The independence of language as a cognitive system. Unpublished paper, UCLA, 1979.

Curtiss, S., Fromkin, V., & Yamada, J. How independent is language? On the question of formal parallels between grammar and action. *UCLA Working Papers on Cognitive Linguistics,* 1981, *1,* 131–157.

Daden, I. Conversational analysis and its relevance to TESL. M.A. thesis, UCLA. 1974.

Dalrymple-Alford, E., & Aamiry, A. Language and category clustering in bilingual free recall. *Journal of Verbal Learning and Verbal Behavior,* 1969, *8,* 762–768.

D'Amico-Reisner, L. Expressions of disapproval. Unpublished paper, University of Pennsylvania, 1981.

d'Anglejan, A., & Tucker, R. The acquisition of complex English structures by adult learners. *Language Learning,* 1975, *25,* 2, 281–296.

Das, J. P. Structure of cognitive abilities: evidence for simultaneous and successive processing. *Journal of Educational Psychology,* 1973, *65,* 1, 103–108.

d'Asaro, L. Comprehension of certain syntactic structures in five to ten year old children. Ph.D. dissertation, California School of Professional Psychiatry, 1973.

DeBeaugrande, R. Design criteria for process models of reading. *Reading Research Quarterly,* 1981, *2,* 261–315.

dePaulo, B., & Bonvillian, J. The effect of the special characteristics of speech addressed to children. *Journal of Psycholinguistic Research,* 1978, *7,* 3, 189–211.

deVilliers, J., & deVilliers, P. A cross-sectional study of the acquisition of grammatical morphemes in child speech. *Journal of Psycholinguistic Research,* 1973, *2,* 267–278.

deVilliers, J., & deVilliers, P.*Language acquisition.* Cambridge, Mass.: Harvard University Press, 1978.

Dickerson, L. The learner's Interlanguage as a system of variable rules. *TESOL Quarterly*, 1975, *9*, 401–407.

Drach, K. The language of the parent. *Working Paper 14*. Language Behavior Research Laboratory, University of California, Berkeley, 1979.

Dulay, H., & Burt, M.K. Should we teach children syntax? *Language Learning*, 1973, *23*, 245–258.

Dunkel, H. B., & Pillett, R.A. A second year of French in the elementary school. *Elementary School Journal*, 1957, *58*, 143–151.

Eckman, F. Markedness and the contrastive analysis hypothesis. *Language Learning*, 1977, *27*, 2, 315–330.

Eckstrand, L. H. Evaluation of teaching techniques and results on the basis of recorded tests from pupils in grades, 1, 2, 3, and 4. Swedish National Board of Education, 1964.

Eckstrand, L. H. Age and length of residence as variables related to the adjustment of migrant children, with special reference to second language learning. Paper presented at AILA, Stuttgart, 1975.

Efron, R. Temporal perception, aphasia and deja vu. *Brain*, 1963, *86*, 403.

Egan, O. Intonation and meaning. *Journal of Psycholinguistic Research*, 1980, *9*, 1, 23–39.

Eilers, R., Wilson, W., & Moore, J. Speech discrimination in the language innocent and the language wise: a study in the perception of voice onset time. *Journal of Child Language*, 1979, *6*, 1–18.

Eimas, P. Linguistic processing of speech by young infants. In R. Schiefelbusch & L. Lloyd (eds.), *Language perspectives: acquisition, retardation, and intervention*. Baltimore: University Park Press, 1974.

Ervin-Tripp, S. On sociolinguistic rules: alternation and co-occurrence. In J. Gumperz & D. Hymes (eds.), *Directions in sociolinguistics*. New York: Holt, Rinehart & Winston, 1972, 213–250.

Ervin-Tripp, S. Wait for me, rollerskate! In S. Ervin-Tripp & C. Mitchell-Kernan, *Child discourse*. New York: Academic Press, 1977.

Fanselow, J. Beyond Rashomon—conceptualizing and describing the teaching act. *TESOL Quarterly*, 1977, *11*, 1, 17–40.

Farhady, H. Justification, development and validation of functional language testing. Ph.D. dissertation, UCLA, 1980.

Farwell, C. The language spoken to children. *Papers and Reports in Child Language Development*. Stanford University, 1973, *5*, 31–62.

Fathman, A. Language background, age and order of acquisition of English structures. Paper presented at TESOL, Los Angeles, Calif., 1975a.

Fathman, A. The relationship between age and second language production ability. *Language Learning*, 1975b, *25*, 2, 245–254.

Ferguson, C. A. Absence of copula and the notion of simplicity: a study of normal speech, baby talk, foreigner talk and pidgins. In D. Hymes (ed.), *Pidginization and creolization of languages*. London: Cambridge University Press, 1971.

Ferguson, C. A. Towards a characterization of English foreigner talk. *Anthropological Linguistics*, 1975, *17*, 1–14.

Florander, J., & Jensen, M. Skoleforsog i engelsk, 1959–1965. Institute of Education, Copenhagen, 1969.

Fodor, J. A., & Bever, T. The psycholinguistic validity of linguistic segments. *Journal of Verbal Learning and Verbal Behavior*, 1965, *4*, 414–420.

Fraser, B. *The verb particle combination in English*. New York: Academic Press, 1976.

Fraser, B. On apologizing. In F. Coulmas (ed.), *Conversational routines*. The Hague: Mouton, 1980.

Fraser, B., Rintell, E., & Walters, J. An approach to conducting research on the acquisition of pragmatic competence. In D. Larsen-Freeman (ed.), *Discourse analysis in second language research*. Rowley, Mass.: Newbury House, 1980, 75–91.

Freed, B. Foreigner talk: a study of speech adjustments made by native speakers of English in conversations with non-native speakers. Ph.D. dissertation, University of Pennsvlvania, 1978.

Fromkin, V. Slips of the tongue. *Scientific American,* December 1973*a*, *229*,6, 110–117.

Fromkin, V. *Speech errors as linguistic evidence.* The Hague: Mouton, 1973*b*.

Fromkin, V. The wheres and whyfores of preach seduction. *UCLA Working Papers in Phonetics,* 1976, *31*, 22–26.

Fromm, E. Age regression and unexpected reappearance of repressed childhood language. *International Journal of Clinical Experimental Hypnosis,* 1970, *18*, 2, 79–88.

Fuller, J. An investigation of natural and monitored sequences by non-native adult performers of English. Paper presented at TESOL, Mexico City, April, 1978.

Gaies, S. The nature of linguistic input in formal second language learning. In H. Brown, C. A. Yorio & R. H. Crymes (eds.), *On TESOL 77.* Washington, D.C.: TESOL, 1977.

Galloway, L. Contributions of the right cerebral hemisphere to language and communication. Ph.D. dissertation, UCLA, 1981.

Galván, J., & Campbell, R. An examination of the communication strategies of two children in the Culver City Spanish immersion program. In R. Andersen (ed.), *The acquisition and use of Spanish and English as first and second languages.* Washington, D.C.: TESOL, 1979, 133–150.

Garnica, O. Some prosodic and paralinguistic features of speech to younger children. In C. Snow & C. Ferguson (eds.), *Talking to children.* New York: Oxford University Press, 1977.

Garrett, M. F. The analysis of sentence production. In G. Bower (ed.), *The psychology of learning and motivation, Vol. 9.* New York: Academic Press, 1975.

Garrett, M.F. Levels of processing in sentence production. In B. Butterworth (ed.), *Language production, Vol. 1.* New York: Academic Press, 1980.

Garrett, M. F., Bever, T. G., & Fodor, J. A. The active use of grammar in speech perception. *Journal of Perception and Psychophysics,* 1966, *1*, 30–32.

Gary, N. A discourse analysis of certain root transformations in English. Indiana University Linguistics Club, Bloomington, Ind., 1976.

Gaskill, W. Correction in native speaker–non-native speaker conversations. In D. Larsen-Freeman (ed.), *Discourse analysis in second language research.* Rowley, Mass.: Newbury House, 1980, 125–137.

Gasser, M. Suprasegmental meaning in English. M.A. thesis, UCLA, 1979.

Gatbonton, E. Patterned phonetic variability in second language speech: a gradual diffusion model. *Canadian Modern Language Review,* 1978, *34*, 3, 335–347.

Gazzaniga, M. S., Bogen, J. E., & Sperry, R. W. Dyspraxia following divisions of the cerebral commissures. *American Medical Association Archives of Neurology,* 1969, *16*, 806–812.

Genesse, F. Comparison of early and late immersion. Paper presented at Second Language Acquisition Research Forum, Los Angeles, 1980.

George, H. V. *Common errors in language learning.* Rowley, Mass.: Newbury House, 1972.

Gerbault, J. The acquisition of English by a five-year-old French speaker. M.A. thesis, UCLA, 1978.

Geschwind, N. Specialization of the human brain. *Scientific American,* September 1979, *241*, 3, 180–201.

Giddens, D. An analysis of the discourse and syntax of oral complaints. MA-TESL thesis, UCLA, 1981.

Givon, T. From discourse to syntax: grammar as a processing strategy. In T. Givon (ed.), *Syntax and semantics, Vol. 12, Discourse and syntax.* New York: Academic Press, 1979, 81–112.

Godfrey, D. A discourse analysis of tense in adult ESL monologues. In D. Larsen-Freeman (ed.), *Discourse analysis in second language research.* Rowley, Mass.: Newbury House, 1980, 92–110.

Goffman, E. Replies and responses. *Language in society,* 1976, 5, 3, 254–313.

Gough, J. Wagner. Comparative studies in second language learning. *CAL-ERIC/CLL Series on Languages and Linguistics, 26,* 1975.

Greenfield, P. Structural parallels between language and action in development. In A. Locke (ed.), *Action, gesture and symbol: the emergence of language.* New York: Academic Press, 1978.

Greenfield, P., Nelson, K., & Salzman, E. The development of rule-bound strategies for manipulating seriated cups: a parallel between action and grammar. *Cognitive Psychology,* 1972, *3,* 291–310.

Grice, H. P. Logic and conversation. In P. Cole & J. Morgan (eds.), *Syntax and semantics: Vol. 3, Speech acts.* New York: Academic Press, 1975, 41–58.

Grinder, R., Otomo, A., & Toyota, W. Comparisons between second, third, and fourth grade children in the audiolingual learning of Japanese as a second language. *Journal of Educational Research,* 1962, *56,* 4, 463–469.

Guilford, J. P. Three faces of intellect. *American Psychologist,* 1959, *14,* 469–479.

Gumperz, J. Sociocultural knowledge in conversational inference. *Georgetown University Roundtable on Languages and Linguistics.* Washington, D.C.: Georgetown University Press, 1977, 191–211.

Hakuta, K. A report on the development of the grammatical morphemes in a Japanese child learning English as a second language. *Working Papers on Bilingualism,* OISE, 1974*a, 3,* 18–44.

Hakuta, K. Prefabricated patterns and the emergence of structure in second language acquisition. *Language Learning,* 1974*b, 24,* 2, 287–297.

Halliday, M. A. K. *Explorations in the Functions of Language.* London: Edward Arnold, 1973.

Halliday, M. A. K. *Learning how to mean: explorations in the development of language.* London: Edward Arnold, 1975.

Halliday, M. A. K., & Hassan, R. *Cohesion in English.* London: Longman, 1976.

Hanania, E. Acquisition of English structure: a case study of an adult native speaker of Arabic in an English speaking environment. Ph.D. dissertation, Indiana University, 1974.

Harkness, S. Mother's language. In R. Hoops & Y. LeBrun (eds.), *Baby talk and infant speech: neurolinguistics,* 5. Amsterdam: Swets & Zeitlinger, 1976, 110–111.

Hartnett, D. The relation of cognitive style and hemispheric preference to deductive and inductive second language learning. M.A. thesis, UCLA, 1975.

Hartnett, D. The relationship of analytic and holistic cognitive styles to second language instructional methods. Ph.D. dissertation, UCLA, 1980.

Harwood, F. W. Quantitative study of the syntax of speech of Australian children. *Language and Speech,* 1959, *2,* 236–271.

Hatch, E. Four experimental studies in syntax of young children. Technical Report 11, Southwest Regional Laboratory, Los Alamitos, Calif., March, 1969.

Hatch, E. Studies in language switching and mixing. In W. McCormack & S. A. Wurm (eds.), *Language and man: anthropological issues.* The Hague: Mouton, 1976, 210–216.

Hatch, E., & Farhady, H. *Research design and statistics for applied linguistics.* Rowley, Mass.: Newbury House, 1982.

Hatch, E., Shapira, R., & Gough, J. Foreigner talk discourse. *ITL Review of Applied Linguistics,* 1978, *39–40,* 39–60.

Heckler, E. E. The acquisition of English verb morphology by non-native speakers. Ph.D. dissertation, Michigan State University, 1975.

Heidelberger Forschungsprojekt. The acquisition of German syntax by foreign migrant workers. In D. Sankoff (ed.), *Linguistic variation: model and methods.* New York: Academic Press, 1978*a,* 1–22.

Heidelberger Forschungsprojekt. *Pidgin Dutch. The unguided learning of German by Spanish and Italian workers: a sociolinguistic study.* Paris: UNESCO, 1978*b.*

Henning, G. H. A research study in vocabulary learning: literature, experimentation, and ESL lessons. M.A. thesis, UCLA, 1973.

Henzl, V. Linguistic register of foreign language instruction. *Language Learning,* 1974, *23,* 2, 207–222.

Henzl, V. Speech of foreign language teachers; a sociolinguistic register analysis. Paper read at AILA, Stuttgart, Germany, 1975.

Hildyard, A., & Olson, D. R. Memory and inference in the comprehension of oral and written discourse. *Discourse Processes,* 1978, *1,* 91–117.

Holzman, M. The use of interrogative forms in the verbal interactions of three mothers and their children. *Journal of Psycholinguistic Research.* 1971, *1,* 311–336.

Hopper, P. J. Aspect and foregrounding in discourse. In T. Givon (ed.), *Syntax and semantics: discourse & syntax, Vol. 12.* New York: Academic Press, 1979, 213–242.

Hopper, P. J., & Thompson, S. A. Transitivity in grammar and discourse. *Language,* 1980, *56,* 2, 251–300.

Huang, J. A Chinese child's acquisition of English syntax. MA-TESL thesis, UCLA, 1970.

Huang, J., & Hatch, E. A Chinese child's acquisition of English. In E. Hatch (ed.), *Second language acquisition.* Rowley, Mass.: Newbury House, 1978, 118–131.

Huebner, T. Order of acquisition vs. dynamic paradigm: a comparison of methods in Interlanguage research. *TESOL Quarterly,* 1979, *13,* 1, 21–28.

Hunt, K. Grammar structures written at three grade levels. *Research Report 3.* Urbana, Ill.: NCTE, 1965.

Hyltenstam, K. Implicational patterns in Interlanguage syntax variation. *Language Learning,* 1977, *27,* 383–411.

Hyman, L. M. *Phonology: theory and analysis.* New York: Holt, Rinehart & Winston, 1975.

Hymes, D. Models in the interaction of language and social life. In J. Gumperz & D. Hymes (eds.), *Directions in sociolinguistics: the ethnography of communication.* New York: Holt, Rinehart & Winston, 1972.

Ilyin, D. *Ilyin oral interview.* Rowley, Mass.: Newbury House, 1979.

Ioup, G., & Kruse, A. Interference vs. structural complexity as a predictor of second language relative clause acquisition. Paper presented at Second Language Acquisition Research Forum, Los Angeles, 1980.

Itoh, H., & Hatch, E. Second language acquisition: a case study. In E. Hatch (ed.), *Second language acquisition.* Rowley, Mass.: Newbury House, 1978.

Jackendoff, R. Morphological and semantic regularities in the lexicon. *Language,* 1975, *51,* 3, 639–671.

James, D. English interjections. *Papers in Linguistics,* University of Michigan, Ann Arbor, 1974.

Johansson, F. A. *Immigrant Swedish phonology: a study in multiple contact analysis.* Lund, Sweden: CWK Gleerup, 1973.

Johnson, G. Vocabulary acquisition in ESL. M.A. thesis, UCLA, 1977.

Johnson, N. A. A psycholinguistic study of bilingual language acquisition. Ph.D. dissertation, University of Texas, 1973.

Johnston, M. V. Observations on learning French by immersion. Paper for Psycholinguistics 260K, UCLA, 1973. Abstract in E. Hatch (ed.), *Second language acquisition.* Rowley, Mass.: Newbury House, 1978.

Jordan, B., & Fuller, N. On the non-fatal nature of trouble: sense-making and trouble managing in Lingua Franca talk. *Semiotica,* 1975, *13,* 1, 11–32.

Jordens, P , & Kellerman, E. Investigation into the strategy of transfer in second language learning. Paper presented at AILA, Hamburg, Germany, 1978.

Justman, J., & Nass, M. L. The high school achievement of pupils who were or were not introduced to a foreign language in elementary school. *Modern Language Journal,* 1956, *XL,* 120–123.

Katz, E., & Brent, S. Understanding connectives. *Journal of Verbal Learning Verbal Behavior,* 1968, *17,* 501–509.

Katz, J. Foreigner talk input in child second language acquisition: its form and function over time. In C. A. Henning (ed.), *Proceedings of the First Second Language Research Forum,* UCLA, 1977.

Kelkar, A. Marathi baby talk. *Word,* 1964, *20,* 40–54.

Keller-Cohen, D., & Gracey, C.A. Repetition in the non-native acquisition of discourse. Paper presented at Stanford Child Language Forum, 1976.

Kellerman, E. Giving learners a break: native language intuitions as a source of predictions about transferability. *Working Papers on Bilingualism,* 1978, *15,* 59–92.

Kemp, M. K. A study of English proficiency levels of the composition errors of incoming students at the University of Cincinnati during 1969–1974. Ph.D. dissertation, Ohio State University, 1975.

Kempen, G., & Hoenkamp, E. A procedural grammar for sentence production. *Internal Report 81 FU.03, 81 SO.07.* Vakgroep psychologische functieleer, Psychologisch laboratorium, Katholieke Universiteit, Nijmegen, the Netherlands, 1981.

Kennedy, G. D. Children's comprehension of English sentences comparing quantities of discrete items. Ph.D. dissertation, UCLA, 1970.

Kenyeres, A. Comment une petite Hongroise apprend le francais. *Archives de Psychologie,* 1938, *26,* 321–366.

Kernan, K., & Blount, B. Acquisition of Spanish grammar by Mexican children. *Anthropological linguistics,* 1966, *89,* 1–14.

Kernan, K. T., & Sabsay, S. Pragmatics of narrative use by the mildly retarded. Paper presented at the 77th Annual American Anthropological Society, Los Angeles, 1978.

Kessler, C., & Idar, I. The acquisition of English syntax structure by a Vietnamese child. In C. Henning (ed.), *Proceedings of the Second Language Acquisition Forum,* 1977, 295–307.

Kessler, C., & Idar, I. The acquisition of English syntax structure by a Vietnamese mother and child. *Working Papers on Bilingualism,* June 1979, *18,* 15 pages.

Kimura, D. Cerebral dominance and the perception of verbal stimuli. *Canadian Journal of Psychology,* 1961, *15,* 166–171.

Kolers, P. Interlingual word associations. *Journal of Verbal Learning and Verbal Behavior,* 1963, *2,* 291–300.

Krashen, S. The development of cerebral dominance and language learning: more evidence. In D. Dato (ed.), *Developmental psycholinguistics: theory and application.* Washington, D.C.: Georgetown University Press, 1975, 209–233.

Krashen, S. Cerebral asymmetry. In H. Whitaker & H. Whitaker (eds.), *Studies in neuro-linguistics, Vol. 2.* New York: Academic Press, 1976.

Krashen, S. Some issues related to the monitor model. In H. D. Brown, C. A. Yorio & R. H. Crymes (eds.), *On TESOL 77: Teaching and learning ESL, trends in research and practice.* Washington, D.C.: TESOL, 1977.

Krashen, S. The input hypothesis. In J. Alatis (ed.), *Current issues in bilingual education.* Georgetown Roundtable on Languages and Linguistics, Washington, D.C.: Georgetown University Press, 1980, 168–180.

Krashen, S. The role of input (reading) and instruction in developing writing ability. Paper presented at AILA, Lund, Sweden, 1981.

Krashen, S., Long, M., & Scarcella, R. Age, rate and eventual attainment in second language acquisition. *TESOL Quarterly,* 1977, *13,* 4, 573–582.

Labov, W., & Fanshel, D. *Therapeutic discourse.* New York: Academic Press, 1977.

Ladefoged, P. Cross linguistic studies of speech production. *UCLA Working Papers in Phonetics,* 1980, *51,* 94–104.

Ladefoged, P., & Broadbent, D. Information conveyed by vowels. *Journal of Acoustical Society of America,* 1957, *29,* 98–104.

Ladefoged, P., & Broadbent, D. Perception of sequence in auditory events. *Quarterly Journal of Experimental Psychology,* 1960, *12,* 162–170.

Lambert, W. E., Ignatow, M., & Krauthamer, M. Bilingual organization in free recall. *Journal of Verbal Learning and Verbal Behavior,* 1968, *7,* 207–214.

Lance, D. M. A brief study of Spanish-English bilinguals: final report. Research project ORR-Lib. Arts, 15504, Texas A&M University, 1969.

Landes, J. Speech addressed to children: issues and characteristics of parental input. *Language Learning,* 1975, *25,* 2, 355–379.

Larsen-Freeman, D. The acquisition of grammatical morphemes by adult ESL students. *TESOL Quarterly,* 1975, *9,* 4, 409–419.

Larsen-Freeman, D. The importance of input in second language acquisition. Paper presented at LSA, Los Angeles, 1980.

Larsen-Freeman, D., & Strom, V. The construction of a second language acquisition index. *Language Learning,* 1977, *27,* 1, 123–134.

Leopold, W. *Speech development of a bilingual child, Vol. 1* (Vocabulary). Evanston, Ill.: Northwestern University Press, 1939.

Levinson, S. E., & Liberman, M. Speech recognition by computer. *Scientific American,* 1981, *244,* 4, 64–87.

Levy, J., Nebes, R. D., & Sperry, R. W. Expressive language in the surgically separated minor hemisphere. *Cortex,* 1971, *7,* 49–58.

Levy-Agresti, J., & Sperry, R. Differential perceptual capacities in major and minor hemispheres. *Proceedings of the National Academy of Science,* 1968, *61,* 1151.

Lewis, M., & Cherry, L. Social behavior and language acquisition. In M. Lewis & L. Rosenblum (eds.), *Interaction, conversation, and the development of language.* New York: Wiley, 1977, 227–247.

Linde, C. Focus of attention and choice of pronouns in discourse. In T. Givon (ed.), *Syntax and semantics, Vol. 12, Discourse and syntax.* New York: Academic Press, 1979.

Linde, C., & Labov, W. Spatial networks as a site for study of language and thought. *Language,* 1975, *51,* 924–939.

Linde, R. A diagnosis of grammar errors made by Japanese persons speaking English. Ph.D. dissertation, American University, 1971.

Long, M. H. Teacher feedback on learner error: mapping cognition. In C. Yorio & R. Crymes, *On TESOL 76.* Washington, D.C.: TESOL, 1976, 137–153.

Long, M. H. Input, interaction and second language acquisition. PH.D. dissertation, UCLA, 1980.

Long, M. H. Input, interaction and second language acquisition. Paper presented at the N.Y. Academy of Sciences, New York, January 1981*a.* To appear in *Annals of the New York Academy of Sciences.*

Long, M. H. Question in foreigner talk discourse. *Language Learning,* 1981*b, 31,* 1, 135–157.

Longacre, R. The warp and woof of discourse. Mimeo paper, University of Texas, Arlington, 1978.

Loos, D. Functional language testing of complaints. MA/TESL thesis, UCLA, 1981.

Lord, C. Variation in the acquisition of negation. *Papers and Reports on Child Language Development,* 1974, *8,* Linguistics Department, Stanford University, Stanford, Calif.

Luria, A. R. *Human brain and psychological process.* Translated by B. Haigh. New York: Harper & Row, 1966.

Luria, A. R. *The mind of a mnemonist: a little book about a vast memory.* Translated by L. Solotaroff. New York: Basic Books, 1968.

Luria, A. R., & Tsvetkova, D. The mechanisms of dynamic aphasia. *Foundations of Language,* 1968, *4,* 296–307.

Ma, R., & Herasimchuk, E. The linguistic dimensions of a bilingual neighborhood. In J. A. Fishman (ed.), *Bilingualism in the barrio.* Bloomington, Ind.: Indiana University Press, 1971, 349–479.

MacLeod, C. M. Bilingual episodic memory: acquisition and forgetting. *Journal of Verbal Learning and Verbal Behavior,* 1976, *15,* 347–364.

Maitre, S. On the representation of second languages in the brain. M.A. thesis, UCLA, 1974.

Manes, J., & Wolfson, N. The compliment formula. In F. Coulmas (ed.), *Conversational routine.* The Hague: Mouton, 1981.

Maratsos, M. New models in linguistics and language acquisition. In M. Halle, J. Bresnan, & G. A. Miller (eds.), *Linguistic theory and psychological reality.* Cambridge, Mass.: MIT Press, 1978.

Marchand, H. *Studies in syntax and word formation.* Munchen: Verlag, 1974.

Martinez-Bernal, J. Children's acquisition of Spanish and English morphological systems and noun phrases. Ph.D. dissertation, Georgetown University, 1972.

Mazeika, E. J. A description of the language of a bilingual child. Ph.D. dissertation, University of Rochester, 1971.

McCurdy, P. L. Talking to foreigners: the role of rapport. Ph.D. dissertation, University of California, Berkeley, 1980.

McNeil, D., & McNeil, N. What does a child mean when he says "no"? In E. M. Zale (ed.), *Language and language behavior.* New York: Appleton-Century-Crofts, 1968, 51–62.

Meisel, J. M. Linguistic simplification: a study of immigrant workers' speech and foreign talk In S. P. Corder & E. Roulet (eds.), *Actes du 5eme de linguistique appliquee de Neuchatel,* 1977.

Merritt, M. On questions following questions. *Language in Society,* 1976, *5,* 3, 315–357.

Mikes, M. Acquisition des categories grammaticales dans le langage de l'enfant. *Enfance,* 1967, *20,* 289–297.

Miller, G. A., & Isard, S. Free recall of self embedded English sentences. *Information and control,* 1964, *7,* 292–303.

Miller, G. A. *Language and speech.* San Francisco: W. H. Freeman & Co., 1981.

Milner, B., Corking, S., & Teuber, H. L. Further analysis of the hippocampal amnesia syndrome: a fourteen year followup study of HM. *Neuropsychologia,* 1968, *6,* 215–234.

Milon, J. P. The development of negation in English by a second language learner. *TESOL Quarterly,* 1974, *8,* 2, 137–143.

Moerk, E. *Pragmatics and semantic aspects of early language development.* Baltimore: University Park Press, 1977.

Moerman, M., & Sachs, H. On understanding in the analysis of natural conversation. In M. Kinkade (ed.), *Relations of anthropology and linguistics.* The Hague: Mouton, 1978.

Moscovitch, M. The development of lateralization of language function and its relation to cognition and language development. In S. J. Segalowitz & F. S. Gruber (eds.), *Language development and neurological theory.* New York: Academic Press, 1977.

Mulford, R., & Hecht, B. Learning to speak without an accent: acquisition of a second language phonology, *Papers and reports in child language development,* 1980, *18.* Linguistics Department, Stanford University, Stanford, Calif.

Mylov, P. *School experiments in English.* Copenhagen: Nunksgaard, 1972.

Naiman, N., Frolich, M., Stern, H. H., & Todesco, A. *The good language learner.* Toronto: OISE, 1978.

Natalicio, D.C., & Natalicio, L.F. A comparative study of English pluralization by native and non-native English speakers. *Child Development,* 1971, *42,* 1302–1306.

Nebes, R. Superiority of the minor hemispheres in commissurotomized man for the perception of part-whole relations. *Cortex,* 1971, *7,* 333–349.

Neisser, U. *Cognitive psychology.* Englewood Cliffs, N. J.: Prentice-Hall, 1967.

Nemser, W. Approximative systems of foreign language learners. *IRAL,* 1971, *1,* 115–123.

Neumann, R. An attempt to define through error analysis an intermediate ESL level at UCLA. M.A. thesis, UCLA, 1977.

Newport, E. The speech of mothers to young children. In N. Castellan, D. Pisoni, & G. Potts (eds.), *Cognitive theory, Vol 2.* Hillsdale, N. J.: Lawrence Erlbaum Associates, 1976.

Nooteboom, G. G. Some regularities in phonemic speech error. Institut voor Perceptie Onderzoek. Annual Progress Report, 2, Eindhoven, 1967.

Obler, L., Albert, M., & Gordon, H. Asymmetry of cerebral dominance in Hebrew-English bilinguals. Paper presented at 13th Annual Meeting of Academy of Aphasia, Victoria, British Columbia, 1975.

Ochs, E. Planned and unplanned discourse. In T. Givon (ed.), *Syntax and semantics, Vol. 12, Discourse and syntax.* New York: Academic Press, 1979, 51–80.

Ochs, E. Talking to children in Western Samoa. Unpublished paper, Linguistics Department, University of Southern California, 1980.

Ochs, E., & Bennet, T. (eds.). Discourse across time and space. *Southern California Occasional Papers in Linguistics, 5,* May 1977.

Ochs Keenan, E. Conversational competence in children. *Journal of Child Language, 1,* 1974, 163–183.

Ochs Keenan, E., & Klein, E. Coherency in children's discourse. *Journal Psycholinguistic Research, 1975, 4,* 365–378.

Ochs Keenan, E., & Schieffelin, B. Topic as a discourse notion. In C. Li (ed.), *Subject and topic.* New York: Academic Press, 1976, 337–385.

Ochs Keenan, E., Schieffelin, B., & Platt, M. Questions of immediate concern. In E. Goody (ed.), *Questions and politeness.* Cambridge: Cambridge University Press, 1978.

Ojemann, J. A., & Whitaker, H. Bilingual brain. *Archives of Neurology,* 1978, *35,* 409–412.

Olds, H. F. An experimental study of syntactic factors influencing children's competence of certain complex relationships. Report 4, Harvard Research & Development, 1968.

Oller, D. K. Toward a general theory of phonological processes in first and second language learning. Paper presented at the Western Conference on Linguistics, Seattle, Washington, 1974.

Oller, J. The factorial structure of language proficiency: divisible or not. In J. Oller, *Language tests at school.* London: Longmans, 1979.

Olmsted, D. *Out of the mouths of babes.* The Hague: Mouton, 1971.

Olshtain, E. The acquisition of English progressive: a case study of a seven-year-old Hebrew speaker. *Working Papers on Bilingualism,* 1979, *18,* 81–102.

Olshtain, E., & Cohen, A. Discourse analysis and language learning: speech event sets. Paper presented at AILA, Lund, Sweden, 1981. To appear in N. Wolfson & E. Judd (eds.), *TESOL and sociolinguistic research.* Rowley, Mass.: Newbury House, in press.

Olson, L., & Samuels, S. The relationship between age and accuracy of foreign language pronunciation. *Journal of Educational Research,* 1973, *66,* 263–267.

Owens, J., Bower, G. H., & Black, J. B. The "soap opera" effect in story memory. Unpublished paper, Stanford University, 1977. Also described in G. H. Bower, Experiments on story comprehension and recall, *Discourse Processes,* 1978, *3,* 211–232.

Oyama, S. C. A sensitive period for the acquisition of a phonological system. *Journal Psycholinguistic Research,* 1976, *5,* 3, 261–283.

Paivio, A. *Imagery and verbal processes.* New York: Rinehart & Winston, 1971.

Paradis, M. Bilingualism and aphasia. In H. Whitaker & H. Whitaker (eds.), *Studies in neurolinguistics, Vol. 3.* New York: Academic Press, 1977.

Pask, G., & Scott, B. Learning strategies and individual competence. *International Journal of Man-machine Studies.* 1972, *4,* 217–153.

Patkowski, M. The sensitive period for the acquisition of syntax in a second language. Ph.D. dissertation, New York University, 1980.

Peck, S. Child-child discourse in second language acquisition. In E. Hatch (ed.), *Second language acquisition.* Rowley, Mass.: Newbury House, 1978, 383–400.

Penfield, W., & Roberts, R. *Speech and brain mechanisms.* Princeton: Princeton University Press, 1959.

Peterson, J., & Lehiste, I. Duration of syllable nuclei in English. *Journal Acoustical Society of America,* 1960, *32,* 6, 693–703.

Phillips, J. Syntax and vocabulary of mother's speech to young children: age and sex comparisons. *Child Development,* 1973, *44,* 182–185.

Phillips, S. The invisible culture. communication in classroom and community on the Warren Springs reservation. Ph.D. dissertation, University of Pennsylvania, 1974.

Plann, S. The Spanish-immersion program: towards native-like proficiency or a classroom dialect? M.A. thesis, UCLA, 1976.

Plann, S. Morphological problems in the acquisition of Spanish in an immersion classroom. In R. Andersen (ed.), *The acquisition and use of Spanish and English as first and second languages.* Washington, D.C.: TESOL, 1979.

Pomerantz, A. A sequential analysis of interpreting absences. Unpublished paper, Sociology Department, UCLA, 1978.

Praninskas, J. *Rapid review of English grammar.* Englewood Cliffs, N. J.: Prentice-Hall, 1959.

Rader, M. Complaint letters: when *is* conflicts with *ought.* Unpublished paper, University of California, Berkeley, 1977.

Ramamurti, R. How do Americans talk to me? Paper for *Folklore*, University of Pennsylvania, 1977. See discussion in Long, M.H., 1980.

Ravem, R. Second language acquisition. Ph.D. dissertation, University of Essex, 1974.

Reiff, R., & Scheerer, M. *Memory and hypnosis age-regression: developmental aspects of cognition explored through hypnosis.* International Universities Press, 1959.

Remick, H. The maternal environment of linguistic development. Ph.D. dissertation, University of California, Davis, 1971.

Richards, J. C. (ed.). *Error analysis: perspectives on second language acquisition.* London: Longman, 1974.

Rintell, E. Getting your speech act together: the pragmatic ability of second language learners. *Working Papers on Bilingualism, 17,* 1979.

Roeper, T., & Siegel, M. A lexical transformation for verbal compounds. *Linguistic Inquiry,* 1978, *9,* 199–260.

Ronjat, J. *Le developpement du langage observe chez un enfant bilingue.* Paris: Campion, 1913.

Rosansky, E. Methods and morphemes in second language acquisition. Paper presented at the Child Language Research Forum, Stanford, Calif., 1976.

Rumelhart, D.E. Notes on a schema for stories. In D. G. Bobrow & A. Collins (eds.), *Representation and understanding: studies in cognitive science.* New York: Academic Press, 1975.

Rutherford, W. *Modern English.* New York: Harcourt, Brace, 1968.

Rutherford, W. Markedness in second language acquisition. Unpublished paper, Linguistics Department, USC, 1981.

Sachs, H., Schegloff, E., & Jefferson, G. A simplest systematics for the organization of turn-taking in conversations. *Language, 1974, 50,* 696–735.

Sachs, J. Recognition memory for syntactic and semantic aspects of connected discourse. *Perception and psychophysics,* 1967, *2,* 437–442.

Sachs, J., & Devin, J. Young children's use of age-appropriate speech styles in social interaction and role playing. *Journal of Child Language,* 1976, *3,* 1, 81–98.

Sachs, J., & Johnson, M. Language development of communication skills: modifications in the speech of young children as a function of listener. *Monographs of Society of Research in Child Development,* 1973, *38,* 5.

Salisbury, R. F. Notes on bilingual and language change in New Guinea. *Anthropological Linguistics,* 1962, *4,* 7, 1–13.

Savin, H. B., & Perchonock, E. Grammatical structure of the immediate recall of English sentences. *Journal of verbal learning and verbal behavior,* 1965, *4,* 348–353.

Scarcella, R. On speaking politely in a second language. In C. Yorio, K. Perkins, & J. Schachter (eds.), *On TESOL 79.* Washington, D.C.: TESOL, 1979a.

Scarcella, R. Watch up! Prefabricated routines in adult second language performance. *Working Papers on Bilingualism,* Toronto, OISE, 1979b, *19,* 79–88.

Scarcella, R., & Higa, C. Input and age differences in second language acquisition. In S. Krashen, R. Scarcella, & M. Long (eds.), *Child-adult differences in second language acquisition.* Rowley, Mass.: Newbury House, in press.

Schachter, J. An error in error analysis. *Language Learning,* 1974, *24,* 2, 205–214.

Schachter, J., & Rutherford, W. Discourse function and language transfer. Paper presented at Los Angeles Second Language Forum, 1978.

Schaefer, E. An analysis of the discourse and syntax of oral complaints in English. MA-TESL thesis, UCLA, 1982.

Schane, S. *Generative phonology.* Englewood Cliffs, N.J.: Prentice-Hall, 1973.

Schegloff, E., Jefferson, G., & Sachs, H. The preference for self-correction in the organization of repair in conversation. *Language,* 1977, *53,* 361–382.

Schegloff, E., & Sachs, H. Opening up closings. *Semiotica,* 1973, *8,* 289–327.

Schiffrin, D. Tense variation in narrative. *Language,* 1981, *57,* 1, 45–62.

Schlue, K. An inside view of Interlanguage: consulting the adult learner about the second language process. MA-TESL thesis, UCLA, 1976.

Schmidt, R. W. Sociolinguistic variation and language transfer in phonology. *Working Papers on Bilingualism.* January 1977, *12,* 79–95.

Schmidt, R. W., & Richards, J. C. Speech acts and second language learning. *Applied Linguistics,* in press.

Schumann, J. The acculturation model for second language acquisition. In R. C. Gingras (ed.), *Second language acquisition and foreign language learning.* Washington, D.C.: Center for Applied Linguistics, 1978*a*.

Schumann, J. The acquisition of English relative clauses by native speakers of Spanish. Paper presented at the Second Language Acquisition Forum, Los Angeles, 1978*b*.

Schumann, J. The acquisition of English negation by speakers of Spanish: a review of the literature. In R. Andersen (ed.), *The acquisition and use of Spanish and English as first and second languages.* Washington, D.C.: TESOL, 1979, 3–32.

Schwartz, J. The negotiation of meaning: repair in conversations between second language learners of English. In D. Larsen-Freeman (ed.), *Discourse analysis in second language research.* Rowley, Mass.: Newbury House, 1980, 138–153.

Scollon, R. A real early stage: an unzippered condensation of a dissertation on child language. In E. Ochs & B. Schieffelin (eds.), *Developmental pragmatics.* New York: Academic Press, 1979.

Scott, M., & Tucker, G. R. Error analysis and English language strategies of Arab students. *Language Learning,* 1974, *24,* 1, 69–97.

Searle, J. R. *Speech acts: an essay in the philosophy of language.* Cambridge: Cambridge University Press, 1969.

Searle, J.R. A classification of illocutionary acts. *Language in Society,* 1976, *5,* 1, 1–23.

Selinker, L. Interlanguage. *IRAL,* 1972, *10,* 210–231.

Selinker, L., Todd-Trimble, M., & Trimble, L. Presuppositional rhetorical information is EST discourse. *TESOL Quarterly,* 1976, *10,* 3, 281–290.

Shapira, R. G. The non-learning of English: a case study of an adult. In E. Hatch (ed.), *Second language acquisition.* Rowley, Mass.: Newbury House, 1978, 246–255.

Sharrock, W., & Turner, R. On a conversational environment for equivocality. In D. Schenkein (ed.), *Studies in the organization of conversational interaction.* New York: Academic Press, 1978.

Shatz, M., & Gelman, R. The development of communication skills. *Monographs of the Society of Research in Child Development,* 1973, *38,* 5.

Sheldon, A. The role of parallel function in the acquisition of relative clauses in English. *Journal of Verbal Learning and Verbal Behavior,* 1974, *13,* 272–281.

Sher, A. Symmetric predicates: a theoretical and empirical study. M.A. thesis, UCLA, 1975.

Shugar, G. W. Text analysis as an approach to the study of early linguistic operations. In N. Waterson & C. Snow (eds.), *The development of communication.* Chichester: Wiley & Sons, 1978, 227–251.

Simms, S. Speech and language modifications as a function of communicative need. CD562 paper, California State University, Northridge, 1978.

Sinclair, J. M., & Coulthard, R. M. *Towards an analysis of discourse: the English used by teachers and pupils.* London: Oxford University Press, 1975.

Sinclair-de Zwart, H. Language acquisition and cognitive development. In T. Moore (ed.), *Cognitive development and the acquisition of language.* New York: Academic Press, 1973, 9–25.

Slobin, D. I. Grammar transformations and sentence comprehension in childhood and adulthood. *Journal Verbal Learning and Verbal Behavior,* 1966, *5,* 219–227.

Slobin, D. I. Cognitive prerequisites for the development of grammar. In C. Ferguson & C. Snow (eds.), *Studies of child language development.* New York: Holt, Rinehart & Winston, 1973, 175–208.

Snow, C. Mother's speech to children learning language. *Child Development,* 1972, *43,* 549–565.

Snow, C. The development of conversations between mothers and babies. *Journal Child Language,* 1977, *4,* 1, 1–22.

Snow, C. Conversations with children. In P. Fletcher & M. Garman (eds.), *Language acquisition: studies in first language development.* Cambridge: Cambridge University Press, 1979, 363–375.

Snow, C., Arlman-Rupp, A., Hassing, Y., Jobse, J., Joosten, J., & Vorster, J. Mothers' speech in three social classes. *Journal of Psycholinguistic Research,* 1976, *5,* 1–20.

Snow, C., & Hoefnagel-Hohle, M. The critical period for language acquisition. *Child Development,* 1978*a, 49,* 1114–1128.

Snow, C., & Hoefnagel-Hohle, M. Age differences in second language acquisition. In E. Hatch (ed.), *Second language acquisition.* Rowley, Mass.: Newbury House, 1978*b,* 333–346.

Snow, C., & Hoefnagel-Hohle, M. The linguistic environment of school-age second language learners. *Language Learning,* 1982, in press.

Snow, C., van Eeden, R. Y., & Muysken, P. The international origins of foreigner talk. *International Journal of Sociology of Language,* 1981, *28,* 81–92.

Sorenson, A. Multilingualism in the Northwest Amazon. *American Anthropologist,* 1967, *69,* 670–684.

Spearman, C. *The abilities of man.* New York: Macmillan, 1927.

Stern, C., & Stern, W. *Die Kindersprache: Eine psychologische und sprachtheoretische Untersuchung.* Leipzig: Barth, 1907. Translated quotation appears in A. Blumenthal, *Language and psychology.* New York: Wiley & Sons, Inc., 1970.

Stern, H. H. Optimal age: myth or reality. *Canadian Modern Language Review,* 1976, *32,* 3, 283–294.

Stewart, J. M., & Barach, C. A brief memory strategy with distinctive features. *Journal Psycholinguistic Research,* 1980, *9,* 4, 391–406.

Steyaert, N. A comparison of the speech of ESL teachers to native and non-native speakers of English. Paper presented at LSA, Chicago, 1979.

Stockwell, R., Bowen, J., & Martin, J. *The sounds of English and Spanish.* Chicago: University of Chicago Press, 1965*a.*

Stockwell, R., Bowen, J., & Martin, J. *The grammatical structures of English and Spanish.* Chicago: University of Chicago Press, 1965*b.*

Street, R. F. A gestalt completion test --a study of a cross-section of intelligence. *Contributions to Education, No. 481.* Teachers College, Columbia University, 1931.

Swain, M., Naiman, N., & Dumas, G. Aspects of the learning of French by English-speaking five-year-olds. In E. Hatch (ed.), *Second language acquisition.* Rowley, Mass.: Newbury House, 1978, 297–312.

Syngle, B. Second language (English) acquisition strategies of children and adults: a cross-sectional study. Ph.D. dissertation, Louisiana State University, 1973.

Tannen, D. A direct/indirect look at misunderstandings. Working paper, Institute of Human Learning, University of California, Berkeley, 1976.

Tannen, D. Ethnicity as conversational style. Paper presented at the American Anthropological Association, Los Angeles, November, 1978.

Tarone, E. Some influences on Interlanguage phonology. *Working Papers on Bilingualism,* 1976, *8,* 87–111.

Tavakolian, S. L. *Language acquisition and linguistic theory.* Cambridge, Mass.: MIT Press, 1981.

Taylor, B. The use of overgeneralization and transfer learning strategies by elementary and intermediate students in ESL. *Language learning,* 1975, *25,* 73–107.

Thompson, S. On the issue of productivity in the lexicon. *UCLA Papers in Syntax, 6,* 1974.

Thorndike, E., & Lorge, I. *The teacher's wordbook of 30,000 words.* New York: Columbia University, 1952.

Thurstone, L. L., & Thurstone, T. G. Factorial studies of intelligence. *Psychometric monographs,* 1941, *2.*

Trager, S. The language of teaching: discourse analysis in beginning, intermediate and advanced ESL students. M.A. thesis, University of Southern California, 1978.

Trubetzkoy, N. *Principles of phonology.* Translated by C. Baltaxe. Los Angeles & Berkeley: University of California Press, 1969.

Turner, E., & Rommetveit, R. Focus of attention in recall of active and passive sentences. *Journal of Verbal Learning and Verbal Behavior,* 1968, *7,* 543–548.

Uyekubo, A. Language switching of Japanese-English bilinguals. M.A. thesis, UCLA, 1972.

Valdman, A. L'effet de modeles culturels sur l'elaboration du langage simplifie. Paper presented at the Neuchatel conference, 1976.

van Ek, J.A. *The threshold level for modern language teaching in schools.* London: Longman, 1976.

van Lancker, D. Heterogeneity in language and speech: neurolinguistic studies. *Working Papers in Phonetics,* 1975, *29,* UCLA.

van Mettre, P.D. Syntactic characteristics of selected bilingual children. Ph.D. dissertation, University of Arizona, 1972.

Vihman, M. The acquisition of morphology by a bilingual child: a whole word approach. Paper presented at the 5th Annual Conference of Language Development, Boston University, October, 1980.

Vorster, J. Mommy linguist: the case of motherese. *Lingua,* 1975, *37,* 281–312.

Walters, J. The perception of politeness in English and Spanish. In C. Yorio, K. Perkins, & J. Schachter (eds.), *On TESOL 79.* Washington, D.C.: TESOL, 1979, 288–296.

Warren, R. M., & Warren, R. P. Auditory illusions and confusions. *Scientific American,* 1970, *223,* 30–36.

Weber-Olsen, M., & Ruder, K. Acquisition and generalization of Japanese locatives by English speakers. *Applied Psycholinguistics,* 1980, *1,* 2, 183–198.

Wechsler, P. *The measurement of adult intelligence.* Baltimore, Md.: Wilkins & Wilkins, 1944.

Weeks, T. E. Discourse, culture and instruction. Paper presented at AERA, 1976.

Weir, R. *Language in the crib.* The Hague: Mouton, 1962.

Weitan, W., & Etaugh, C. Lateral eye movements as related to verbal and perceptual motor skills and values. *Perceptual and Motor Skills,* 1973, *36,* 423–428.

Wernicke, C. *Der aphasische Symtonenkomplex.* Breslau: Cohn & Weigart, 1908. Translated in *Boston Studies in the Philosophy of Science, 4,* 34–97.

Whitaker, H. A case of isolation of the language function. In H. Whitaker & H. Whitaker (eds.), *Studies in neurolinguistics, Vol. 2,* New York: Academic Press, 1976.

Wiggins, B. Syntax and discourse analysis: an approach to the teaching of scientific English. M.A. thesis, University of Hawaii, 1977.

Williams, F., Cairns, H., Cairns, C., & Blosser, D. Analysis of production errors in the phonetic performance of school age standard English speaking children. Austin, Texas: Center for Communication Research, 1971.

Willerman, B., & Melvin, B. Reservations about the keyword mnemonic. *Canadian Modern Language Review,* 1979, *35,* 3, 443–453.

Willis, M. Affixation in English word formation and application for TESOL. M.A. thesis, UCLA, 1975.

Witkin, H. A., Moore, C. A., Godenough, D. R., & Cox, P. W. Field dependent and field independent cognitive styles and their educational implications. *Review of Educational Research,* 1977, *47,* 1–65.

Wittrock, M. C. Education and the cognitive processes of the brain. *77th Yearbook of the N.S.S.E., Part II.* Chicago: University of Chicago Press, 1978.

Wittrock, M. C., Doctorow, M. J., & Marks, C. B. Reading as a generative process. *Journal of Educational Psychology.* 1975, *67,* 484–489.

Wolfson, N. A feature of performed narrative: the conversational historical present. *Language in Society,* 1978, *7,* 2, 215–238.

Wolfson, N. "Let's get together sometime." Perceptions of insincerity. Paper presented at TESOL, Boston, 1979.

Wolfson, N. Compliments in cross-cultural perspective. *TESOL Quarterly,* 1981*a, 15,* 2, 117–124.

Wolfson, N. The descriptive analysis of rules of speaking. Paper presented at AILA, Lund, Sweden, 1981*b.*

Wolfson, N., & Judd, E. (eds.). *TESOL and sociolinguistic research.* Rowley, Mass.: Newbury House, in press.

Wong-Fillmore, L. The second time around: cognitive and social strategies in second language acquisition. Ph.D. dissertation, Stanford University, 1976.

Yamada, J. On the independence of language and cognition: evidence from a hyperlinguistic retarded adolescent. Paper presented at the International Congress of Child Language, University of British Columbia, Vancouver, August, 1981.

Yarmey, A. D. I recognize your face but I can't remember your name: further evidence on TOT phenomena. *Memory and Cognition,* 1973, *1,* 3, 287–290.

Yorkey, R. C. *Study skills for students of English as a second language.* New York: McGraw-Hill, 1970.

Yoshida, M. The acquisition of English vocabulary by a Japanese speaking child. In E. Hatch (ed.), *Second language acquisition.* Rowley, Mass.: Newbury House, 1978.

Young, D. The acquisition of English syntax by three Spanish-speaking children. M.A. thesis, UCLA, 1974.

Zaidel, E. Linguistic competence in the right cerebral hemisphere of man following commissurotomy and hemispherectomy. Ph.D. dissertation, California Institute of Technology, 1973.

Zaidel, E. Lexical organization in the right hemisphere. In P. Buser & A. Rougeul-Buser (eds.), *Cerebral correlates of unconscious experience.* Amsterdam: Elsevier, 1978*a,* 177–197.

Zaidel, E. Concepts of cerebral dominance in the split brain. In P. Buser & A. Rouguel-Buser (eds.), *Cerebral correlates of unconscious experience.* Amsterdam: Elsevier, 1978*b.*

Zelinker, T., & Jeffrey, W. E. Reflective and impulsive children. *Monograph of the Society for Research in Child Development,* 1976, *41,* 1–52.

Zimmer, K. Affixal negation in English and other languages. *Word,* Monograph 5, 1964, *20,* 2, supplement, 3–101.

Zimmer, K. Some general observations about nominal compounds. *Working Papers on Language Universals, No. 5.* Stanford University, 1971, C1–21.

Author Index

Subject Index